Scott's Novels and the Counter-Revolutionary Politics of Place

Scottish Cultural Review of Language and Literature

VOLUME 27

The titles published in this series are listed at *brill.com/scrl*

Scott's Novels and the Counter-Revolutionary Politics of Place

By

Dani Napton

BRILL

RODOPI

LEIDEN | BOSTON

Cover illustration: Old Woodstock Palace, Old Woodstock, Woodstock, Oxfordshire. Reproduced by permission of Historic England Archive.

The Library of Congress Cataloging-in-Publication Data is available online at http://catalog.loc.gov
LC record available at http://lccn.loc.gov/2018011068

Typeface for the Latin, Greek, and Cyrillic scripts: "Brill". See and download: brill.com/brill-typeface.

ISSN 1571-0734
ISBN 978-90-04-35277-3 (hardback)
ISBN 978-90-04-35278-0 (e-book)

Printed by Printforce, the Netherlands

For Tony who has always been the inspiration

and

*for Muti, Shelley and Peter, Juliette, and Benjamin
who have always been the incentive*

∵

Contents

Acknowledgments

Many people have accompanied me on this journey, which would have been a much poorer and far less joyful experience without them. It is a pleasure to acknowledge my many debts.

A.D. Cousins has been a beacon of knowledge, wisdom, generosity of spirit and encouragement. His insights and scholarship have improved the arguments in this book immeasurably, while I alone am responsible for its flaws. I am grateful to Christine Alexander, Clara Tuite and Joanne Wilkes for their reviews of, and valuable advice on, an earlier draft of this monograph, which is also the better for Masja Horn's and Ronnie Young's suggestions. Kim Fiona Plas, Jan van Waarden and SPi Global's sterling work has added considerably to this monograph. Thanks are also due to the Macquarie University library staff for their sustained efforts to procure essential research material.

I am indebted to Lynn Williams whose companionship and intellectual curiosity have influenced this work so positively and in so many ways. My especial thanks go to Margo Lanagan (that evocative sorcerer), Jim Abel and Juliette Napton for their careful review of this work. My gratitude extends to Lee Griggs for nurturing my literary passion over many years, and to John and Collette Napton for their encouragement from afar throughout this endeavour. Thanks also go to Les Vance for challenging my paradigms and arguments with forthright good humour; they are the better for his doing so.

For their unstinting support and friendship, I am grateful to Sandra Abel, Brad Anderson, Sarah Archer, Jennifer Arculus, Nic Astudillo, Penny Blythman, Helen Campbell, Vanessa Cavagnaro, Melanie Clarke, Anne and Catriona Coote, Jo Defries, Lauren Fine, Elizabeth and Geoffrey Fisher, Elsa Hill, Patrick Hung, Amy Jones, Sophie Khouchaba, Marlya MacNeill, Jo Miles, Jane Smith, Rachael Smith, Jodi Staunton Smith, Wen Ming Tan, Clare Thurling, Sarah Van Cooten, Kim Virtue-Wilson, Shelley Walder, Jane Wakeling, Joy Wright and Sara Wright.

Finally I am deeply grateful to Shelley, Peter, Tony, Juliette and Benjamin, who have been such a constant source of love, encouragement and support.

Earlier and different versions of material in this book have appeared in: AUMLA: *Journal of the Australasian Universities Language and Literature Association* (parts of Chapter 1); SEL: *Studies in English Literature, 1500–1900* with Stephanie Russo (parts of Chapter 2); *The French Revolution and the British Novel in the Romantic Period* (Peiterlen, Switzerland: Peter Lang, 2012) and *Home and Nation in British Literature from the English to the French Revolutions* (Cambridge: Cambridge University Press, 2015) (parts of Chapter 4); and *The Explicator* with A.D. Cousins (parts of Chapter 5).

Permissions

I am grateful to Edinburgh University Press for permission to quote from the respective editors' commentary from the Edinburgh Edition of the Waverley Novels (EEWN).

Introduction

Few would deny that politics—contemporary as well as past—play a significant role in Scott's novels. Indeed, many of the truisms of Scott criticism refer
primarily to the political conservatism and attachment to the notion of monarchy that inform his writings. Yet although Scott was attached to the politics
of the past, he was also firmly committed to considered political progress.
Given the complexities inherent in the politically volatile situations he explores in the Waverley Novels, and those he was involved in or commenting
upon while writing his canon, there has been ongoing critical inquiry into the
specific nature of Scott's political stance. That Scott was fascinated by social
and political history is well known. Critics have also focused on how Scott's
writings explore or project viewpoints, precedents and possibilities that touch
on, resonate with, or are triggered by issues connected with his immediate political involvements or concerns. However, I want to take this position further
and suggest that within the context of a Toryism that is consistently, if not constantly, evident in Scott's fiction, his position is that of a counter-revolutionary.

The exploration of this argument—and its ramifications—is best realized
through understanding the sophisticated nature of Scott's counter-revolutionary stance, as well as the historical and contemporaneous situations informing
that stance. It is further served by establishing an overarching framework that
involves concepts of reimaging, reconstruction and representation of political systems by means of which to consider Scott's reactionary position. In the
broad context of that framework, I suggest that exploring Scott's use of space
and place in his fiction exposes his adroit appropriation of locales to position
his political stance. While I contend that the Waverley Novels, by and large,
demonstrate Scott's counter-revolutionary leanings, there is especial value in
focusing on novels set during periods that grapple particularly with notions of
revolution, with the possibilities of alternative political institutions and governance being established in volatile times and environments, and that also
encompass the transition between monarchical dynasties. This reveals the fact
that in these novels exists a continuum of counter-revolution, one that offers a
cumulative critique of individual monarchs and their rules.

That Scott was politically conservative and a staunch Tory is widely
agreed, although debate about the extent and nature of that conservatism re-
curs throughout the critical assessment of his work.[1] Here I shall argue that

---

1 See, as examples, the following commentary on the nature of Scott's conservatism and political stance in the context of his writings (fiction, history, and political tracts) and his involvement in contemporaneous political activities: Anna Faktorovich's *Rebellion as Genre in the*

within the context of the Toryism and political conservatism so consistently, if not constantly, evident in Scott's fiction, he offers a sophisticated, counter-revolutionary interpretation of Britain past and present. However, if Scott develops a counter-revolutionary position throughout various novels in the Waverley canon, it is therefore useful to consider the following as a point of departure. Any definition of Scott as a counter-revolutionary has to begin by evaluating the nature of his political thought in relation to that of Burke.

Burkean discourse, as we know, underpinned and shaped the framework of conservative thinking from 1790 (when *Reflections on the Revolution in France* was first published). Not only did it influence Scott particularly, but the entire conservative debate was shaped by this tract.[2] Given Scott's known abhorrence of radicalism and its violent enthusiasms (and despite his own comfort with

---

Novels of Scott, Dickens and Stevenson (Jefferson, NC: McFarland, 2013); Katrin Berndt's 'Civic Virtues in the Restless Polity: Sir Walter Scott's Fergusonian vision of British civil society in *Redgauntlet* (1824),' *Studies in Eighteenth-Century Culture*, 41 (2012), 115–35; Samuel Baker's 'Scott's Worlds of War,' Tara Ghoshal Wallace's 'Monarchy and the Middle-Period Novels,' and Alexander Dick's 'Scott and Political Economy' in *The Edinburgh Companion to Sir Walter Scott*, ed. Fiona Robertson (Edinburgh: Edinburgh University Press, 2012), severally at 70–81, 106–17, and 118–30; Norman Arthur Fischer's 'The Modern Meaning of Georg Lukács' Reconstruction of Walter Scott's Novels of Premodern Political Ethics' in *Georg Lukács Reconsidered: Critical Essays in Politics, Philosophy and Aesthetics*, ed. Michael J. Thompson (London: Continuum, 2011), 128–50; Anthony Jarrells' chapter 'Bloodless Revolution and the Form of the Novel' in his *Britain's Bloodless Revolutions: 1688 and the Romantic Reform of Literature* (Basingstoke and New York: Palgrave Macmillan, 2005), 170–95; Caroline McCracken-Flesher's *Possible Scotlands: Walter Scott and the Story of Tomorrow* (Oxford: Oxford University Press, 2005); Thomas R. Mockaitis' 'Sir Walter Scott and the Problem of Revolutions' in *Scott in Carnival*, ed. J.H. Alexander and David Hewitt (Aberdeen: Association for Scottish Literature Studies, 1993), 419–33; Bruce Beiderwell's 'Romantic Enlightenment: Sir Walter Scott and the Politics of History,' *European Romantic Review*, 13 (September 2002), and David Hewitt's '*The Heart of Mid-Lothian* and "the People"' in *European Romantic Review*, 13 (September 2002), 299–309 and 223–4 respectively.

2   For further readings about Burkean discourse and his counter-revolutionary position, see specifically: Edmund Burke, 'Reflections on the Revolution in France,' *The Writings and Speeches of Edmund Burke, Volume VIII: The French Revolution 1790–1794*, ed. L.G. Mitchell (1998; rpt. Oxford: Oxford University Press, 2007), 53–293; David Bromwich's *The Intellectual Life of Edmund Burke: From the Sublime and Beautiful to American Independence* (Cambridge MA: Belknap Press Harvard, 2014); Ian Hampsher-Monk's 'Edmund Burke's Changing Justification for Intervention,' *The Historical Journal*, 48 (2005), 65–100; Yoon Sun Lee's *Nationalism and Irony: Burke, Scott, Carlyle* (Oxford: Oxford University Press, 2004); Bruce Mazlish's 'The Conservative Revolution of Edmund Burke,' *The Review of Politics*, 20 (1958), 21–3; and Jeff Spinner's 'Constructing Communities: Edmund Burke on Revolution,' *Polity*, 23 (1991), 395–421.

quelling rebellion by force), Burke's mythologizing of the Glorious Revolution as the non-violent and 'bloodless' revolution—emphatically distinct from the regicide and violence of the 1640s—would have held distinct appeal for Scott, committed as he was to the belief that measured societal progress towards a shared and unified future would effect lasting improvement of existing social conditions.

In the *Reflections*, Burke foresaw the French Revolution's disastrous transition into a military dictatorship, which occurred under Napoleon some two years after Burke's death. Burke's ongoing concern was that, unlike the American revolutionaries in their battle for freedom for all, or indeed the English in their peaceful transition to a new monarchy in the Glorious Revolution, the avowed principles of the French Revolution were not being realized, but rather corrupted. As a longstanding Whig, he rejected the notions of the divine right of kings and supported the populace's right to depose an oppressive government. Within this framework, however, he argued for gradual and sustained constitutional reform. His interest in abstract principles of government was disdainful and wary of the opportunity for corruption of these ideals in their application. He placed far greater credence in the embedment of the people's specific, concrete liberties and rights in the constitution to afford protection against monarchical and governmental oppression.

There is much in Burke's counter-revolutionary tract with which Scott had sympathy. Despite Burke's Whiggery and Scott's Toryism, both rejected the extreme radicalism they feared would corrupt the government of society and desolate society itself. While they differed in their thoughts on the role of the monarchy—with Scott being more convinced of the importance of the monarch as individual and as body politic than Burke—each supported gradual and sustained constitutional reform. Both were firmly opposed to the airy theoretical constructs of politics, preferring tangible, practical steps towards viable solutions to effect social benefit and progress. Yet while Scott looked, with Burke, across the Channel to the French Revolution, his counter-revolutionary position was also influenced by contemporary domestic political experiences and the debates associated with them. Of particular interest for Scott were the lingering tensions in Scotland and Ireland, and the Peterloo massacre in the post-French Revolutionary period—all associated with questions of sovereignty, nationalism and unification.[3]

---

3 Evan Gottlieb raises a number of pertinent points regarding the complexities inherent in and existing between Scottish and British nationalism in *Feeling British: Sympathy and National Identity in Scottish and English Writing, 1707–1832* (Lewisburg: Bucknell University Press, 2007). Julie Kipp also provides an analysis of Scott's responses to the tumultuous events

Unification as a means of simultaneously respecting national difference yet creating an umbrella of integrated progress for a nation is a constant theme in Scott's Waverley Novels, his political writings and his personal correspondence. Indeed, Scotland's entrance into the Union in 1707 served him as evidence of the apparent success of the notion that a separate state could simultaneously co-exist as a sovereign equal within a broader unification. This, as Leith Davis notes, was despite "Scotland's anomalous position after the Union as a nation without the political apparatus of nationhood".[4] Evan Gottlieb makes the further point that:

> [t]here are compelling historical reasons for inquiring after the literary and cultural formation of modern Britishness [...]. Beginning just before the Union and ending with the death of Walter Scott, the period 1707–1832 comprehends the construction of Anglo-British national identity from its modern inception to the passage of the First Reform Bill, after which the political constitution of Great Britain changed considerably.[5]

Scott, as an heir to David Hume and Adam Smith, could thus interpret the Act of Union as a means of transforming the long-disputed narrative regarding Scotland's independence from England.[6] However, in the 1790s, he viewed with increasing disquiet the emergence of the 'Friends of Reform' movement in Scotland (1793–94) and then the Irish Rebellion (1798). These events threatened his belief in the adoption of steady and sustained political—and thus societal—progress that explicitly informed his attempts to reconcile the merging of conflicting cultures and sometime combatants. Ireland's step towards political progress by entering the Union in 1801 was, for Scott, reassuring evidence of the success of unification and proof that "cultural distinctiveness might be celebrated and safeguarded within a broader unionist design".[7] However, two decades later, in 1819–20, he witnessed again widespread political agitation and fears concerning a populist rising. In Scotland rioting took place in the wake of

---

across England, Scotland and Ireland between the 1790s and 1820s in her 'Back to the Future: Walter Scott on the Politics of Radical Reform in Ireland and Scotland,' *European Romantic Review*, 16 (2005), 231–42.

4 Leith Davis, *Acts of Union: Scotland and the Literary Negotiation of the British Nation, 1707–1830* (Stanford, CA: Stanford University Press, 1996), 6–7.

5 Gottlieb, *Feeling British*, 15.

6 Hume, in his moderate and pragmatic assessment of Whig and Tory ideology and in his defence of prerogative, especially informed Scott's own Tory narrative, as Douglas S. Mack argues in *Scottish Fiction and the British Empire* (Edinburgh: Edinburgh University Press, 2006), 43–87.

7 Kipp, 'Back to the Future,' 233.

the Peterloo massacre in 1819, followed by the Radical War in 1820. In Ireland political resentment regarding restrictions on the right to assemble and the refusal of George III to grant Catholic Emancipation continued to smoulder in various forms, with the uprising of the populace an ongoing fear. In Scott's opinion, the principles of the Enlightenment such as societal progress and organic constitutional reform being premised on the rational advancement of the common good were again being co-opted and corrupted by radical reformers in both Scotland and Ireland just as they had been in the 1790s. Thus the historical narrative to which he was committed was under increasing stress.

Scott's fears concerning radical associations, now in Ireland, Scotland and England herself, were played out in his counter-revolutionism insofar as that appears both in his fiction and his non-fiction (it appears as well, of course, in his correspondence and his desire to be involved in defending the peace in Scotland). He remained committed to achieving and maintaining a pragmatic peace, despite the strength and attraction of Scots-Irish radical alliances at that time. As Julie Kipp points out:

> Scott liked to turn in this way to the Highlands as a testament to history's unfolding linear narrative: remember that things have been worse and that they will eventually be better. Peace and tranquility become the markers of a more mature stage of historical development as well as proving to be a key factor in economic stability.[8]

This classical liberal position of Scott's underpinned, of course, his belief in a narrative of historical advancement, a view of societal progress occurring harmoniously, whereby separate cultures and identities could be encompassed in a greater whole without divisiveness or irreconcilable conflict.

In the context of what has been outlined above—chiefly, the idea that Scott's counter-revolutionism existed within, was associated with, yet was not merely identical to, his political conservatism and Toryism—I want to emphasize the concept of a 'pragmatic nationalism.' By that I mean "a nationalism that, far from being impracticably sentimental, did not so much yield concessions as accept realities in order to sustain a Scottish cultural identity within the broader British context".[9] As Gottlieb states, "Scott may fantasize about the possibilities for Scottish independence had the Stuart house been restored to

---

8   Ibid., 237.

9   I am indebted to A.D. Cousins, not only for the term and definition of 'pragmatic nationalism' (in private communication), but for the development of my argument regarding the nature of Scott's counter-revolutionary position as a result of the generous sharing of his insights and scholarship.

the British throne, [but] he nevertheless pledges a rational allegiance to the current Hanoverian line".[10] In relation to that concept I shall argue the following: Scott's portrayal of the institutions as well as social practices of law and justice operating in various past eras is the means by which he explores various governing mechanisms and the political threats to them—to social stability, the enactment of justice, and so on—generated by the fact or possibility of revolution. In short, I suggest that in his historical fiction, within the broader context of but somewhat removed from his Tory sympathies and political conservatism, lies a sophisticated and sustained counter-revolutionary position that has not as yet been adequately identified or interpreted.

Scott is thus not at all to be regarded as a cardboard cut-out reactionary, one-dimensional in the regurgitation of specious and sweeping political platitudes. Rather, his counter-revolutionary position is both wary and qualified, seeking to grapple with the subtleties arising from the political, societal and financial changes affecting Britain (that is, England and Scotland), both historically and at the time of his writing. To illuminate more distinctly what I take to be Scott's nuanced counter-revolutionism, I want now to consider his tactics for representation of the monarchy and of the various political alternatives once proposed to it.

An illuminating approach to Scott's counter-revolutionary thought in the Waverley Novels is offered by Kevin Sharpe's study of how political authority was imaged from Tudor to Hanoverian times.[11] This timescale frames the Glorious Revolution, which is intrinsic to the Burkean mythology of counter-revolution. Sharpe contends that the image of political regimes was created through the notion of performance of rulership, that is (for example), by means of poetry, prose, paintings, speeches, rituals, ceremonies, homilies and pageantry. Thus, the power of images was an intrinsic and critical factor in establishing, legitimizing and sustaining political authority. He focuses on the relative successes and failures of both the Stuart monarchy (and specific Stuart monarchs) and the Protectorate to position and shore up their respective images and actual relationships with the populace over whom they governed and from whom they sought to gain dynastic legitimacy. Sharpe identifies a number of legitimating discourses at work across this period, and enables the

---

10   Gottlieb, *Feeling British*, 173.

11   See: Kevin Sharpe, *Selling the Tudor Monarchy: Authority and Image in Sixteenth-Century England* (New Haven and London, 2009); *Image Wars: Promoting Kings and Commonwealths in England, 1603–1660* (New Haven and London: Yale University Press, 2010); and *Rebranding Rule: The Restoration and Revolution Monarchy, 1660–1714* (New Haven and London: Yale University Press, 2013).

recognition of Scott's use of many of these in the Waverley Novels as a means of exploring the political regimes he scrutinizes.

Although a more detailed analysis of the Stuart-Hanoverian transition occurs in a later chapter, the centrality of the Stuarts and the Hanoverians to the argument of this book necessitates an outlining of some important features of the respective dynasties and consideration—in light of Sharpe's research—of what Scott sought to interpret and defend. There was, of course, an ideological divide between the two royal dynasties. Whereas the Stuarts were Scottish and Catholic-affiliated, the Hanoverians were German and Protestant. Religion was then indisputably a cornerstone of monarchy. Hence, Catholic sympathies were an inescapably problematic issue to be managed by the Stuarts, given that Protestant orthodoxy, spiritual leadership and personal piety were fundamental to any British monarchical authority. The obvious alignment of Catholicism (and not it alone, as we know) with foreign regimes and their political interests made this aspect of governance especially difficult to position and thence to image appropriately. Similarly, the court with which a monarch surrounded himself was an extension of that individual as body politic. This proved difficult for the Stuarts, as Scott indicates, with their particular fondness for the Villiers family, most notably the two Dukes of Buckingham whose morals, behaviours and amatory affairs drew so much and so often hostile attention. A key concern was, then, the ability of a monarch to master and manage "the need at one and the same time for distance and popularity".[12] This is another aspect of monarchical image, as identified by Sharpe, that Scott likewise focuses on. The ability to marry suitable distance with appropriate accessibility, inspiring awe while maintaining the 'common touch,' was something each of the Stuart monarchs struggled with—not least, perhaps, because of the earlier Stuart adherence to the notion of kingship by divine right.

One must, however, see this latter concern as metonymic of a larger one. Scott was intrigued by how various monarchs sought to establish, consolidate and legitimate authority in dynamic politico-religious environments that were effecting widespread social instability. Here we might focus again on the Stuarts. Despite his penchant for representing his monarchical claims via the theatre of the court, James' general preference for written rather than visual representation of his authority led to some diminution of acknowledgment of his kingliness (as indeed did his personal habits and the activities—or proclivities—of his court).[13] Scott considers these aspect of James' rule

---

12   Sharpe, *Image Wars*, 280.

13   See: Sharpe, *Image Wars*, 58–60 for his discussion on James' preference for literary forms of representation; and Chapter 3 '"Masquing" the Body Politic of Britain' and Chapter 4

in one of his novels, in which he also assesses Charles as heir to the throne. It is not surprising, in the context of building positive images of the monarchy, that Scott places only one of his novels during the reign of Charles I— and that Charles is not the focus but rather part of the setting of this novel. After the fall of Charles, Sharpe contends, Cromwell assumed many of the "regal cultural forms" of traditional authority including "modes of language, visual representations and public performances that made [him] appear quasi-monarchical".[14] Scott also considers this imagery in the context of Cromwell's longing for and reluctance to assume kingship in the one Scott novel in which both Cromwell and a young Charles II are foregrounded. Further, Sharpe notes that Cromwellian imagery involved appropriating rather than replacing motifs and significances. Scott, to his anger and dismay, saw the same technique being used by the radical reformers in Scotland and Ireland to convince the populace of the authenticity of their cause.

It is interesting to consider how Sharpe and Scott share their similar fascination with Charles II. Scott, in a pair of novels, considers Charles II in two lights: directly as a monarch-in-waiting with nascent authority; and specifically as a royal authority after 1660. Of particular interest here is that fact that neither Sharpe nor Scott engages in detailed consideration of how the Scots or Irish portrayed Charles II, focusing rather on his representations and images in England. Charles II's image, Sharpe argues, was primarily recreated by Tories during his reign and after, which is of course exactly what happens in Scott's novels involving Charles II, given Scott's own politics. James II's image was also constructed positively during his monarchy, but was thereafter revisited by the Whigs who questioned both the legitimacy and, indeed, the divine right of his kingship once his period of rule had ended. Understandably, although Scott sets fifteen of his Waverley Novels between the reigns of James I and George III, none of them is set during James II's rule. Upon William and Mary's ascending the English throne (she being notionally a Stuart via her father, James I), two sets of images of monarchy were being positioned throughout the country. While Whig supporters sought to create an authentic image of monarchical legitimacy for the new king and queen, Jacobites drew heavily on the historical legitimacy of the (unadulterated) Stuart dynasty. Tangentially

---

'Landscaping the Body Politic of the British State' of Kenneth R. Olwig's *Landscape, Nature, and the Body Politic: From Britain's Renaissance to America's New World* (Madison: University of Wisconsin Press, 2002), 62–79, 80–98 respectively, which argue that James' use of landscape in the theatre to position the sovereign body politic as a geopolitical ideal in unifying Scotland and England was a more effective mechanism than his writings.

14   Sharpe, *Image Wars*, 467.

Scott considers the ramifications of the rival images co-existing in two novels set after the Glorious Revolution during William and Mary's rule. Sharpe argues that Queen Anne, as the last ruling Stuart, sought to create an image in a world where monarchical imagery fashioned on behalf of the crown was no longer automatically and unquestioningly consumed. As much as she was able in this situation, she located herself as ruling by God's will but aware of the nature of her position as a constitutional monarch. This movement from centrality of influence over Britain is replicated in the ancillary role of Anne in the one novel Scott sets during her reign.

In this broader context, it is interesting to note Scott's interest in the specific use of portraiture, which reflects Sharpe's views about the links between portraiture and power. It is, for Scott, an ongoing means of enhancing characterizations in his novels—through his descriptions of portrait paintings and his own detailed depiction of various monarchs and important, related characters. This is of particular value when one seeks to position monarchical images and their respective causes—current and retrospective—within the broader significances of the physical, political and social landscapes of the novels. Sharpe's scholarship, therefore, helps clarify how Scott represents royalty.[15]

A major aspect of my argument in what follows is that Scott's imaging and re-branding of monarchy (and thus the two monarchies and various monarchs) is effected by his use of landscape, space and place. Sharpe's work, in other words, encourages us to read, in light of recent theories of 'place' and 'space,' how Scott's counter-revolutionism relates to questions of justice, law and the notion of monarchy itself. With that in mind, I am concerned with how Scott consciously makes use of a long tradition of developing image and brand through built environments and changes to the landscape. This general issue has long been the focus of architectural, political and cultural historians. Penny Fielding, in her work on literary and artistic interpretations of regionality, comments on "acts of curation that imagine strong connections between art, local history and geography," suggesting that to "think of a region as 'curated' opens up questions of how it is delimited, and how its contours are shaped".[16] In this vein, Scott's use of place(s) and space(s) enables him to produce his own interpretation of the mutability of the individual monarch and

---

15   It is unfortunate that Sharpe's work concludes with the ascension of the Hanoverians to the throne of England. His commentary would no doubt have added much to our understanding of those seven novels wherein Scott dealt with the period of Hanoverian dynastic rule.

16   Penny Fielding, 'Curated Regions of the North: Art and Literature in the "Scottish Border" and the "Transpennine Corridor,"' *Visual Culture in Britain*, 15 (2014), 159.

the monarchy's status. In his novels, I shall argue, these concepts are crucially contextualized by place: landscape and setting transmit vital political meaning to the story. Place is surely one of the most consistently important elements of the Waverley canon. Indeed, along with identifying other techniques and rhetoric favoured by Scott, the commentary across *The Edinburgh Edition of the Waverley Novels* draws attention to Scott's use of place to emphasize particular aspects of the hero or heroine's journey towards justice effected by the respective monarch, and to the importance of place and politics in Scott's act of writing.[17] As Tony Inglis, J.H. Alexander, David Hewitt and Alison Lumsden point out, Scott, in his *Journal*, details his experience of writing as being

> just the same case as I used to be when I lost myself in former days in some country to which I was a stranger—I always pushed for the pleasantest road and either found or made it the nearest [...] it is a perilous stile I grant but I cannot help [it]—when I chain my mind to ideas that are purely imaginative—for arguments are a different thing—it seems to me that the sun leaves the landscape, that I think away the whole vivacity and spirit of my original conception, and the results are cold, tame and spiritless.[18]

---

17   See, for example: Frank Jordan's 'Essay on the Text' in Walter Scott's *The Fortunes of Nigel*, ed. Frank Jordan (Edinburgh: Edinburgh University Press, 2004), 415–6, where Scott's revisions to the manuscript to emphasize the atmosphere and significance of specific locales are examined; P.D. Garside's tracing of Scott's travels through the Scottish Highlands and the evolution of the *Waverley* manuscript in 'Essay on the Text,' specifically 371, 372 and 377, and his analysis of the myriad topographies in 'Historical Note,' 509–14, in Walter Scott's *Waverley*, ed. P.D. Garside (Edinburgh: Edinburgh University Press, 2007); and G.A.M. Wood and David Hewitt's comments on the 'personal' nature of *Redgauntlet* for Scott and the links to his own life, including characters and locales: "his education in law and preparation for the bar in 1789–92; his tour of Cumbria and the Lakes in August 1797 when he met his wife; and his visit to Dumfries in 1807" in 'Essay on the Text' in Walter Scott, *Redgauntlet*, ed. G.A.M Wood and David Hewitt (Edinburgh: Edinburgh University Press, 1997), 382.

18   Scott quoted in Inglis, et al. 'Essay on the Text,' *Woodstock*, 430. Tony Inglis, J.H. Alexander, David Hewitt and Alison Lumsden comment on Scott's use of landscape as metaphor with regards his memories and processes of writing in their 'Essay on the Text' in Walter Scott's *Woodstock*, 419 and 430; Alison Lumsden's 'Historical Note' in Walter Scott's *Peveril of the Peak*, 612–7 considers specifically the significance of topography throughout the novel; Alison Lumsden and David Hewitt's 'Essay on the Text,' *The Heart of Mid-Lothian*, 474–5 focuses on the physical environment of Edinburgh and its redesign being an inspiration for Scott.

Similarly, Kenneth M. Sroka notes that "[i]n Scott's fiction generally, places are valuable in themselves as literal, palpable realities. They are important too as symbols of stability, inheritance, and the endurance of familial and national tradition amid the turmoil of personal and public change".[19]

It is hardly surprising that several recent critics have focused on the role and importance of place in Scott. Through the concept of place—often realized through specifically and laboriously described locales—Scott introduces social conflicts and issues, develops character and plot, and links the past with the present within his novels.[20] Furthermore, Scott's choice of locales and the significance with which he imbues them are frequently pivotal to his exploration of the broader political and cultural issues in his novels. My suggestion here is precisely that the use of spatial theory can shed light on many of the mechanisms by which Scott seeks to rehabilitate the various sovereigns, and thus delineate his counter-revolutionary stance within a number of the Waverley Novels.[21]

Here I want to focus on a number of overarching concepts that provide a useful entry point to the discussion in this book about Scott's use of place,

19 Kenneth M. Sroka, 'Fairy Castles and Character in Woodstock,' *Essays in Literature*, 14 (Fall 1987), 190.

20 The following concepts of place are useful. Martin Heidegger theorizes that "[t]he idea of place [...] is not [...] the idea of that in which entities are merely 'located;' rather [...] place is that open, cleared, yet bounded region in which we find ourselves gathered together with other persons and things, and in which we are opened up to the world and the world to us" (Jeff Malpas, *Heidegger's Topology: Being, Place, World* (Cambridge: MIT Press, 2007) 221). With regard to the notion of locale, I find the reference to and emphasis on the Latin term *locus* by Hubbard, Kitchin and Valentine, and by Janice Hewlett Koelb useful in that it acknowledges the dual significance of "a physical place and an intellectual position or outlook (both position and outlook of course are spatial metaphors)" (See Phil Hubbard, Rob Kitchin and Gill Valentine, eds. *Key Thinkers on Space and Place*, 2nd edition (London: Sage, 2011), 6, and Janice Hewlett Koelb. *The Poetics of Description: Imagined Places in European Literature* (New York: Palgrave Macmillan, 2006), 12).

21 Reference to the texts of Scott's novels is from *The Edinburgh Edition of the Waverley Novels* 30 vols, ed. David Hewitt (Edinburgh: Edinburgh University Press, 1993–2015). References from these editions of the novels are included in the text as follows: *The Fortunes of Nigel*, hereafter (*Nigel*), *Woodstock*, hereafter (*Woodstock*), *Peveril of the Peak*, hereafter (*Peveril*), *The Heart of Mid-Lothian*, hereafter (*Mid-Lothian*), *Waverley*, hereafter (*Waverley*), *Redgauntlet*, hereafter (*Redgauntlet*), with the citation of page numbers. Reference to Scott's 'Tales of a Grandfather' is from *The Prose Works of Sir Walter Scott* (Edinburgh: Robert Caddell, 1836), hereafter ('Tales'); to his journal is from *The Journal of Sir Walter Scott* (New York: Burt Franklin, 1890), hereafter (*Journal*) and to his letters is from *Letters of Sir Walter Scott*. 12 vols, ed. H.J.C. Grierson (London: Constable, 1932–37), hereafter (*Letters*).

spatial perception, embodiment and the built environment. My starting point is Edward S. Casey's phenomenological approach to space and place, which relates to how our embodied existence is located in place and is explored through the Bachelardian concept of 'topoanalysis'—the concept of memories of a place and its various parts being not something merely remembered but rather entwined with the ongoing experience of that place.[22] Casey is focused on locating topoanalysis through the relationship between the body and place. His placement of individuals within the broader experience of place—meaning our experience is embedded in place, rather than space or time—is a valuable way to approach how Scott explores the relationship between characters (including the monarch as both individual and body politic) and the significances of various locales in his novels. Similarly, Casey's illustration of how buildings intrinsically incorporate nature, and his study of gardens as a form intermediate between built place and natural place, is useful when exploring Scott's representations of familial and monarchical history through dwellings, gardens and the surrounding landscapes. Valuable too is Casey's focus on undiscovered and transitional parts of buildings and their relationships to their surrounds. This notion is used by Scott as a means of exploring the spirit of places and the complementary, rather than dichotomizing, effects of the relationship between the dwelling and the immediate landscape surrounding it. While it is, of course, tempting to limit the analysis of space and place in Scott to one theorist, interpreting the novels through several different spatial theorists allows the illumination of the novel's representations of place and space—and hence, the diversity in Scott's registering of those phenomena—via a range of recent theoretical insights (given the theoretical investigations of the last several decades). Thus, although I begin with reference to Casey's work, I subsequently investigate how other spatial theorists also serve to illuminate Scott's fictions.

Considerable critical analysis has been focused, as has been mentioned above, on the myriad significances of place in the Waverley canon, which spans centuries, continents and cultures. For a number of reasons, however, it is valuable to focus specifically on those Waverley Novels set in the reigns of the Stuart and Hanoverian monarchies, and which concentrate specifically on the role of the monarch (or his representative) in effecting both individual

---

22   See: Edward S. Casey's *Getting Back into Place: Toward a Renewed Understanding of the Place-World* (Bloomington: Indiana University Press, 1993) and *The Fate of Place: A Philosophical History* (Berkeley, Los Angeles and London: University of California Press, 1998). For a more detailed discussion of place in this capacity, see Gaston Bachelard's *Poetics of Space: The Classic Look at How We Experience Intimate Places*, trans. Maria Jolas (1969; rpt Boston: Beacon Press, 1994).

justice and social order across the united Scotland and England. It is in these novels that the subtleties and challenges of Scott's counter-revolutionary position are most comprehensively explored, both in isolation and collectively. This is especially true if one considers that Scott's stance is realized not only by the rehabilitation of the Stuarts and the endorsement of the Hanoverians, but also via the transition from the one monarchy to the other. *The Fortunes of Nigel* (1822), *Woodstock* (1826), *Peveril of the Peak* (1823), *The Heart of Mid-Lothian* (1818), *Waverley* (1814) and *Redgauntlet* (1824) are therefore crucial novels to consider, for throughout these six novels Scott conducts a rehabilitation of both the Stuart and Hanoverian dynasties, the constant re-affirmation of which constitutes a staunchly counter-revolutionary critique.[23] Certainly they are not the only novels in which Scott focuses on Stuart monarchs or regents, or posits a qualified, careful support of that dynasty while wrestling with an awareness of the inherent flaws contributing to its political demise. However, in *The Abbot* (1820) and *The Monastery*, (1820) both set in sixteenth-century Scotland and thus prior to the union of Scotland and England, Scott confines his analysis of notions of rightful sovereignty and justice to Stuart rulership in Scotland alone. Nor are *The Fortunes of Nigel, Woodstock, Peveril of the Peak, The Heart of Mid-Lothian, Waverley* and *Redgauntlet* the only novels in which he adopts an inherently counter-revolutionary position; such a position is integral to most, if not all, of the Waverley canon. But these six together provide a historical landscape in which various forms of political instability and unrest—republicanism, restoration, riots and rebellions—occur, against which Scott can assemble a coherent political argument.[24]

---

23   *Rob Roy* (1817) takes place during the sovereignty of the House of Hanover, against the backdrop of the Jacobite Rebellion of 1715, and it is distinctly similar to *Waverley* and *Redgauntlet*, most notably tracing the journey of a young English protagonist to the Borders where fanatical Jacobites plot the return of the Stuart monarchy. However, the significance of the royal presence is not central to the novel, nor does the sovereign body politic or its representative effect any major instance of natural justice, as occurs in *Waverley* and *Redgauntlet*. Hence, it has not been included in the novels I am addressing as primary texts.

24   There is, of course, a not insignificant lacuna in the Waverley canon. Scott, drawing on a broad expanse of history and the associated monarchs (from the Byzantine Empire in 1096 when *Count Robert of Paris* (1832) is set, to nineteenth-century England in *St Ronan's Well* (1824)), chooses not to attempt a novel in which Charles I or James II play a central role. Even the most optimistic of counter-revolutionaries would quail at the idea of attempting to re-frame either of these monarch's rules as beneficent (regardless of Scott's opinion of Charles I's or James II's personal characteristics), and this attempt would significantly compromise the more successful, if not unequivocal, rehabilitation of James I, Charles II, Caroline, George II (both implicitly and overtly), and George III on whom this analysis

   Although I will be focusing primarily on those six novels, there are a number
of others to which I will of course refer for elucidation by way of comparison
and contrast. These include the novels Scott set between the reigns of James
I and George III. As Alison Lumsden points out, Scott "had been immersed in
the seventeenth century for much of his writing career [... and had] visited the
period of the Civil Wars in a Scottish context in *The Tale of Old Mortality* (1816)
and as a backdrop to *The Heart of Mid-Lothian* (1818)".[25] In addition, *A Legend
of Montrose* (1819) is set in Charles I's reign, *The Bride of Lammermoor* (1819)
and *The Pirate* (1822) after the Glorious Revolution under William and Mary,
The Black Dwarf (1816) under Anne, *Rob Roy* (1817) in George I's reign, and *Guy
Mannering* (1815), *The Antiquary* (1816) and *St Ronan's Well* (1824) in George
III's.[26] Several of these are concerned with monarchic legitimacy and the legitimate exercise of monarchic power. Nevertheless, as I shall demonstrate, the
six Waverley Novels that focus on the British monarch, resident in England and
effecting justice from there, best demonstrate the scope and cohesiveness of
Scott's counter-revolutionary views.
   The Fortunes of Nigel considers the nature of James VI and I's intervention
in the restoration of a Scottish subject's estate in the latter, troubled years of
his reign over England. *Woodstock* explores the role of the fugitive monarch,
Charles II, in the healing of bitter Cavalier and Roundhead divisions during the
final years of the Commonwealth. *Peveril of the Peak* takes as its subject Charles
II's capacity for achieving justice for an English subject caught in the hysteria surrounding the Popish Plot of 1678.[27] *The Heart of Mid-Lothian* considers
the intervention of Caroline, as George II's regent, in the injustices of the laws

------

focuses. Cf. Fiona Robertson, *Legitimate Histories: Scott, Gothic, and the Authorities of
Fiction* (Oxford: Clarendon Press, 1994), 230. Throughout the discussion I make use of Ernst
Hartwig Kantorowicz's concepts of 'political theology' and of the 'King's two bodies'—the
body politic and the body natural—as outlined in his *The King's Two Bodies: A Study in
Mediaeval Political Theology* (Princeton, New Jersey: Princeton University Press, 1957).

25   'Essay on the Text,' *Peveril of the Peak*, ed. Alison Lumsden (Edinburgh: Edinburgh University Press, 2007), 498.

26   Scott's original title for this was *A Legend of the Wars of Montrose*, but it was altered in the
face of both Constable and Ballantyne's dislike to *A Legend of Montrose*. The Edinburgh
Edition of the novel (Edinburgh: Edinburgh University Press, 1995) edited by J.H. Alexander reinstates Scott's first title.

27   Stuart Kelly notes that these three novels—*The Fortunes of Nigel*, *Woodstock* and *Peveril
of the Peak* in "chart[ing] the reigns of James VI and I, the Commonwealth and Charles
II [...] concentrate on the emerging 'British' identity [...] and are united by concerns
over London's financial supremacy and underground criminality; the moral laxity of the
court; the persisting divisions between Parliamentarians and Royalist, Roundheads and
Cavaliers, Catholics and Protestants. They also explore the relationship of the regions

operating within Scotland during the Porteous Riots of 1736. *Waverley*, set in the second Jacobite Rebellion of 1745, juxtaposes George II and Charles Edward Stuart, bringing George II into indirect view through Edward Waverley's royal pardon. *Redgauntlet*, surely Scott's ultimate counter-revolutionary novel, juxtaposes the presence of both the Stuart and Hanoverian sovereign bodies politic with the physical presence of Charles Edward Stuart's natural body and the absence of George III's during the (fictitious) rebellion of 1765 during that monarchy's reign.

Taken together, these novels cover nearly 150 years of English history and present a continuum of counter-revolutionary and politically conservative interpretations of history. Each novel posits its own representations of—and unique arguments supporting—the presiding monarch, but there is especial value in considering the dialogue between Scott's counter-revolutionary arguments and positions in the different novels, and their continuities with, and variations from, each other. Comparing and contrasting the six works shows how Scott saw his themes playing out in each king's reign, while also forming a larger, coherent and cumulative argument spanning the period as a whole.

Frederick Burwick usefully draws attention to Scott's focus on this period of history in these novels:

> The novels were published during the years that saw the fall of Napoleon and the restoration of the Bourbon kings in France, events that had political reverberations throughout Europe. They were also events that strangely echoed that era of British history which Scott made the subject of seven of the twenty-seven novels. One hundred and forty years before the French Revolution, Britain had experienced a revolution of its own. Charles I, of the Scottish House of Stuart, was beheaded in 1649; Oliver Cromwell ruled as military dictator for the ensuing decade. Following the restoration of Charles II in 1660, many of the old conflicts between the Church of England and the Puritans and other dissenting factions persisted. The British had a sense of historical *déjà vu* in witnessing the events unfolding in France, [including Louis XVI's beheading in 1793, Napoleon's ascendancy, Louis XVIII's restoration and the aftermath]. Scott's novels exploit that *déjà vu* and give emphasis to frictions between Scotland and England.[28]

(Derbyshire, Oxfordshire, the Isle of Man) to the capital and the idea of the court" (Stuart Kelly, *Scott-Land: The Man Who Invented a Nation* (Edinburgh: Polygon, 2010), 174).

28   Frederick Burwick, 'Competing Histories in the Waverley Novels,' *European Romantic Review*, 13 (September 2002), 262.

I am not suggesting that Scott wrote these novels deliberately to present an integrated, historically consecutive and authorially coordinated argument. For a start, he wrote them in a different order from that in which I have placed them, interspersed with other novels written and published in this period of tumultuous political activity. *Waverley*, the astronomical literary success that simultaneously captured the public's interest in the past and redefined the very nature of the novel as genre, was published anonymously in 1814. *The Heart of Mid-Lothian* (1818) was Scott's seventh Waverley novel, *The Fortunes of Nigel* (1822) his fifteenth, *Peveril of the Peak* (1823) his sixteenth, *Redgauntlet* (1824) his nineteenth and *Woodstock* (1826) his twenty-second.

I believe there is significant value in deliberately departing from considering the novels in their chronological order of publication and exploring them rather in the sequential order of their historical settings. This enables one to acknowledge and draw attention to issues germane to the order of their writing as they arise, while considering overarching themes of image, portraiture and what I am calling a pragmatic nationalism. These novels consistently endorse the monarchy, effecting, exploring, and embellishing that endorsement in myriad ways.[29] Considering each in turn, I want to explore the different ways in which Scott suffused these with (the generally) positive implications of the two monarchical dynasties and thus his counter-revolutionary politics.

Following this procedure, I shall thus present the overarching argument in this volume, namely, that Scott develops a cumulative, but highly critical and inherently qualified, counter-revolutionary critique throughout these six novels that moves from portraying the personal involvement of the monarch's natural body and body politic so as to effect justice, to portrayal of the sovereign's instituting a degree of social stability that no longer requires the royal presence in order for justice to be effected.[30]

---

29   On the same premise, as Caroline McCracken-Flesher also notes, at least one reviewer has bemoaned the order in which *The Black Dwarf* (1816) and *Old Mortality* (also 1816) were published: "There is [...] a defect in their arrangement, for *The Black Dwarf* refers to the state of Scotland in the reign of Queen Anne, while *Old Mortality* speak of its condition during the struggles by the Presbyterians in favour of 'the solemn league and covenant,' in the latter end of the reign of Charles II. For this reason, we wish that the order had been reversed—that as far any difference exists, not only the historical transactions, but the manners and habits of the people might have been displayed chronologically" ('*The Black Dwarf* and *Old Mortality*: Unsigned Review (1816)' in John O. Hayden's *Scott: The Critical Heritage* (London: Routledge and Kegan Paul, 1970), 107). See also McCracken-Flesher's 'Scott's Jacobitical Plots,' *The Edinburgh Companion to Sir Walter Scott*, ed. Fiona Robertson (Edinburgh: Edinburgh University Press, 2012), 47–58.

30   Of the wealth of critical commentary on Scott and issues of historicity, law and justice, Georg Lukács' *The Historical Novel* (London: Merlin Press, 1989) is seminal with E. Garcia

In the subsequent chapters, my argument will unfold in this way:

Chapter 1 focuses on notions of compromised authority and of confinement in *The Fortunes of Nigel* and *Woodstock*, applying concepts from Edward W. Said's work that are still viable (primarily from *Culture and Imperialism* but also *Orientalism*) and from David Sibley's *Geographies of Exclusion: Society and Difference in the West*.[31] This chapter focuses on the roles and historical significances of two very different Stuart monarchs, James I and Charles II. James' reign precedes the tumultuous and revolutionary times of Charles I's downfall and regicide. Charles II seeks to establish his sovereignty in a society still unreconciled to Charles I's beheading, and teetering between revolution and counter-revolution. In this chapter I suggest that, despite the many differences between the two novels, Scott uses various notions and representations of 'otherness' to explore the role of the monarchy.

In *The Fortunes of Nigel*, the multi-layered and multi-faceted representation of Scotland as an essentially 'other' place, in Saidian terms, facilitates Scott's cautious approval of James and his reign. In *Woodstock* and at Woodstock, Scott's depiction of the relationships existing among the various Royalist, Parliamentarian and Independent characters, and their respective and negative representations of each other as spiritually 'other' in that limited environment (and here I use Sibley), expresses his argument in support of Charles' restoration to the English throne. Scott is preoccupied in both novels with the centrality of authority. In *The Fortunes of Nigel*, he considers the notion of compromised authority, and by doing so establishes the qualified nature of his support for James as a Stuart and as a monarch. In *Woodstock*, Scott juxtaposes Charles' compromised authority with other, more defiled forms of authority present during the Interregnum, and thus presents Charles' sovereignty as at least having superior potential to those alternatives. Notions of 'otherness' and of authority therefore inform and preface Scott's engagement with Jacobean and Caroline history, acting as a critical, if not immediately explicit, way to interpret and assess Scott's counter-revolutionary representations of history in both novels.

Diaz's recent 'An Overview of Justice in Sir Walter Scott's Waverley Novels: *The Heart of Mid-Lothian*,' *Oñati Socio-legal Series* [online], 4 (2014), 1167–72 being especially useful in its consideration of specific issues of justice affecting both Scotland and England in *The Heart of Mid-Lothian*. Stuart Ferguson's argument in 'The Imaginative Construction of Historical Character: What Georg Lukács and Walter Scott Could Tell Contemporary Novelists,' *Scottish Studies Review*, 6 (Autumn 2005), 32–48 analyses various Scott characters in the context of Lukács' theories and concepts of historical consciousness.

31 See: Edward W. Said, *Orientalism* (London: Penguin, 1995) and *Culture and Imperialism* (New York: Vintage Books, 1994); David Sibley's *Geographies of Exclusion: Society and Difference in the West* (London and New York: Routledge, 1995).

The concept of locale, as formulated in Jeff Malpas' *Place and Experience: A Philosophical Topography*, is fundamental to Chapter 2 and the analysis of governance and agency in *Woodstock* and *Peveril of the Peak*.[32] Although it may appear that Scott uses locale very differently in these two novels, I suggest that there are intrinsic similarities in its uses to depict experiences of governance and of sovereignty. In *Woodstock* the action takes place primarily in Woodstock itself; in *Peveril of the Peak* the protagonist, Julian Peveril, traverses a number of locales—the Isle of Man, London, Newgate and Martindale—in his quest for justice. But in both novels Scott realizes his argument supporting the restoration of Charles II through his representation of locale and of the various experiences of governance and sovereignty embedded in each locale. My argument draws on three Malpasian concepts: topographical surveying as a metaphor and as a framework for exploring locales; the significance of 'nesting' or the embedding of smaller locales within larger ones; and the importance of considering locale in the context of embodiment. Through these concepts of regional mapping, nesting and embodiment, Scott juxtaposes failed and successful sites of governance and sovereignty, and in doing so positions Charles II as the embodiment of natural justice in both novels.

Iris Marion Young's work on oppression provides the framework for the discussion in Chapter 3 which centres on concepts of oppression, justice and monarchy in *Peveril of the Peak* and *The Heart of Mid-Lothian*.[33] These are by no means the only Waverley Novels to chart a heroic protagonist's quest culminating in the monarch's effecting justice.[34] However, these two novels are of particular interest because, viewed one after the other in terms of their historical settings, they allow us to compare Scott's representation of the late Stuart and early Hanoverian monarchies. Young's framework of the "five faces of oppression" (exploitation, marginalization, powerlessness, cultural imperialism and violence) and her "conceptualizations of spatio-temporal relations" illuminate how Scott positions his counter-revolutionary argument to incorporate both dynasties and the shortcomings of the individual monarchs in *Peveril of the Peak* and *The Heart of Mid-Lothian*.[35] This enables him to assign primary responsibility for the various oppressions portrayed in the novels to the court, to

---

32 See: Jeff Malpas, *Place and Experience: A Philosophical Topography* (Cambridge: Cambridge University Press, 1999).

33 See: Iris Marion Young, *Justice and the Politics of Difference* (Princeton: Princeton University Press, 1990).

34 Other Waverley Novels in which the monarch is personally engaged in effecting a form of justice include *The Fortunes of Nigel*, *Woodstock*, *The Abbot*, and *Ivanhoe* (1820).

35 Felicity Callard. 'Iris Marion Young,' *Key Thinkers on Space and Place*, 484, 485.

institutions of (supposed) justice, or to the revolutionary elements of society. Ultimately it also enables his adroit rehabilitation of both monarchies, Stuart and Hanoverian.

Chapter 4, with its focus on landscaping justice and politics in *The Heart of Mid-Lothian*, *Waverley* and *Redgauntlet*, explores those three novels, drawing from Kenneth R. Olwig's exploration of the use of landscape to position the sovereign body politic as a geopolitical ideal, which enables us to analyse how Scott represents Scotland and England under successive Hanoverian monarchs. This chapter focuses primarily on the nexus of landscape, politics and sovereignty. It is valuable to consider how Scott, in *The Heart of Mid-Lothian*, constructs a positive representation of the sovereign body politic as landscape in two locales, Richmond and Knocktarlitie. Moreover, Scott positions both places as sites of natural justice premised on Tory notions of landscape. In doing this, Scott reconciles the fraught political relationship between England and Scotland which is presented—at one level—as a conflict between natural and customary law. It is then useful to explore Scott's representations, both artistic and political, of rebellion as failure, which he does through specific characters, dynasties and landscapes in *Waverley* and *Redgauntlet*. Olwig's notion of landscape functioning as the monarch's body geographical is especially valuable in relation to this, for it is through concepts of space, place and geography that Scott depicts the dwindling importance of the Stuart sovereign body politic, and thus the Hanoverian monarchy's consolidation of its political stature and stability. While Olwig's study is, as he himself says, "a historical geography of ideas, mentalities, and narrations," I suggest that *Waverley* and *Redgauntlet* each contain a *geographical history* of those various 'ideas, mentalities, and narrations' that affirm the futility of rebellion.[36]

In exploring through individual sovereigns the arguable rehabilitation of the Stuart and Hanoverian monarchies, Chapter 5 is predicated on the notion that the most important locale in each of the six novels is in fact that of the royal presence. As such, the chapter weaves together concepts of image, notions of place, and Scott's qualified but sustained counter-revolutionary position in (re)presentation of each monarch as both individual sovereign and the site of the body politic. Sharpe's focus on image is helpful here for the revisiting of Scott's use of portraiture—through his descriptions of portrait paintings and his own detailed depiction of various monarchs and key characters—in the novels. This is of particular value when positioned within the novels' broader physical, political and social landscapes. Scott explores the character of each

---

36   Olwig, *Landscape, Nature, and the Body Politic*, xxvii.

sovereign, constructing a historically recognizable and ultimately positive representation of James I, Charles II, Queen Caroline, George II and George III.

The significance of Scott's depiction of the respective royal presences extends, however, beyond this. Individually and collectively, the six novels explore a broad range of notions of sovereignty throughout the monarchical dynasties. In *The Fortunes of Nigel* Scott considers questions of decorum and sovereignty using his portrait of James I, that most indecorous of English monarchs. Drawing on an extensive array of historical representations of James, Scott adroitly posits a rehabilitation of both the king and his reign. Furthermore, James is not the only figure of sovereignty that Scott depicts in *The Fortunes of Nigel*. While his primary focus is indeed the "wisest fool in Christendom," he also considers that tragic future king, Charles I (*Nigel*, 67). Indeed, in both *Woodstock* and *Peveril of the Peak* he references not only Charles I's reign, but also that of his son, Charles II. By exploring the two monarchs' reigns, Scott traces the path of the diminishing, absent and finally restored sovereign body politic leading up to, during and after the Interregnum. In *The Fortunes of Nigel*, *Woodstock* and *Peveril of the Peak* the king ultimately effects a form of natural justice and also an emblem of lasting social order by enabling the protagonist's marriage.

It should be added here that in *The Heart of Mid-Lothian*, Queen Caroline plays a significantly reduced role. Her involvement in the restoration of justice is limited by contrast with that achieved by her male counterparts in *The Fortunes of Nigel*, *Woodstock* and *Peveril of the Peak*. As such, Scott appears to harbour some discomfort in that novel with the notion of women holding and executing monarchical power. In *Waverley* and *Redgauntlet*, Scott portrays an increasing distance from the processes of justice effected by the natural body of the sovereign when contrasted with those in *The Fortunes of Nigel*, *Woodstock*, *Peveril of the Peak* and *The Heart of Mid-Lothian*.

Considered together, the six novels trace a recession of the sovereign's engagement in effecting justice, and a correlative lessening of the need for the monarch personally to establish representative examples of social order, now that society is stable, government effective, and the monarchy's authority robust and enduring. A counter-revolutionary argument can thus be seen to accumulate throughout the six novels, moving from the necessity for the personal involvement of the sovereign's natural body to the monarch's instituting a degree of social stability that negates the need for the royal presence to effect justice. Scott's support for the notion of monarchy is grounded in the historicity of the various periods in which the novels are set and, as we have seen, encompasses both the Stuart and the Hanoverian monarchies. In *The Fortunes of Nigel*, *Woodstock* and *Peveril of the Peak*, he constructs an argument supporting the Stuart monarchy; he repositions his rehabilitation of the concept of legitimate monarchy to incorporate specifically the Hanoverian dynasty in *The Heart of Mid-Lothian, Waverley,* and *Redgauntlet.* It is in the context of legitimate sovereignty that each of the monarchs is portrayed as a 'character,' and Scott labours relentlessly to represent them positively within their respective reigns. He astutely creates a historically recognizable visage for each sovereign. Doing so presents him with unique challenges; in response, he expounds on the particular virtues of each monarch, foregrounds and shadows specific qualities, attributes and behaviours, and thereby finally positions each (although at times with heavy qualifications) as an emblem of justice realized.

G.A.M. Wood and David Hewitt argue that "*Redgauntlet* concludes the series of remarkable Jacobite novels, *The Tale of Old Mortality, The Bride of Lammermoor, The Black Dwarf, Rob Roy* and *Waverley,* in which Scott ponders the history of his own country, and considers fundamental problems like political legitimacy, political freedom and responsibility, and political justice".[37] In this study, I suggest those same issues are located in another, differently classified series of which *Redgauntlet* is again the culminating novel. Viewed in chronological historical sequence, *The Fortunes of Nigel, Woodstock, Peveril of the Peak, The Heart of Mid-Lothian, Waverley* and *Redgauntlet* engage, individually and collectively, with issues of 'political legitimacy, political freedom and responsibility, and political justice,' exploring against sweeping historical and geographic landscapes questions of monarchical governance, socio-political instability, nationalism and unification.

---

37   G.A.M. Wood and David Hewitt, 'Historical Note' in Walter Scott, *Redgauntlet,* ed. G.A.M
      Wood and David Hewitt (Edinburgh: Edinburgh University Press, 1997), 442–3.

CHAPTER 1

Compromised Authority and Confinement in *The Fortunes of Nigel* and *Woodstock*

A stateless nation in a nationless state[1]

∵

For all their differences in plot, theme, locale and characterization, *The For-tunes of Nigel* and *Woodstock* both focus on the role and historical significance of a Stuart monarch. The two novels depict different monarchs—James I and Charles II—at very different stages of their reigns: James is firmly ensconced on the English throne (though not to universal approbation) while Charles, having lost the Battle of Worcester, remains the unrecognized king in Crom-well's Interregnum. James' reign precedes (and arguably contributes to) the revolutionary times of Charles I's downfall and execution; Charles II seeks to establish his sovereignty in an environment residually riven by political and religious strife, and struggles to reconcile notions of appropriate leadership, spiritual rectitude and moral authority.

Despite the myriad differences between the two novels, Scott uses various notions and representations of 'otherness' to explore the role of the monarchy in both. Sharpe argues in *Image Wars* that James I represented himself both through his writings (which were widely published and read) and his (rela-tively) few official portraits as the successful and recognized symbol of English and Scottish unity. Scott, however, demonstrates in *The Fortunes of Nigel*, through his own construction of royal images, the fraught imbalance existing in the English-Scot political and social relationships. Conversely, Sharpe, in his *Rebranding Rule*, notes the unusual nature of Charles II's representation as (literally and metaphorically) unrecognized monarch. Charles had, "especially in the weeks after flight from Worcester in September 1651 while incognito, to

---

1 Evan Gottlieb, *Feeling British: Sympathy and National Identity in Scottish and English Writing, 1707–1832* (Lewisburg: Bucknell University Press, 2007), 20.

© KONINKLIJKE BRILL NV, LEIDEN, 2018 | DOI 10.1163/9789004352780_003

suffer indignities, discomforts and taunts quite unbefitting a king: innkeepers, boatmen, servants."[2] This accords with Scott's depiction of the marginalized nature of Charles' sovereignty in *Woodstock*, through the absence of those built and ceremonial symbols that traditionally manifest the public representation of a monarch. It can be added here that a number of Casey's conceptualizations of place are useful when one considers how Scott demonstrates the 'otherness' and relative lack of Scottish identity in *The Fortunes of Nigel* through the absence of images of built environments. Similarly, Casey's ideas about the intermediary significance of gardens and immediate surrounds in relation to the buildings they encompass and the nature to which they link are especially relevant to Woodstock Lodge and its environs in the context of Scott's representations of familial and monarchical history.

With these various concepts in mind, I want to focus initially on Scott's use of place as a political construct. In *The Fortunes of Nigel*, the multi-layered representation of Scotland as an essentially 'other' place (as we would now understand that 'otherness' in Saidian terms) facilitates Scott's cautious approval of James and his reign. In *Woodstock* and at Woodstock, Scott depicts the relationships existing among the Royalist, Parliamentarian and Independent protagonists. The tracing of these different combatants, and their respective and negative representations of each other as spiritually 'other' in that limited environment (as we would now appreciate that via Sibley), enable Scott to mount a counter-revolutionary argument supporting Charles' restoration to the English throne.

Scott also seeks, in both novels, to position each king's reign as a positive epoch in English history by considering the specific concepts of authority operating at the time. In *The Fortunes of Nigel*, he explores the notion of compromised authority, and in doing so establishes the qualified nature of his support for James as a Stuart and as a monarch. In *Woodstock*, Scott juxtaposes Charles' compromised authority with other, defiled forms of authority present during the Interregnum, and thus presents Charles' sovereignty as having superior potential to those alternatives. While not immediately explicit, these notions of 'otherness' and of authority inform and preface Scott's engagement with Jacobean and Caroline history, and are critical to Scott's counter-revolutionary representations of history in both novels.

---

2   Kevin Sharpe, *Rebranding Rule: The Restoration and Revolution Monarchy, 1660–1714* (New Haven and London: Yale University Press, 2013), 7.

The Otherness of Scotland in *The Fortunes of Nigel*

When one reads *The Fortunes of Nigel*, it is valuable to consider the broad landscape of the novel, and the significance of the two primary locales operating
within the text—namely, London and Scotland. Scott, in juxtaposing London-
as-England and Scotland, and in his depiction of the relationship operating
between them at all levels of the social order, posits Scotland and the Scots
as "other".[3] However, the multiplicity of intertwined, interdependent and convoluted dialogues that take place between England and Scotland throughout
the novel negates any attempt to interpret Scotland as a simple representation
of what we might call a subordinate Saidian otherness. Scott uses primarily
two concepts to illustrate Scotland's otherness and the complex nature of the
English-Scottish relationship under James VI and I: lack of presence (as opposed to absence) and the notion of compromised authority. Through these
two concepts, he seeks ultimately to position the reconstruction of Glenvarloch, to consider the significance of this reconstruction at James' (and others')
hands, and to comment on the efficacy of James as sovereign of both Scotland
and England.

Said makes specific reference to Scott when explaining his concept of otherness in *Orientalism*. As we would anticipate, he considers Scott's portrait of
Muslim otherness in *The Talisman* with regard to the depiction of the otherness of cultures (and locales) less powerful than the dominant Western culture.[4] Using the meeting between Sir Kenneth (of the Crouching Leopard) and
his Muslim opponent (Saladin in disguise) during which "the Christian discovers his Muslim antagonist to be not so bad a fellow after all," Said reveals the
evident limitations inherent in Scott's portrayal of the West's encountering the
East.[5] However, Scott depicts far more complex relationships existing between

---

3   I am of course not the first to note the complex nature of the Scottish–English relationship
    in *The Fortunes of Nigel*. See, for example: George A. Drake, "'The Ordinary Rules of the Pave:'
    Urban Spaces in Scott's '*Fortunes of Nigel*,'" *Studies in the Novel*, 33 (Winter 2001), 416–29;
    Hugh C. Holman, '*Nigel* and the Historical Imagination,' *The Classic British Novel*, ed. Howard
    M. Harper, Jr. and Charles Edge (Athens: University of Georgia Press, 1972), 65–84; and Yoon
    Sun Lee, 'Time, Money, Sanctuary, and Sociality in Scott's *The Fortunes of Nigel*,' *European
    Romantic Review*, 14 (June 2003), 233–8.
4   Said makes the important point that "[i]n time, culture comes to be associated almost ag-
    gressively, with the nation or the state [...] Culture in this sense is a source of identity, and a
    rather combative one at that" (Edward W. Said, *Culture and Imperialism* (New York: Vintage
    Books, 1994), xiii).
5   Edward W. Said, *Orientalism* (London: Penguin, 1995), 101. For a summary of the criticism
    of Said's simplistic representations of the 'other,' see Karen M. Mornin's 'Edward W Said,'
    Key Thinkers on Space and Place 2nd edn, ed. Phil Hubbard, Rob Kitchin and Gill Valentine

England and Scotland in *The Fortunes of Nigel* than the one-dimensional West-East interactions he traced in *The Talisman*. Scott achieves a representation of Scotland's (and indeed Scottish) otherness in this novel that is, by contrast to his caricature of Muslim difference (and inferiority) in *The Talisman*, sophisticated and nuanced.

The concept of Scotland as 'other' is fundamentally complicated by Scott's own nationality, his nationalist loyalties, and his authorial role. Like Rudyard Kipling in Said's penetrating post-colonial analysis of *Kim*, Scott is 'of' the other culture about which he writes, seeking to "juxtapose the meritorious traditions and manners of the Scots against the fading relics of [the] past".[6] However, unlike Kipling, Scott in his depiction of Scotland is not writing from "the dominating viewpoint of a white man in a colonial possession [or] from the perspective of a massive colonial system whose economy, functioning, and history had acquired the status of a virtual fact of nature".[7] As David Blair argues:

> In his whole address to Scottish history through his novels Scott's project participates *in part* in [...] anglocentrism [... and] Scott, as a pro-Union Tory, identifies ideologically with rule from London [...] foster[ing] an equivocation between that assertion of difference and the simultaneous assertion of accommodation between 'Scotland' and 'Britannia.'[8] (my emphasis)

As such, Scott demonstrates the internal changes occurring in Scotland in response to the joining of the crowns. Fielding, writing on Scott's *Minstrelsy of the Scottish Border* (1802), focuses on "regions that have emerged in a process of cultural identification that uses a complex mixture of assimilation and

---

(London: Sage, 2011), 342. James Watt explores interesting notions of orientalism in Romantic fiction in his chapter 'Orientalism and Empire', *The Cambridge Companion to Fiction in the Romantic Period*, ed. Richard Maxwell and Katie Trumpener (Cambridge: Cambridge University Press, 2008), 129–42.

6 Said refers to the authority of the author as "someone writing out the processes of society in an acceptable institutionalized manner, observing conventions, following patterns, and so forth" (Said, *Culture and Imperialism*, 92). I see authorial authority somewhat differently, building on Said's definition (and perhaps covered by him in the phrase "and so forth") by adding a further dimension of controlling the representation of individual, personal, public and cultural relationships operating within the text. In the light of this, I suggest that Scott exerts deliberate authorial authority in his depiction of two cultures co-existing with varying degrees of respective power in *The Fortunes of Nigel*. There is value in comparing Scott's treatment of Scotland in *The Heart of Mid-Lothian* with that in *The Fortunes of Nigel*.

7 Said, *Culture and Imperialism*, 162.

8 David Blair, 'Scott, Cartography, and the Appropriation of Scottish Place,' *Literature and Place, 1800–2000*, ed. Peter Brown and Michael Irwin (Bern: Peter Lang, 2006), 93–4.

homogenization on the one hand, and diversification and fluid process, on the other".[9] In that context, I suggest that Scott's fascination with graduated experiences of regional acculturation and separatism displays constantly throughout *The Fortunes of Nigel*.[10] In one of several instances, through the re-defined relationship between Lord Huntinglen and Nigel Olifaunt, he illustrates how James' ascension to the English throne has, at one level, resulted in the Scots uniting as representatives of a Scotland identified as an entity rather than as a conglomeration of regions and clans:

> "By my saul, my lord, this is strange," said the King; "ye are pleading for the son of your enemy!"
> "Of one who *was* my enemy till your Majesty made him my friend," answered Lord Huntinglen.
> NIGEL, 113

Yet Scott does not depict the same unification occurring between the English and the Scottish.

Linda Colley writes of the external forces that generated some of the superficial 'sameness' of the newly formed and post-Union Britain.[11] Gottlieb, on the other hand, questions that simplicity and depth of shared identity. "By force of sheer xenophobia, Colley contends that the English and Scottish learned to define themselves as similar primarily by virtue of not being French or Catholic".[12] I suggest that the enmity between France and England, the British suspiciousness of the French Catholicism and the wars between those two countries which Colley references as having created a form of British nationalism is not captured or referenced by Scott in *The Fortunes of Nigel*. Rather he

---

9   Penny Fielding, 'Curated Regions of the North: Art and Literature in the "Scottish Border" and the "Transpennine Corridor,"' *Visual Culture in Britain*, 15 (2014), 162.

10   This fascination is not limited to *The Fortunes of Nigel*. Fielding's insights regarding *Minstrelsy of the Scottish Border* can be applied to illuminate, in different ways and to varying degrees, Scott's representations of 'regions,' locales and landscapes as a means of exploring Scottish-English political, legal and social relationships in, for example, *The Heart of Mid-Lothian*, *Waverley* and *Redgauntlet*, as well as the myriad political and religious issues dividing England in the wake of Charles I's regicide, both during the Interregnum and the Restoration in *Woodstock* and *Peveril of the Peak*.

11   See Linda Colley's *Britons: Forging the Nation, 1707–1837* (New Haven: Yale University Press, 1992), especially Chapters 1, 3 and 4 (11–54, 55, 100 and 147–94), and her 'Britishness and Europeanness: Who Are the British Anyway?,' *Journal of British Studies*, 31 (Oct 1992), 309–29.

12   Gottlieb, *Feeling British*, 17. For a detailed exploration of Gottlieb's thoughts of critical analysis of Anglo-Scottish relationships, see 17–22.

depicts the many difficulties in reconstructing Scotland as part of Britain, given the multiplicity of divisions separating both the aristocracies and the working classes of England and Scotland.

Therefore, what one could call Scott's authorial authority, though arguably not compromised as such, signals a (self-) conscious benevolence towards 'his' culture that—although England presides throughout the novel as the dominant culture—precludes the simple positioning of Scotland as unequivocally subordinate and subject to the unilateral imposition of England's influence and perceptions. Indeed, this could not be so, given that the two locales and their respective cultures exist within the one meta-culture of Britishness. The most immediate and striking illustration of Scotland's otherness is its lack of physical presence in the novel. As a locale, it frames the novel: it is seen that Nigel has come directly from Scotland in the opening chapters, and the novel concludes with Dalgarno's attempted return to Scotland via Enfield Chase and the presumption of Nigel's triumphant homecoming. For all that, Scotland exists in the novel as that Saidian concept which Karen M. Mornin defines as "imaginative geography [... and] the invention and construction of geographical space beyond a physical territory".[13] Thus Scotland, as place, exists at a distance, often referenced but curiously 'presence-less' and literally never on stage. It is a locale of historical but dwindling importance, that has produced the English Stuart monarch—James VI and I—who is himself a conflict of Scottish and English loyalties and a deeply flawed sovereign. England, by contrast—or rather London, the metropolis representing 'England'—dominates the novel, physically and culturally, accommodating within its boundaries the splintered othernesses of, and the associated tensions and "inveterate national prejudices" percolating between, the countrymen of the "sister kingdoms" (*Nigel*, 19). As Scott's narrator observes:

> These prejudices were, of course, most inveterate during the reign of King James. His English subjects accused him of partiality to those of his

---

13   Karen M. Mornin, 'Edward W Said,' *Key Thinkers on Space and Place* 2nd edn, ed. Phil Hubbard, Rob Kitchin and Gill Valentine (London: Sage, 2011), 339. Said himself makes reference to the notion of the authority of the community "whose representative most often is the family but also is the nation, the specific locality, and the concrete historical moment" (Said, *Culture and Imperialism*, 92). This concept further supports the argument that Scott creates a complex othering of Scotland in *The Fortunes of Nigel*. The individual representative of the family is Nigel (of Scottish nobility), and James I is, of course, the head of the nation, that being the wider Scottish and English communities. London is the primary locale in the novel; however, the "concrete historical moment" is that of a yoking together of the disparate and, at times, combative Scottish and English cultures.

ancient kingdom; while the Scots, with equal injustice, charged him with having forgotten the land of his nativity, and with neglecting those early friends to whose allegiance he had been so much indebted.

The temper of the King, peaceable even to timidity, inclined him perpetually to interfere as mediator between the contending factions, whose brawls disturbed the court. But, notwithstanding all his precautions, historians have recorded many instances, where the mutual hatred of two nations, who, after being enemies for a thousand years, had been so very recently united, broke forth with a fury which menaced a general convulsion; and, spreading from the highest to the lowest classes, as it occasioned debates in council and parliament, factions in the court, and duels among the gentry, was no less productive of riots and brawls amongst the lower orders.

        NIGEL, 19–20

Said's concept of otherness enhances understanding that the tension caused by stereotyping and prejudice informs, frames and explains the experience of cultural intercourse Scott is exploring throughout *The Fortunes of Nigel* in various Scottish-English and Scottish-Scottish interactions across the social spectrum—at Court, in Temple Bar, even in the royal kitchens.[14] Scott explores those interactions and establishes the consequent position of Scotland-as-other using the idea of compromised authority, which occurs when legitimate authority is undermined by the shortcomings of the person wielding it, when positional authority is not recognized, or when authority exists out of context—that is, remotely from the source of its legitimacy.

The opening chapter of the novel focuses immediately on London and on Scotland-as-other. Richie Moniplies (surely the epitome of the dour Scottish servant) is taunted with racial gibes by the English apprentice, Vincent Jenkins, who is himself employed by a Scot residing in the commercial area of London. Thus, Jenkins' actions represent two aspects of compromised authority—Moniplies is not granted the respect due to him as a nobleman's servant and Jenkins simultaneously ignores his own subordinate status as apprentice and degrades his loyalty to his (notionally) Scottish master.

Scott's depiction of other Scots throughout the novel reinforces and elaborates upon this notion of compromised authority. George Heriot, whose worthy character, good heart and strength of principle would not initially seem emblematic of compromised authority, embodies many of Scott's juxtapositions

---

14   It is curious that the only locale in the novel where Nigel is presented as the sole Scot-in-residence is in Alsatia; perhaps Scott could not support the notion of embedding Scottishness in that place.

of cultural dominance and subordination. His financial dexterity and wealth, James' (and thus Baby Charles and Steenie's) resultant dependence on him, and Heriot's influence across the social spectrum, coupled with his principled uprightness, position him as a dominant force, even a moral barometer, within the novel. However, this status (if not his rectitude) is undermined by his being both Scottish and an artisan, as opposed to English and of the aristocracy— doubly other, so to speak. He is literally barred from the presence-chamber at Court and unable to accompany Nigel: "'Master Heriot's name will pass cur- rent for much gold and silver, my lord,' replied Maxwell, with a civil sneer, 'but not for birth and rank'" (*Nigel*, 108). Similarly, Laurie Linklater is a subordinate cultural identity operating in a menial role in the royal kitchens; the legitimacy of his status is questioned by his English peers on the grounds of his Scottish heritage (and qualities), even as he asserts to the unfortunate nobleman, Nigel, that he is in fact a person of consequence in his own sphere:

> But nobody amongst these brave English cooks can kittle up his Majesty's most sacred palate with our own gusty Scottish dishes. So I e'en betook myself to my craft and concocted a mess of friar's chicken for the soup, and a savoury hachis, that made the whole cabal coup the crans; and in- stead of disgrace, I came by preferment. I am one of the clerks of the kitchen now—make me thankful—with a finger in the purveyor's office, and may get my whole hand in by and by.
>
> *NIGEL*, 301

Furthermore, while it is common for villainy to be depicted as 'other,' Scott's representation of Dalgarno is an interesting twist to the notion of compro- mised authority. Dalgarno's superior knowledge of and position at Court natu- rally establish him as an authority for Nigel, and his villainous motives and actions of course compromise that authority. But he is also a means by which the compromised authority of Charles and Buckingham (their misuse of pub- lic institutions and persons of authority to fulfil private desires—the Scottish Chancellor, for one) can be registered and also displaced. While Charles and Buckingham are complicit in wanting to acquire Glenvarloch as a hunting ground, and Buckingham is (honourably) involved in Dalgarno's mistreatment of Lady Hermione, it is Dalgarno's iniquities that are foregrounded. James chortles, "it was grand to hear Baby Charles laying down the guilt of dissimula- tion, and Steenie lecturing on the turpitude of incontinence!," to which George Heriot replies, "I am afraid [...] I might have thought of the old proverb of Satan reproving sin" (*Nigel*, 362).

James is obviously the most important Scottish character in *The Fortunes of Nigel* through whom Scott presents Scotland as other using the notion of compromised authority. James' Scottishness—which Scott is at pains to emphasize through the monarch's speech and his (at times, inappropriate) recollections of his Scottish ancestry—invests Scotland with a degree of sovereignty and cultural strength that forms no part of Said's traditional concept of otherness.[15] However, the inherent primacy of the sovereign over the dominant English culture is subverted by James himself—a monarch derided, mocked (albeit *sotto voce*) and overtly manipulated by his own Court, including his son, Charles, and his favourite, Buckingham. Scott shows one instance of such manipulation when Lord Huntinglen begs James to grant a royal boon:

> "[L]ook at the placet of Lord Glenvarloch, and do upon it what your own just and royal nature shall think meet and just, without reference to your Secretary or any other of your Council." [...]
>
> "Weel spoken, my lord!" said the King; "and with a true Christian spirit. And, respecting the Supplication of this young man, I partly guess where the matter lies; and in plain troth I had promised to George Heriot to be good to the lad—But then, here the shoe pinches. Steenie and Baby Charles cannot abide him—neither can your own son, my lord; and so methinks, he had better go down to Scotland before he comes to ill luck by them."
>
> "My son, and it please your Majesty, so far as he is concerned, shall not direct my doings," said the Earl, "nor any wild-headed young man of them all."
>
> "Why, neither shall they mine," replied the Monarch; "by my father's saul, none of them all shall play Rex with me—I will do what I will, and what I aught, like a free king."
>
> *NIGEL*, 113–4

Scott's simultaneous representation of James VI and I as Scotland-as-dominant-culture and Scotland-as-other is interesting, furthermore, when considered with reference to the mediaeval politico-theological concept of the monarch's having two bodies; the body politic and the body natural.[16]

---

15   See, as examples, James' nostalgic reminiscing with two Scotsmen, George Heriot and Lord Huntinglen (*Nigel*, 64–5, 106–7).

16   The landmark discussion of the 'two bodies' theory and the monarch as natural body and incarnation of the body politic is Ernst Hartwig Kantorowicz's *The King's Two Bodies: A Study in Mediaeval Political Theology* (Princeton: Princeton University Press, 1957). See also: Louise Olga Fradenburg's *City, Marriage, Tournament: Arts of Rule in Late Mediaeval Scotland* (Madison: University of Wisconsin Press, 1991) and Kenneth R. Olwig's

James, the British sovereign body politic incarnate and representative, in that role, of the history and culture of Scotland, carries great authority. It speaks strongly of the extent of this monarch's personal inadequacies that they can so comprehensively undermine the august authority in his (quasi-divine) official and political stature as monarch. Scott represents James' various compromised authorities in many ways. These include his vacillations between the "right" and the "politic," the influence of Babie Charles and Buckingham over him and the emptiness of his erudition. There is also the juxtaposition of his desire for pompous ceremony (note especially his instruction to George Heriot about the proper submission of a supplication) and his frequent indulgence in appallingly inappropriate behaviour—for example, his use of the "lugg" in the Tower and his hiding of Richie Moniplies behind a curtain. Most significantly, Scott explores this undermining process by describing James' treatment of Nigel's supplication. And Scott deftly contrasts the past James-as-monarch-of-Scotland with the present James-as-monarch-of-England by having James recognize his own Scottish loyalty in response to Lord Huntinglen's boon request, and simultaneously derogate Nigel's inheritance in terms of English values. Scott has James remark:

> And so the lad only wants payment of the siller due from us, in order to reclaim his parental estate? But then, Huntinglen, the lad will have other debts—and for what burther himsell with sae mony acres of barren woodland? let the land gang, man, let the land gang; Steenie has the promise of it from our Scottish Chancellor—it is the best hunting ground in Scotland—and Baby Charles and Steenie want to kill a buck there this next year—they mun hae the land—they mun hae the land—and our debt shall be paid to the young man plack and bawbee and he may hae the spending of it at our court; or if he has such an eard hunger, oons! man, we'll stuff his stomach with English land, which is worth twice so much, ay, ten times so much, as these accursed hills and heughs, and mosses and muirs, that he is so keen after.
>
> *NIGEL*, 114[17]

It is notable that James appears to greatest advantage in his portrait as sovereign of Scotland and when his public and private personae are aligned. The Earl of Huntinglen overtly distinguishes between James' earlier sovereignty over Scotland and his current rule over England, and also draws attention more

---

Landscape, Nature, and the Body Politic: From Britain's Renaissance to America's New World (Madison: University of Wisconsin Press: 2002).

17   Refer to *Fortunes of Nigel*, 113–5, for James' full discussion with Lord Huntinglen.

than once to James' success as monarch when he governs in accordance with
his (James') own judgment:

> "O my poor master!" groaned the Earl of Huntinglen. "When you were in
> your own cold country, you had warmer blood in your veins. [...]"
>   "You are my own native and noble Prince [...] just and generous, when-
> ever you listen to the workings of your own heart."
>   *NIGEL*, 114; 115

By depicting the chasm that exists between James as monarch (and body politic) and James as private individual, Scott explores another aspect of the convoluted otherness of Scotland central to the novel—the Glenvarloch estate. Just
as the two bodies of the monarch, the political and the personal, are distinct,
so are the physical property of the house of Glenvarloch and the House of
Glenvarloch as the estate that transcends the individual, Nigel, and encompasses the heritage and lineage of the Glenvarlochs together with their traditional role and responsibilities. Linklater is conscious of this duality: "God for-
give them that would sacrifice an honourable house for their own base ends!"
(*Nigel*, 301). Scott emphasizes Scotland's inherent otherness by keeping it out
of view in *The Fortunes of Nigel*, and he renders the Glenvarloch estate similarly
invisible. The House of Glenvarloch is freighted with symbolism, with notions
of history, loyalty, identity, honour and nobility; it informs and influences Nigel's varied receptions in London. Yet this House—and the determinants of its
fate—are represented throughout the novel by nothing more substantial than
papers charting its status and ownership: the mortgage or "wadset," Nigel's
Supplication to James, and James' sign-manual for payment of the King's debt.
These documents, around which the novel's conspiracies, characters and plots
swirl bewilderingly, are curiously ephemeral yet robustly metaphorical constructs, especially as a representation of that most tangible of entities and most
contested aspect of cultural dominance in the nineteenth century—land.[18]

In *The Fortunes of Nigel*, Scotland is represented as a convoluted and splintered otherness, a representation effected by its being denied a presence as a
setting and by its various representatives' authorities being compromised. Now
the question arises: what is Scott's purpose in representing Scotland in this
complicated way, exposing the multi-layered tensions existing between the

---

18   Indeed Natasha Tessone emphasizes how Scott, in writing *The Antiquary* (1816), set in the
      final years of the eighteenth century, was preoccupied with the cultural and financial sig-
      nificance of Scottish property and entail in the context of "Scotland's participation within
      the larger British union [and] how to preserve a distinct cultural and national legacy and
      still remain a part of the larger nation". (Natasha Tessone, 'Entailing the Nation: Inheri-
      tance and History in Walter Scott's *The Antiquary*', *Studies in Romanticism*, 51 (Summer
      2012), 152.)

two cultures that warily, tenuously and, at times, combatively coexist with the now "united crown of England and Scotland" that is the result of James VI and I's ascension to the English throne? (*Nigel*, 19). Scott uses this complex representation of Scotland to consider James' efficacy as a sovereign, and his ability to effect natural justice. George A. Drake, in his analysis of space in *The Fortunes of Nigel*, focuses on London as a Lefebvrian concept of a hybridized urban space.[19] I would argue that Scott depicts London accommodating various splintered othernesses in dynamic adjacency, rather than evolving into an integrated hybridity, to show that James is not capable of wielding monarchic authority efficaciously enough to direct such an evolution. London is, however, the dominant locale from which James is able to reconstruct the House of Glenvarloch; his actions can affect a minority site, but not the dominant environment of London.

Even that reconstruction of Glenvarloch is a qualified achievement. James, despite being morally obliged to effect the natural justice required to restore the Glenvarloch estate to Nigel, and having signed the sign-manual to secure its future, is unable to achieve financial restoration of the estate. The multiplicity of compromises to his authority means that he cannot effect wholly Nigel's realization of justice. It is Richie Moniplies and Martha Trapbois (*in absentia*) who reinstate Nigel as the publicly recognized and lawful owner of the Glenvarloch estate. James' role is limited (reflecting his personal limitations) to promoting the marriage of Nigel and Margaret and reinventing Margaret Ramsay.[20] However, even the restoration of the Glenvarloch estate is an 'other' occurrence: a bastion of Scotland is reconstructed in London, the dominant locale, where it has no public importance. Caroline McCracken-Flesher, in her analysis of 'circulation' in *The Fortunes of Nigel* and George IV's visit to Scotland in 1822, suggests, in the broader issue of the 'value' of Scotland as a nation, that "at the end of *Nigel* the hero has recovered and seems likely to withdraw there with his wife. By the intervention of the King, romance overcomes money and delimits play. Circulation has ceased because value is achieved".[21] While this may well be the case, this locale's greater significance lies in the importance to Scotland and to the House (and house) of Glenvarloch of replacing the stagnating, precariously owned, backward-looking Glenvarloch estate with a more nuanced, stable, financially secure, forward-looking and revitalized locale.

Similarly, James' recreation of Margaret's ancestry is limited, as Frank Jordan comments, to his "strategy of justifying the commoner Margaret Ramsay's

---

19   Drake, "'The Ordinary Rules of the Pave,'" 416–29.

20   Cf. Drake, "'The Ordinary Rules of the Pave,'" 426–7, who interprets their marriage somewhat differently.

21   Caroline McCracken-Flesher, *Possible Scotlands: Walter Scott and the Story of Tomorrow* (Oxford: Oxford University Press, 2005), 72.

marriage to Lord Glenvarloch by concocting an aristocratic genealogy for her and then signifying it by creating a new coat of arms turning on the contrast between time and eternity".[22] This manufacture of a minor Scottish aristocracy is, of course, insignificant within English culture and thus far less politically sensitive than would be the creation of an English aristocratic title (such as, say, the Duke of Buckingham's). James' limited capacity to achieve public good is made clear by this example of justice existing under, but not through, his monarchical authority and being confined to the other 'presence-less' land that produced him as sovereign of Britain, but not the united kingdom over which he reigns. Upon the financial restoration of Glenvarloch by Richie Moniples and Martha Trapbois, James' involvement in the marriage of Nigel and Margaret is shown to have been a marginal achievement by a compromised authority that reconstructs an essentially private place lacking physical presence and existing for the reader only through various symbolic legal documents. If, as Gottlieb argues, "new discourses had to be constructed and deployed to facilitate the hegemonic dissemination of a new national identity," this was by no means a wholesale endorsement of James' achievement as depicted by Scott in *The Fortunes of Nigel*.[23]

The Political Significance of Locale and Language in *Woodstock*

While Scott set *The Fortunes of Nigel* in a sweeping landscape encompassing two primary locales—London and Scotland—and a wealth of sub-locales within London itself, *Woodstock* is confined essentially to its titular locale. Although the Glenvarloch estate exists as arguably the most thematically significant locale in *The Fortunes of Nigel*, it is a static and distant symbol, represented by various legal documents and awaiting Nigel (and Margaret's) return in order to restore its symbolic and actual worth. By contrast, the locale of Woodstock is spatially present, clearly visible to the reader, and is invested with a wealth of immediate and dynamic symbolic values—past, present and future. The shadows of both mediaeval history (Henry II and Rosamund's relationship) and more immediate history (the Civil Wars) stretch across Woodstock, and Charles II's restoration is forecast, and indeed premised, on his escape from this locale.[24]

22   Frank Jordan, 'Essay on the Text,' *The Fortunes of Nigel*, ed. Frank Jordan (Edinburgh: Edinburgh University Press, 2004), 420.

23   Gottlieb, *Feeling British*, 17.

24   As Bachelard suggests, "[p]ast, present and future give the house different dynamisms, which often interfere, at times opposing, at others, stimulating one another." See Gaston Bachelard, *The Poetics of Space* (1969; rpt Boston: Beacon Press, 1996), 6.

Two of Kevin Sharpe's concepts are useful means by which to examine Scott's counter-revolutionary stance throughout the novel. The first is the significance of monarchical symbolism located within Woodstock and throughout *Woodstock*. While Woodstock, the building and the locale, are physically and metaphorically the centre of the novel, the myriad traditional representations of kingship—the poetry, prose, speeches, rituals and ceremonies of which Sharpe makes mention—are noticeably missing throughout the novel. This absence underlines Charles' actual physical presence (albeit in disguise) but more significantly the absence of his recognized monarchical role. This lack of authoritative symbolism extends to Cromwell too, referencing—no doubt—the dour Puritan edicts of his governance but also subtly positioning his authority as inherently illegitimate. It is in this dual context that the pageantry and symbolism of the concluding chapters, where Charles travels the road to that centre of recognized and authority—London—to assume his sovereignty, proclaim his ceremonial change in status and legitimate monarchical authority. The second is the importance of Scott's focus on portraiture in *Woodstock*, which is best understood through Sharpe's concept of pictorial representation's importance in constructing political authority.

It is in this context of imaging sovereignty that Scott's construction of authority in the novel is so effective. In *The Fortunes of Nigel*, Scott used the concept of compromised authority to indicate Scotland's otherness, and the complex English-Scottish relationships operating under James' sovereignty to comment on the efficacy of James as monarch. This technique is applied differently in *Woodstock* as Scott seeks to establish and assert his supportive position of Charles II and his anticipated and eventual sovereignty. Scott makes use of the concept of compromised authority in *Woodstock* as he did in *The Fortunes of Nigel*. It is helpful at this point to recognize that this premise of compromised authority does not only occur in *The Fortunes of Nigel* and *Woodstock*. It is a recurring issue for Scott and therefore a central feature of the Waverley Novels. Scott's various representations of this concept of compromised authority occur primarily, though not exclusively, through the paradigms of law(lessness), (il)legitimacy and (il)legality in each of the Waverley Novels from his first, *Waverley* (1814), to his last, *Castle Dangerous* (1831).

However, it is in *Woodstock* that Scott introduces the notion of defiled authority, juxtaposing various operations of both compromised and defiled authority throughout the novel. He then, having suffused the novel with the language of spiritual defilement and infection, aligns the omniscient narrator's sympathies with the mischievous 'devilry' practised upon the Independent sequestrators by the Royalists, and simultaneously associates Parliamentary and Independent principals with the ultimate defiled authority, the Devil himself.

In doing so, he posits an implicit yet consistent argument supporting the Royalist assumption of (relative) moral rectitude and integrity during the historical period depicted in the novel, hence portraying Charles II's restoration as a generally positive chapter in English history.

Given Scott was crafting *Woodstock* concurrently with writing his *Life of Napoleon*, Tony Inglis, J.H. Alexander, David Hewitt and Alison Lumsden make the point that

> it seems highly likely that his initial subject, the preliminary history of the French Revolution, sparked *Woodstock*. Scott was turning from the French Revolution to the English, from the aftermath of the execution of Louis XVI to the aftermath of the execution of Charles I. There were both parallels and differences and Scott, with his philosophical view of the patterning of history, was always aware that human nature was constant, and yet never exactly the same.[25]

In that context of revolution, Gary Kelly considers *Woodstock* to be "perhaps the best of the later Waverley Novels, [...] present[ing] Scott's mature deliberations on politics, language, and power, subjectivity, authority, and literature, with particular reference to British society in a post-revolutionary, or perhaps a pre-revolutionary age".[26] Indeed, I would suggest that Scott's "deliberations on" and resultant representations of the politics, language, power and authority operating specifically in the context of this historical period in fact constitute a covert argument supporting Charles' restoration at *Woodstock*'s close.[27] Of course, he uses the political and religious nexus that dominates both the novel *Woodstock* and the locale Woodstock to explore issues of authority and power.

---

25   Tony Inglis, J.H. Alexander, David Hewitt and Alison Lumsden's 'Essay on the Text,' *Woodstock*, ed. Tony Inglis, J.H. Alexander, David Hewitt and Alison Lumsden (Edinburgh: Edinburgh University Press, 2009), 424.

26   Gary Kelly, *English Fiction of the Romantic Period, 1789–1830*, Longman Literature in English Series (Harlow: Longman, 1989), 165. Fiona Robertson concurs, suggesting that "[w]ithin Woodstock itself, characters both exemplify and explicitly debate the relationship between language and political opinion. They also consider the part played in revolution— and, by implication—by works of literature" (Fiona Robertson, *Legitimate Histories: Scott, Gothic, and the Authorities of Fiction* (Oxford: Clarendon Press, 1994), 272).

27   The significance of the closing scenes of *Woodstock* has occasioned some critical dispute. See Judith Wilt, *Secret Leaves: The Novels of Walter Scott* (Chicago: University of Chicago Press, 1985), 175–6 and Robertson, *Legitimate Histories*, 272, who differ in their interpretations. Wilt considers the tableau-scene in the final chapter of the novel to signal the positivity of the Restoration, while Robertson posits that the tableau is a concern in its static representation of restored legitimacy.

Scott has been commended for his 'even-handed' portraits of the various warring individuals and factions in the novel—these being one means of examining "the enduring binary split in British politics and culture, topics which Scott addresses in passing in *Woodstock* but which also shaped his whole *oeuvre* over his lifetime".[28] Bjorn Tysdahl, for example, suggests that "*Woodstock* gives us characters that mirror each other across the political gulf".[29] Similarly, D.J. Trela emphasizes that "[b]ad as these characters [the Commissioners] are, it is important to recall Scott's careful balancing act in *Woodstock*, for the Cavaliers do not themselves come off all that well".[30]

However, I suggest that the notionally balanced representation achieved through the mirroring of characters across the socio-political-religious divides premised on the historical realities of the Interregnum is, in fact, deliberately and skilfully distorted. It is useful to consider three instances of this distortion of characterization through the mirroring mechanism in the novel: Charles II and Cromwell; Sir Henry Lee and the Commissioners; and Joceline Joliffe and Trusty Tomkins. Scott portrays Charles II, Sir Henry Lee and Joceline Joliffe as emblems merely of *compromised* authority: Cromwell, the Commissioners and Trusty Tomkins are shown to be manifestations of *defiled* authority. I have previously defined compromised authority as occurring when legitimate authority is undermined by its own shortcomings—that is, when positional authority is not recognized, or when authority exists out of context. Defiled authority, by contrast, is: when legitimate authority is engaged in unlawful activity; when positional authority is abused to the point of corruption; or when illegitimate authority is accorded legitimate status. I want now to demonstrate how Scott positions each of these six agents of authority as either compromised or defiled, thus embedding implicit approval of Charles and the Royalists in the context of a more invidious alternative.

It can be seen that Scott establishes the compromised nature of Charles' authority in three ways. First, Scott demonstrates how, in Charles, legitimate authority is undermined by its own shortcomings. He forces an adjacency between the portrait of the ideal monarch painted by Alice and the "hard-favoured" reality of this Stuart monarch's character (*Woodstock*, 247). Second, Charles' status as legitimate monarch is unrecognized. At Woodstock, initially

---

28   Inglis, et al. 'Historical Notes,' *Woodstock*, 537.

29   Bjorn Tysdahl, 'Scott's Imagery: The Beast and the Body,' *Excursions in Fiction: Essays in Honour of Professor Lars Hartveit on His 70th Birthday*, ed. Andrew Kennedy and Orm Øverland (Oslo: Novus, 1994), 241.

30   D.J. Trela, 'Sir Walter Scott on Oliver Cromwell: An Evenhanded Royalist Evaluates a Usurper,' *CLIO: A Journal of Literature, History, and the Philosophy of History*, 27 (Winter 1998), 214.

he is physically unrecognizable, disguised as he is, though his identity and sovereignty are ultimately acknowledged: beyond Woodstock's boundaries, he continues to be politically unrecognized until the novel's close. Finally, it becomes apparent that Charles' authority even when recognized—as occurs when he declares his true identity to Markham Everard and Sir Henry—exists out of context. His authority is confined to the locale of Woodstock and to his loyal Royalist subjects. Charles is not in the position of legitimate and recognized authority necessary for him to effect the lasting restoration of a locale, and thus affirm his public capacity to bring about moral justice and order, as does the monarch in *The Fortunes of Nigel* and *Peveril of the Peak*. James, by promoting the marriage of Nigel Olifaunt and Margaret Ramsay in *The Fortunes of Nigel*, achieves the partial restoration of the House of Glenvarloch, and thus is seen to function in his public role as monarch. In *Peveril of the Peak*, Charles' intervention in the abuse of justice surrounding Julian Peveril facilitates the reconstruction of Martindale-Moultrassie, another symbol of the king's effecting the restoration of order in a public capacity. In both instances, the monarch achieves a restoration of justice and order through the reinstatement of the rightful owner and the recreation of a locale that functions as an emblem of moral order. However, in *Woodstock* and at Woodstock, Charles can only facilitate a purely private instance of restoring order by exercising restraint over his private desires, forgoing his ignoble pursuit of Alice, and bringing about the reconciliation between Henry Lee and Markham Everard necessary for the marriage of Alice and Everard.[31]

Scott represents Cromwell's authority in somewhat different terms. As Trela argues, Scott's depiction of Cromwell is surprisingly balanced, especially when viewed in the context of other Tory assessments.[32] Nonetheless, while crafting this adroit portrait of Cromwell's positive and negative characteristics—Inglis, Alexander, Hewitt and Lumsden emphasize the "Old Noll of *Woodstock* [being] a series of paradoxes and contradictions"—Scott also establishes his authority as being not merely compromised, as Charles' is shown to be, but defiled.[33]

---

31   Wilt interprets the public and private significance of Charles' renouncing his amorous pursuit of Alice somewhat differently in *Secret Leaves*, 175. Gary Kelly sees the duel between Everard and Charles as "yet a further example of Charles' failure to govern his private character according to the requirements of his public position and responsibilities." See Kelly, *English Fiction*, 167–8.

32   See Trela, 'Scott on Oliver Cromwell,' 195–220.

33   Inglis, et al. 'Historical Notes,' *Woodstock*, 542. See 542–3 for an insightful assessment of Scott's sources for and construction of Cromwell's character in *Woodstock*.

Indeed, it is interesting to note the similarity of Scott's technique in crafting Charles' and Cromwell's portraits. Scott draws their characters in equivalent depth, focusing on their respective strengths, weaknesses and histories. He even depicts their unprepossessing visages in similar terms. Of Charles he says, "[t]he features of the Wanderer were harsh as ever," while Cromwell is "strong and coarsely made, with harsh and severe features" (*Woodstock*, 242, 81).

Cromwell's authority, although arguably legitimate (and shown to exist and operate beyond the confines of Woodstock by Wildrake's journey to Windsor), is represented as being irretrievably debased by his 'unlawful' act of regicide. Scott's Cromwell is well aware that this regicide was a heinous act, with this awareness made apparent in two instances. The first occurs when, in Wildrake's presence, he unwittingly displays and comments in agitation on the Van Dyck painting of Charles I:

> [...] It was a stern necessity—it was an awful deed! [...]—Who blames him, who, mounted aloft, rides triumphantly amongst the people, for having succeeded, where the unskilful and feeble fell and died?—Verily he hath his reward—Then, what is that piece of painted canvas to me more than others?—No—let him show to others the reproaches of that cold, calm face, that proud yet complaining eye—Those who have acted on higher respects have no cause to start at painted shadows—Not wealth nor power brought me from my obscurity—The oppressed consciences, the injured liberties of England, were the banner that I followed.
>
> *WOODSTOCK*, 94

The second instance takes place as Cromwell seeks to flush the supposed Charles II out from hiding in Woodstock. Cromwell articulates the scorn visited upon him as a result of his role in Charles I's beheading:

> [...] canst thou think it a light thing to me, that, the blood of this lad's father lying in some measure upon my head, I should now put in peril that of the son? [...] I am called parricide, blood-thirsty usurper already [...]. Nevertheless, who has spoke unto me graciously since that high deed? Those who acted in the matter with me are willing that I should be the scape-goat of atonement—those who looked on and helped not, bear themselves now as if they had been borne down by violence; and [...] they look aside to say, 'Ha! ha! the King-killer, the parricide—soon shall his place be made desolate.'
>
> *WOODSTOCK*, 372

Throughout the novel Scott also establishes—both through Markham Everard's commentary and Cromwell's own speech—that Cromwell's personal
hunger for kingship, rather than a disinterested assumption of leadership, further defiles his authority. Judith Wilt—focusing on Cromwell's "forbidden desire to leap into the empty saddle, the high space just vacated by the legitimate
king"—emphasizes that:

> [i]n Oliver Cromwell Scott shows a man maddened by the kingship he
> murdered, well ahead of his time, on January 30, 1642, haunted not only
> by the picture of the dead Charles I but, more terribly, by the desire which
> he must not desire—for kingship.[34]

Thus, Charles' compromised authority is shown to be superior to Cromwell's—
the unrecognized king is ultimately more fit to rule than the aspiring king.
Charles, despite his varied flaws and unlike Cromwell, is shown to be capable
of effecting—and indeed does achieve—a form of salvation as he chooses to
act in accordance with his corporate responsibilities, rather than his baser
instincts.

Scott addresses other aspects of defiled authority: the abuse of positional
authority to the point of corruption and the imbuing of illegitimate authority
with legitimate status. Yet he associates these examples of defiled authority
with Independent, rather than Parliamentarian, characters—specifically, the
Commissioners and Trusty Tomkins. Although Scott is at pains to construct
an ostensible balance between the two supreme authority figures of the novel,
Charles II and Cromwell, he does not seek such a balance in juxtaposing the
two denizens of Woodstock—Sir Henry Lee and the sequestrators, the Commissioners. Sir Henry is fondly drawn, a gallant yet irascible Cavalier of the
old school, idealistic in his loyalty and devoted to his King, his Bible and his
Shakespeare. The Commissioners are not so kindly used:

> Harrison was one of the most cruel and pitiless in Cromwell's army; al-
> ways urging some misapplied text to authorize the continued execution
> of the fugitives, and sometimes even putting to death those who had sur-
> rendered themselves as prisoners.
> *WOODSTOCK*, 115

Bletson is a coward and an atheist who is "quite prepared to submit to Cromwell, or any one else who might be actually possessed of the existing powers"

---

34   Wilt, *Secret Leaves*, 171, 170.

(*Woodstock*, 117). Desborough is Cromwell's brother-in-law, whose body parts "seemed rather to resemble the disputatious representatives of a federative congress, than the well-ordered union of the orders of the state, in a firm and well-compacted monarchy, where each holds his own place, and all obey the dictates of a common head" (*Woodstock*, 114).

It is interesting that Sir Henry Lee and the Commissioners both contravene martial law in their attempts to secure Woodstock as their prerogative.[35] The Commissioners' authority is shown to be defiled by their malfeasance in sequestrating Woodstock and evicting its tenants, in defiance of the precepts of military law. This defilement is worsened by their subsequent abuse and corruption of their (equivocal) positional authority as they seek to profit from their unwarranted tenancy of the Lodge. Scott implicitly contrasts this debased authority with Sir Henry Lee's authority as 'Keeper' of the King's property, an authority founded on his disinterested commitment to the King's cause, and compromised only by his, Sir Henry's, illegal exile (arguably a microcosmic allusion to Charles II's own exile and its questionable legality). By comparison, Sir Henry's violation of martial law is not an example of defiled authority; rather, it is presented as being a perfectly honourable exercising of authority, and is further validated by constituting one of the more effective comedic events in the novel. Sir Henry, together with the deaf old Dame Goody and the terrified Phoebe Mayflower, seeks to defend Woodstock from Cromwell's troop of soldiers—to no avail.

> "Death to all who resist—life to those who surrender!" exclaimed Cromwell, stamping with his foot. "Who commands this garrison?"
>
> "Sir Henry Lee of Ditchley," answered the old knight, stepping forward; "who, having no other garrison than two weak women, is compelled to submit to what he would willingly have resisted."
>
> "Disarm the inveterate and malignant rebel," cried Oliver. "Art thou not ashamed, sir, to detain me before the door of a house which you had no force to defend? Wearest thou so white a beard, and knowest thou not, that to refuse surrendering an indefensible post, by the martial law, deserves hanging?"
>
> "My beard and I," said Sir Henry, "have settled that matter between us, and agree right cordially. It is better to run the risk of being hanged, like honest men that to give up our trust like cowards and traitors."
>
> WOODSTOCK, 376–7

---

35 Both the omniscient narrator and Sir Henry denounce General Harrison for transgressing martial law by putting to death prisoners who had surrendered.

While Sir Henry is indubitably contravening martial law by his defiance of
Cromwell's military authority, again his disinterested loyalty and valour in
seeking to defend Woodstock contrast with the defiled authority of the Commissioners and their ambition to profit from their unlawful appropriation of
the locale. If Charles' sovereignty is a superior alternative to Cromwell's Lord
Protectorate, Sir Henry's stature as an ambassador for the Royalists is far higher
than the Commissioners' as representatives of the Independents.

One other coupling of characters across the political and religious divide of
the novel further demonstrates Scott's contrasting of compromised and defiled
authority. The characters of Trusty Tomkins and Joceline Joliffe are paralleled
comprehensively to demonstrate their inherent differences. The two are boy-
hood friends, of the same lower order in life, and in love with the same woman;
even so, they are political and religious opponents. Again Scott seeks to set the
compromised authority of the Royalist cause against the defiled authority of
the Independents. In this instance, defiled authority is the result of illegitimate
authority being legitimate status. The Independent Trusty Tomkins is "an out-
right hypocrite playing both sides of the political fence as an informer, [...] a
spy who has worked for both rebels and royalists [and] an amoralist without
political allegiance".[36] Nonetheless he inveigles himself into Woodstock as a
trusted and hence legitimated member of the Royalist cause. Joceline Joliffe,
however, is cautious, keeping under careful watch this "discreet seneschal"
(*Woodstock*, 322). Ultimately Trusty Tomkins' attempted rape of Phoebe—yet
another example of the abuse of a position of trust and consequent authority—
results in Joceline Joliffe's inadvertent killing of Tomkins. Although this act of
violence compromises Joceline Joliffe's own authority as Sir Henry's servant
and as trusted recipient of Louis Kerneguy's true identity, Joliffe's gallant and
instinctive motive of protecting Phoebe Mayflower contrasts favourably with
Tomkins' defiled intentions and hypocrisy.

Thus it can be seen that Scott, in his juxtaposition of compromised and
defiled authority at various social levels, seeks to promote the Royalist cause,
and, in so doing, Charles II as a preferable alternative to Cromwell and his cro-
nies. Throughout the novel Scott carefully constructs alternatives to Charles
and his potential to function as a legitimate, acknowledged and reinstated sovereign. Each of these alternatives is shown to operate not as a compromised
authority, but as a defiled one. Nevertheless, notions of defilement are not
confined to Scott's assessment of the various authorities. They are embedded

---

36   Kenneth M. Sroka, 'Fairy Castles and Character in *Woodstock*', *Essays in Literature*, 14 (Fall
      1987), 200–1.

in the novel's territorialization of space as the opposing factions campaign to control the historic built environment of Woodstock. Scott enmeshes concepts of defilement in the language used by the warring parties of Charles II and Cromwell. As we might expect, each attempts to establish his own moral purity and superiority, and to represent the opposing religio-political culture as other, as spiritually and morally polluted. David Sibley argues that stable built environments enable the inclusions of dominant cultures and the exclusion (and control) of subordinate ones. "Socio-spatial exclusion," he says, "[i]s part of the more general question of social control [... which] is the attempted regulation of the behaviour of individuals and groups by other individuals and groups in dominant positions".[37]

Woodstock is not, however, a stable built environment during the Interregnum. It functions as a confined space where the struggle to determine and establish the dominant culture takes place. Hence, the efforts of both the Independents and the Royalists to effect a "socio-spatial exclusion" of their enemies from the confined space of Woodstock constitute an attempt to control those broader social boundaries determined by political and religious alignments. The eviction of the Royalist Lees by Tomkins on behalf of the Commissioners is therefore a means of imprinting Independent dominance on Woodstock by establishing and reinforcing spatial boundaries. It is also the Independents' "attempt to distance themselves [...] from those who are deviant, different and dangerous [...] because of their desire to maintain purity and cleanliness" in both political and religious terms.[38] The Royalists' attempts to reassert their control of Woodstock are premised on the same aspiration.

Sibley argues that "[t]here is a history of imagined geographies which cast others who are seen to pose a threat [...] as polluting bodies or folk devils".[39] Throughout *Woodstock*, both factions can be seen to engage vigorously and enthusiastically in this practice. In the opening chapter, Tomkins, in his self-appointed role as preacher, demands of his Royalist listeners, "wallow[ing] in the mire of monarchy," (*Woodstock*, 15) "[A]re ye not now plotting, or ready to plot, for the restoring of the young Man, the unclean son of the murdered tyrant?" (14). Shortly afterwards, with typical Shakespearean referencing, Sir Henry accuses his daughter of "let[ting] that rebel youth creep into thy heart

---

37   David Sibley, *Geographies of Exclusion: Society and Difference in the West* (London and New York: Routledge, 1995), 81.

38   Minelle Mahtani, 'David Sibley,' *Key Thinkers on Space and Place*, 368. I make use of a number of Sibley-esque concepts regarding the domination and control of space and place, the desire to maintain spatial exclusion of the 'other' and the ambition to establish oneself as clean and the 'other' as polluted, as explored in *Geographies of Exclusion*.

39   Sibley, *Geographies of Exclusion*, 49.

I wot not; perhaps it is a punishment on me, who thought the loyalty of my house was like undefiled ermine. Yet here is a damned spot, and on the fairest gem of all" (23–4). Sir Henry and Trusty Tomkins then energetically trade insults of a similar vein:

> "Friend," said the soldier, "I would willingly be civil, but it consists not with my duty to these godly men, in whose service I am, spoken of after this irreverent and unbecoming fashion. And albeit I know that you malignants think you have a right to make free with that damnation, which you seem to use as your own portion, yet it is superfluous to invoke it against others, who have better hopes in their thoughts, and better words in their mouths."
>
> "Thou art but a canting varlet," replied the knight; "and yet thou art right in some sense—for it is superfluous to curse men who already are damned as black as the smoke of hell itself."
>
> *WOODSTOCK*, 26

Soon after, Sir Henry passes judgment on his nephew, Markham Everard: "Thou has spoken truth in that, Mark, wert thou the blackest Puritan whom hell ever vomited out, to distract an unhappy country" (*Woodstock*, 50). Later, Holdenough insists that "our native country is about to become the very sink and cess-pool of all schisms, heresies, blasphemies, and confusions, as the army of Hannibal was said to be the refuse of all nations" (102). Holdenough also vehemently condemns Woodstock as a source of Royalist pollution and contagion:

> a house of witchcraft and abomination, this polluted den of ancient tyranny and prostitution should be totally consumed by fire, lest Satan [...] should find a garrison and a fastness from which he might sally forth to infest the whole neighbourhood.
>
> *WOODSTOCK*, 187–8

Sometime later, Sir Henry is disgruntled to find that blasphemous republicans can write well:

> "John Milton?" exclaimed Sir Henry in astonishment—"What! John Milton, the blasphemous and bloody-minded author of the *Defensio Populi Anglicani!*—the advocate of the infernal High Court of Fiends; the creature and parasite of that grand impostor, that loathsome hypocrite, that detestable monster, that prodigy of the universe, that disgrace of

mankind, that landscape of iniquity, that sink of sin, and that compendium of baseness, Oliver Cromwell!"

WOODSTOCK, 279

Thus it can be seen that the language of pollution and defilement is harnessed for use by Royalists, Presbyterians and Independents alike—and the more fulsome the insult, the more dogmatic the speaker. The only significant characters at Woodstock who do not make use of this means of disparaging others and establishing their own superior moral credentials are Alice Lee and Markham Everard. These two are the most virtuous individuals in the novel; their marriage is effected by Charles' intervention and "exemplifies the good qualities of moderation and reconciliation that alone deserve perpetuation. Thus out of the crucible of the Civil Wars comes this marriage of Royalist and Puritan, this melding of the best elements of both characters".[40]

It is revealing then, that having established the general descent into the use of language of defilement, and the superior moral qualities of those who do not engage in such badinage, Scott enunciates his own Royalist sympathies throughout the novel in two ways. The first is through the 'devilry' in which the Royalists engage to rid Woodstock of the Commissioners; the second is through the frequent association of the defiled authority figures of the novel—Cromwell, the Commissioners and Tomkins—with the Devil himself.[41] In the opening chapter of the novel, Scott establishes his Royalist sympathies through an authorial voice that resonates with a sense of loss and bereavement at the wanton sullying of legitimate order and decorum. Attention is drawn to the desecration of traditional values through the violence reverberating throughout this chapter which portrays the oppression of Royalist values by the crude display of military power.[42] Scott's Royalist sympathies, already foregrounded in the opening chapter, are further revealed in his careful crafting of "the devil's work" at Woodstock during the Commissioners' tenancy. Sibley suggests that when

---

40   Trela, 'Sir Walter Scott on Oliver Cromwell,' 218.

41   Sroka makes the same point: "The authorities of the Interregnum—the commissioners, their dragoons, and Oliver Cromwell himself—are all repeatedly referred to as 'devils'" (Sroka, 'Fairy Castles,' 193).

42   Sroka argues that "*Woodstock* begins, therefore, with an act of desecration, a church occupied by brute military force, presented as a kind of demonic possession" (Sroka, 'Fairy Castles,' 193). Trela makes the point that "[t]he story opened with a description of the Woodstock parish church, which has seen its effigies smashed, its stained-glass windows shattered, wood carvings broken up, and its sacred aisles used as a stable (1.15–18)" (Trela, "Sir Walter Scott on Oliver Cromwell," 215–6).

a threat to core values [occurs], social and spatial boundaries [...] can become charged and energised. The oppressed, however, have their own strategies which challenge the domination of space by the majority, if only briefly and in prescribed locales. Ultimately, carnivalesque events confirm their subordination.[43]

Scott does not pass judgment on the Royalists' antics at the "possessed" Woodstock locale; rather, his commentary is directed towards the effects of this devilry on the Independent and Parliamentary recipients. The cowardice displayed by the Independent Commissioners is scorned: "Here are Bletson and the brute Desborough, terrified out of their lives, and Harrison raving mad, because the devil will not be civil enough to rise to fight him" (*Woodstock*, 131).

Sroka suggests that the conflict in *Woodstock* is a "conflict between tradition and rebellion, [...] depicted as a dramatized contest between good and evil, between the sacred and the demonic".[44] However, I would argue that the conflict is between compromised and defiled authorities. Thus, as a means of emphasizing the moral turpitude of those defiled authority figures mentioned, Scott juxtaposes the pseudo-devilry of the Royalists with the specific references by a range of characters—both Royalist and Presbyterian—to Cromwell, the Commissioners and Tomkins that link them to the Devil. It is interesting to note how Scott deflects the one exception to this linking. When Albert Lee takes issue with Wildrake's entrenched debauchery, Dr Rochecliffe argues that this is the more the effect of societal disorder occasioned by the Roundhead perversion of hierarchical mores, laying explicit blame for Wildrake's failings at the door of "the lower orders," and suggesting that Charles is similarly affected:

> "Alas!" said the doctor, "it is but too true; but what can you expect? When the higher and more qualified classes are broken down and mingled undistinguishably with the lower orders, they are apt to lose the most valuable marks of their quality in the general confusion of morals and manners—just as a handful of silver medals will become defaced and discoloured if jumbled about among the vulgar copper coin. Even the prime medal of all, which we royalists would so willingly wear next our very hearts, has not, perhaps, entirely escaped some deterioration."
> WOODSTOCK, 239

---

43   Sibley, *Geographies of Exclusion*, 46.
44   Sroka, 'Fairy Castles,' 193.

Again, Scott notes the compromised authority of Charles and his "defaced and discoloured" character, yet differentiates it from the more debased forms of authority existing in the novel. By contrast, Scott links Cromwell—as defiled authority—explicitly with the Devil. Gary Kelly suggests that

> all the characters in the novel are manipulated directly or indirectly by [Cromwell]; he is the *diabolus ex machina*, a real counterpart to the imagined and faked devil-work conducted at Woodstock to frighten off the Parliamentary commissioners and allow Charles to seek temporary refuge there.[45]

Cromwell himself is conscious (and speaks) of the widely held belief that he is in league with the Devil: "Think'st thou, like other fools, that I have made a paction with the devil for success, and am bound to do my work within an appointed hour, lest the spell should lose its force?" (*Woodstock*, 372). Wildrake is one of those "fools"—"Noll hath certainly sold himself to the devil," he advises Markham Everard early in the novel, sometime later adding: "I have seen the devil and hast, as thou say'st, got a warrant from him" (*Woodstock*, 59, 97). References to the Commissioners as embodying or in league with the Devil are equally overt:

> "I say" said the Presbyterian [Holdenough], "there are worse folk may rise than cavaliers; and I will prove what I say. The devil is worse than the worst cavalier that ever drank a health, or swore an oath—and the devil has arisen at Woodstock Lodge! [...] I see not that I may with prudence trust myself with the tossing and goring ox Desborough, or the bloody and devouring bear Harrison, or the cold and poisonous snake Bletson— all of whom are now at the Lodge, doing license and taking spoil as they think meet; and, as all men say, the devil hath come to make a fourth with them."
>
> *WOODSTOCK*, 103

Central therefore to Scott's position throughout *Woodstock* of supporting Charles II and his anticipated, and ultimately realized, sovereignty is the cumulative process of demoting the alternative authorities operating in the Woodstock locale. In that confined space, Scott seeks to denounce implicitly Cromwell, his associates and his henchman as representatives of a defiled authority, against which Charles' compromised authority is favourably situated.

---

45   Kelly, *English Fiction*, 169.

Charles' potential to function as a legitimate, acknowledged and reinstated sovereign is further demonstrated by his being the only authority figure to achieve a positive restoration of order (albeit only a private instance) when he effects the marriage of Alice and Everard. By contrast, Cromwell's equivalent restoration of order at Woodstock is merely the rescinding of his arbitrary and illegal order to put the Royalists—including Bevis, the faithful hound—to death. Although at no time in *Woodstock* does Scott visit unequivocal approval upon Charles' character, ultimately he posits a strong and consistent argument that in the world of the Interregnum, where so much defiled authority is recognized and rewarded, Charles II's legitimate authority, undermined as it is by its own shortcomings, is a superior authority—even when unrecognized, but especially when restored.

CHAPTER 2

Governance and Agency in *Woodstock* and *Peveril of the Peak*

To have a sense of the past is to have a sense of the way in which present and future conditions are embedded within a complex 'history' that is articulated only with respect to particular individuals and concrete objects as they interact within specific spaces and with respect to particular locations.

The past cannot be grasped independently of location in place.

MALPAS[1]

∴

It might seem that Scott uses locale very differently in *Woodstock* and *Peveril of the Peak*. In *Woodstock* the action takes place primarily in Woodstock itself, while in *Peveril of the Peak* the protagonist, Julian Peveril, traverses a number of locales in his quest for justice. Much of Scott's counter-revolutionary argument in *Woodstock* is illustrated through his use of place and the transition between various locales within and around Woodstock; and, in *Peveril of the Peak*, it is conveyed through Julian's visitations of discrete locations—the Isle of Man, London, Newgate and Martindale.[2] Fielding suggests that Scott, in imaging the Scottish Border in *Minstrelsy of the Scottish Border*, effected "a double function—both affirming the singularity of a region not well known to the majority of readers and translating that singularity into general ideas about the

---

1   Jeff Malpas, *Place and Experience: A Philosophical Topography* (Cambridge: Cambridge University Press, 1999), 180.

2   The significance for Scott of the Isle of Man is emphasized in 'Essay on the Text' and 'Historical Note' of *Peveril of the Peak*, ed. Alison Lumsden (Edinburgh: Edinburgh University Press, 2007), 497–8, 603 and 614. Lumsden also discusses the likelihood of "Haddon Hall [being a] prototype for Martindale" but notes that "the fictional castle is only very loosely based on the actual one" (*Peveril*, 613, 614). In addition, she comments on the vibrant representations of London and Newgate Scott creates in the later chapters of the novel in her broader analysis of the significance of topography throughout the novel (*Peveril*, 614–6).

© KONINKLIJKE BRILL NV, LEIDEN, 2018 | DOI 10.1163/9789004352780_004

customs and language of its [...] population".[3] Similarly, he achieves this in the representations of all of those aforementioned sites, for Scott, utilizing what Casey would understand by the phrase 'spirit of place,' positions conflicting and competing mechanisms of governance and the natures of their respective authorities in the two novels.[4] Thus topoanalysis is pertinent here to an appreciation of how Scott places individuals within the experience and history of the various sites within Woodstock in that novel; and those locales through which Julian peregrinates in *Peveril of the Peak* are intrinsic to his counter-revolutionary argument throughout the novel of that name. Topoanalysis sheds light, too, on his placement of Charles II—both unrecognized and restored royal entity, fledgling and mature sovereign, monarchical individual and body politic—into specific locales in this pair of novels. Within that broad context, Malpas' contention that there is a "necessary locatedness of experience in place" illuminates intrinsic similarities between Scott's representations of governance and of sovereignty in both novels.[5] Ultimately it is through Scott's portrayals of locale—of the various experiences of governance and sovereignty that are embedded in each locale—that his argument supporting the restoration of Charles II is realized.[6]

I shall therefore focus on three Malpasian methods of exploring the nexus between place and experience in order to analyse how Scott communicates this argument effectively in both *Woodstock* and *Peveril of the Peak*. The first is the use of topographical surveying as a metaphor and as a framework to "map out that region from within the region itself".[7] When this is done, the

3   Penny Fielding, 'Curated Regions of the North: Art and Literature in the "Scottish Border" and the "Transpennine Corridor,"' *Visual Culture in Britain*, 15 (2014), 163.

4   For a more detailed discussion of place in this capacity, see Edward S. Casey's *Getting Back into Place: Toward a Renewed Understanding of the Place-World* (Bloomington: Indiana University Press, 1993) and *The Fate of Place: A Philosophical History* (Berkeley, Los Angeles and London: University of California Press, 1998). See also Gaston Bachelard's *Poetics of Space: The Classic Look at How We Experience Intimate Places*, trans. Maria Jolas (1969; rpt Boston: Beacon Press, 1994).

5   Malpas, *Place and Experience*, 194.

6   I am grateful to A.D. Cousins for his insights regarding representations of political governance and instability throughout the Interregnum in the context of individual and national, private and public experiences of 'home.' See: A.D. Cousins, 'Home and Nation in Andrew Marvell's Bermudas,' *Home and Nation in British Literature from the English to the French Revolutions*, ed. A.D. Cousins and Geoffrey Payne (Cambridge: Cambridge University Press, 2015), 33–48, and the chapter 'Home and Homeland in *Upon Appleton House, To My Lord Fairfax*' in his *Andrew Marvell: Loss and Aspiration, Home and Homeland* (London; New York: Routledge, 2016), 186–215.

7   Malpas, *Place and Experience*, 40.

respective significance of each locale, and the locales' overarching thematic cohesion, become immediately apparent. Furthermore, Scott's "nesting" or embedding smaller locales within larger ones is neither accidental nor lacking in significance, for "[t]he nesting of events is very similar to the nesting of places. Events are 'located' by inclusion in larger events, just as places are located with reference to larger places".[8] In both novels Scott nests or interconnects various locales and events so as to irradiate the dysfunction of failing forms of law and justice within Britain as a sovereign state. This enables him to contrast different forms of law and justice from locale to locale, and demonstrate their potential impacts on a national rather than merely a parochial landscape, allowing for both "a unifying of diverse elements within a single structure" and for Scott to assert that Charles can effect social order and natural justice more comprehensively than can those inferior systems of justice.[9]

Finally, given that Scott's preoccupation in both novels is undeniably the functioning of various agencies of law and justice, there is value in assessing each locale in the context of embodiment. Malpas argues that "[s]patiality and embodiment—and so, also, the idea of the locality in which action is embedded—are essential to the possibility of agency".[10] Characters such as Sir Henry Lee, the Commissioners, and Cromwell in *Woodstock* and the Countess of Derby and the Duke of Buckingham in *Peveril of the Peak* make it possible for Scott to examine the disparate laws and justice systems operating during the Interregnum and the Restoration. He can therefore position Charles II as the embodiment of natural justice (potentially in *Woodstock* and actually in *Peveril of the Peak*). Scott's use of these locales, when contrasted with, say, the sites of failed governance and sovereignty in *Peveril of the Peak*—the Isle of Man, London and Newgate—demonstrates how his support of Charles II as monarch in both *Woodstock* and *Peveril of the Peak* is ultimately embedded "in the concreteness of an embodied, located, bounded existence".[11]

A Geopolitical Mapping of *Woodstock*

Throughout *Woodstock* and *Peveril of the Peak*, Scott analyses the multiplicity of laws and forms of justice present in Cromwellian and Restoration England. He considers the functioning of various laws (divine, positive, feudal, common,

---

8   Ulric Neisser, quoted in Malpas, *Place and Experience*, 102.
9   Ibid., 104.
10   Ibid., 136.
11   Ibid., 193.

and natural) and justice systems (legal, social, religious, and natural) under different political systems within these historical frameworks in order to present Charles' restoration as a positive chapter in England's history. Intrinsic to his argument is the depiction of both Woodstock and Martindale initially as sites vulnerable to failed systems of governance and sovereignty, and ultimately as sites where the restoration of legitimacy and social order can be, and have been, effected.

To ascertain how successfully Scott uses locale to affirm Charles' reign in these two novels, it is necessary to define what is meant by a locale of failed governance, or of successful sovereignty, in the historical context of the seventeenth century. From one then-familiar, if not of course uncontested, point of view in the seventeenth century, law was understood to exist as a hierarchy, with the highest form of law being eternal law from which all other laws derived. This ultimately Thomist perspective asserts—as it did for Dante—that natural law is "the participation of the rational creature in the Eternal Law".[12] Scott, conversant with and influenced by the Scottish Enlightenment on issues of jurisprudence, supported the natural evolution of law, based on the rational and moral philosophies codified by James Dalrymple, 1st Viscount of Stair and George Mackenzie of Rosehaugh.[13]

Thus, a locale of failed governance and sovereignty is one where inferior forms of law, such as positive law—law "posited or laid down by a particular body of conventions [that is] entirely the product of human design"—prevail and where, as a result, natural law cannot exist.[14] A site of successful sovereignty is, therefore, one where natural law, evidenced by the presence of natural justice—a "justice that does not depend on convention but only on nature, so as to contain within itself a criterion of validity that is independent of positive law"—can be, at the very least, effected and, at best, sustained.[15] Woodstock and Martindale function in each of these capacities, and in doing so facilitate Scott's counter-revolutionary support of Charles II's reign, especially when contrasted with the alternative modes of governance presented in each of the novels.

---

12   For a brief illustration of this, see Dante Alighieri, *The Divine Comedy: Purgatory* (London: Penguin, 1995), 346.

13   For a detailed analysis of the Scottish Enlightenment and issues of jurisprudence including the foundational work by Stair and MacKenzie, see Knud Haakonssen's 'Natural jurisprudence and the theory of justice,' *The Cambridge Companion to the Scottish Enlightenment*, ed. Alexander Broadie (Cambridge: Cambridge University Press, 2003), 205–21.

14   Roger Scruton, *A Dictionary of Political Thought* (London and Basington: Macmillan Press, 1982), 364.

15   Ibid., 316.

There are many aspects to consider when mapping Woodstock from within the region, and it is no simple task. Scott's own preoccupation with the significance of place is clearly signalled by his inclusion in the novel (added to the text as an 'Appendix to the Introduction' by Scott in 1832) of a regional and historical mapping of Woodstock titled 'A Short Survey of Woodstock' which discusses the monarchical history of Woodstock and the physical characteristics of that noble seat and details the Commissioners' experiences while at this site.[16] Indeed, Scott's detailed embedding of the events in specific locations throughout the novel supports Gary Kelly's contention that "Scott had a profoundly political and moral attitude to the material objects of life, state or domestic, and to the shape of the physical environment in which people lived".[17] Woodstock is the primary setting of thirty-four of the thirty-eight chapters in *Woodstock*. If one considers the specific location of each chapter, it becomes clear that Woodstock, itself a unitary locale, encompasses the following sub-locales: St John's Chapel; Woodstock Lodge, including Rosamund's Tower and Love's Ladder; and the environs of Woodstock, incorporating Woodstock Park and Woodstock Chase. Each of these, while contributing to the overarching thematic unity of the novel, also has unique significance. Casey's focus on the importance of undiscovered and transitional parts of buildings and their relationships to their surrounds is thus of particular relevance here. So too is Malpas' view that "the structure of place is further complicated by its character as containing and contained, open but bounded, as folded inwards and outwards, as both concretely experienced and abstractly represented".[18] Their concepts are valuable when one explores Scott's accounts of the spirits of places and of the complementary relationship between a dwelling and the immediate landscape surrounding it. Every one of these sub-locales within Woodstock is invested with dual significance. Each is used to portray a site beleaguered by positive law, and at times literally besieged by representatives of martial law, However, each also exemplifies a site where legitimacy and social order have previously existed, or where the potential for their restoration resides.

---

16   See the Appendix to Introduction in *Woodstock*, xxii–xxxvii, for "Appendix No. II.: The Just Devil of Woodstock; or, A True Narrative of the Several Apparitions, the Frights and Punishments, Inflicted Upon the Rumpish Commissioners Sent Thither to Survey the Mannors and Houses Belonging to His Majesties," including "A Short Survey of Woodstock, Not Taken by Any of the Before-Mentioned Commissioners," (Walter Scott, *Woodstock* (London and Toronto: J.M. Dent & Sons Ltd, 1931), xxxv–xxxvii).

17   Gary Kelly, *English Fiction of the Romantic Period, 1789–1830,* Longman Literature in English Series (Harlow: Longman, 1989), 146.

18   Malpas, *Place and Experience*, 173.

In Chapter 1, I discussed the significance of the opening pages of *Woodstock*, in which Scott establishes the Royalist sympathies that reverberate throughout the novel. Equally important in the novel's beginning is Scott's use of St John's Chapel—these "hallowed precincts [...] made the quarters of a troop of horse"—to establish Woodstock as a site once peaceful and orderly, but now riven by ascendant, destructive governance (*Woodstock*, 8). He says:

> The condition of the church and character of the audience both bore witness to the rage of civil war, and the peculiar spirit of the times. [...] The windows, once filled with stained glass, had been dashed to pieces with pikes and muskets, as matters of and pertaining to idolatry. The carving on the reading-desk was damaged, and two fair screens of beautiful sculptured oak had been destroyed, for the same pithy and conclusive reason. The high altar had been removed, and the gilded railing, which was once around it, was broken down and carried off. The effigies of several tombs were mutilated, and now lay scattered about the church.
>
> WOODSTOCK, 7–8

In this wantonly sullied church, Scott depicts the social, political and religious ramifications of the loss of traditional monarchical governance, and the inherent failings of the replacement sovereignty. He continues:

> The audience, like the building, was abated in splendour. None of the ancient and habitual worshippers during peaceful times, were now to be seen in their carved galleries, with hands shadowing their brows, while composing their minds to pray where their fathers had prayed, and after the same mode of worship [...]. There were among the congregation, however, one or two that, by their habits and demeanour, seemed country gentlemen of consideration, [...]. But, besides these dignified persons, there were in the church a numerous collection of the lower orders, some brought thither by curiosity, but many of them "unwashed artificers," bewildered in the theological discussions of the time, and of as many various sects as there are colours in the rainbow. The presumption of these learned Thebans being in exact proportion to their ignorance, the last was total and the first boundless. Their behaviour in the church was anything but reverential or edifying.
>
> WOODSTOCK, 8–9

It is here in the "place" of God, also, that the chasm is highlighted between the precepts and tenets of divine law—that eternal law revealed in Scripture and in the commandments which express God's will in the Bible—and its application resulting from sectarian (mis)interpretation of that Scripture. The expulsion of the Presbyterian Reverend Holdenough by the Independent Tomkins is a clear example of this misappropriation of divine law; so too is the triumphant eviction of the Presbyterian pastor from the Martindale parish by Sir Geoffrey and the Episcopalian minister, in *Peveril of the Peak.*

It is only once the impact of the Independent regime—social, political, and religious—is witnessed at St John's Chapel that the reader is led to the "symbolic centrality" of the novel that is Woodstock Lodge.[19] Woodstock Lodge—that building, carefully constructed both physically and narratively, which resonates with history, referencing the monarchy from Henry II on—encapsulates the struggle for political and cultural dominance by the warring Royalist and Parliamentarian/Independent parties. The ascendancy of the "scoundrelly roundheads" heralds, for Scott, the fate of common law in a politically unstable environment, especially when it is subject to potential abuse by the imposition of positive and martial laws (*Woodstock*, 278). Common law functions optimally in an established and stable social environment where compromise is possible and legal precedent is recognized.[20] Its vulnerability is demonstrated by the expulsion of the Lees from the Lodge:

> "Expelled—by soldiers!" exclaimed Everard, in surprise—"there is no legal warrant for this."
>
> "None at all," answered the knight, in the same tone of cutting irony which he had all along used, "and yet as lawful a warrant, as for aught that has been wrought in England this twelvemonth and more."
>
> WOODSTOCK, 49

Woodstock is therefore as susceptible to the vagaries of positive law as Martindale is shown to be when the Peveril Pole-star is extinguished in *Peveril of the Peak*, during Julian Peveril's detour on his way to London. The Commissioners' sequestration of Woodstock indicates the potential evils implicit

---

19   Francis R. Hart, *Scott's Novels: The Plotting of Historic Survival* (Charlottesville: University Press of Virginia, 1966), 103.

20   The effectiveness of common law, being "based initially on judicial interpretation of local customs, on judicial and royal decisions in important cases, and on rare acts of formal legislation contained in royal statutes" is limited because of its inability to provide unfailing justice and protection against the potential evils of positive laws, as a result of its innately reactive nature and, therefore, its need for precedent. There is, of course, no precedent for these stirring times of the Interregnum (Robertson, *The Penguin Dictionary of Politics*, 56).

in positive and martial laws when they are carelessly wielded by those with little concern for the effects of their doing so. In Woodstock Lodge, however, there also resides the opportunity to resurrect Cavalier values and traditions that Scott (cautiously and conditionally) aligns with the potential restoration of legitimacy and social order. Within Woodstock—"the perplexed maze of rooms and passages [...] chambers of retreat and concealment [...] trapdoors and hatchways, sliding panels and portcullises [...] strong doors, party-walls, and iron-grates"—lie the inner sanctums of Dr Rochecliffe's study and Victor Lee's apartments (*Woodstock*, 382). Scott positions these as the very heart of Woodstock, from where both the Cavalier "devilry" visited upon the Commissioners and Charles' escape, are planned and executed. Despite their apparent impenetrability, Cromwell, operating under martial law, gains access to both, forcing Phoebe Mayflower to reveal the secret access to Dr Rochecliffe's study via Victor Lee's picture, and sending his soldiers to locate the study. It would appear that the Parliamentary interest is finally and unassailably dominant at Woodstock. However, Scott demonstrates that entry to these apartments does not signal success:

> [I]t seemed they had gained the very citadel of the labyrinth; but though various passages opened from it, they all terminated in places with which they were already acquainted, or communicated with the other parts of the house, where their own sentinels assured them no one had passed.
>
> WOODSTOCK, 384

The same principle ultimately applies to Woodstock Lodge *in toto*, ostensibly made uninhabitable by Cromwell's blowing up the Love's Ladder tower.

Graham McMaster contends that "[w]hen the tower is blown up, it is the monarchy that is demolished, morally if not physically".[21] I would, however, quote 'Appendix II to the Introduction' of Woodstock: "What kings do build, subjects may sometimes shake, but utterly can never overthrow".[22] By attempting to demolish Woodstock, Cromwell is hoisted with his own petard. The building itself is destroyed, but the King has escaped (as has Albert Lee), and Cromwell's own soldier has been killed. Thus, just as forced entry into the heart of Woodstock does not constitute the triumph of the Roundhead cause within the building, the demolition of Woodstock does not signal the demise of the Royalist cause. It is merely an attempt at that demise, and its failure is

21   Graham McMaster, *Scott and Society* (Cambridge: Cambridge University Press, 1981), 128–9.
22   Walter Scott, *Woodstock* (1931), xxxvi.

made concrete nine years later when the latently dominant Royalist culture witnesses Charles' Restoration. Assertion of physical dominance over Woodstock achieves little, for Woodstock Lodge is a symbol of the monarchy's (and England's) history, but not of its future. Its demolition signals the monarchy transcending its past—public and private, political and amorous—and beginning afresh. Therein lies the significance of the Lees removing from Woodstock to live near their Presbyterian kin: the social order Charles effects by bringing about the marriage of Alice and Markham Everard is a reconciliation, a new beginning to be located separately from Royalist history.

McMaster goes on to argue that Rosamund's Tower and Love's Ladder are significant because of their association "with the expression of the King's will, with abuse of power and the corruption of the court".[23] I contended earlier that their significance lies in their past association with previous monarchs and the machinations of their courts. Similarly, Woodstock Park, over which Rosamund's Tower and Love's Ladder cast a long, historic shadow, is the site where Scott explores the public implications of acting on private desires and the need for the public body of the monarch to subdue the private one. Gary Kelly suggests

> [o]ne of the noticeably 'progressive' elements in Scott is his critical treatment of court culture and politics, especially court intrigue, the 'mistress system' or 'backstairs politics,' the selfish and damaging competitiveness of courtiers, and the way these negative social values and practices filter down through the rest of society.[24]

This is borne out by the different degrees of significance with which Woodstock Park and Woodstock Chase are imbued. Here Charles, "first quitting the Lodge of Woodstock, and plunging into the forest," moves—physically and morally—from the constraints of Woodstock Lodge to an environment where "the gay old Norman secluded his pretty mistress [...] Rosamond Clifford" (*Woodstock*, 252, 251). Here, court culture dominates, leading Charles to contemplate the seduction of Alice at the potential cost of his sovereignty.

> His [Charles'] profligate logic, however, was not the result of his natural disposition, nor received without scruple by his sound understanding. It was a train of reasoning which he had been led to adopt from his too close intimacy with the witty and profligate youth of quality by whom

---

23   McMaster, *Scott and Society*, 128–9.
24   Kelly, *English Fiction*, 149.

he had been surrounded. It arose from the evil communication with Villiers, Wilmot, Sedley, and others, whose genius was destined to corrupt that age, and the Monarch on whom its character afterwards so much depended. Such men, bred amidst the licence of civil war, and without experiencing that curb which in ordinary times the authority of parents and relations imposes upon the headlong passions of youth, were practised in every species of vice, and could only recommend it as well by precept as by example, turning into pitiless ridicule all those nobler feelings which withhold men from gratifying lawless passion.

> WOODSTOCK, 252

It is in Woodstock Park that Charles plays "battledore and shuttlecock with his conscience," electing to seduce Alice and embark on a duel with Everard until, despite the risk of being unmasked and captured—and the risk of thus permanently sacrificing his monarchical aspirations—his nobler self gains ascendancy over his baser desires (*Woodstock*, 254).[25] He chooses to assume his public, monarchical role, and, by doing so, effects the marriage between Everard and Alice. It is in this sub-locale that Charles receives what Francis R. Hart terms his "education," marking the transition from an uncertain relationship with his monarchical responsibilities to his "salvation of the heart through recognition of the reality of goodness," whereby he elects to embrace his sovereign duties rather than the object of his personal desire.[26] It is here, too, that he realizes the inherent worth of Sir Henry's fervent, "old school" Royalism and thus his own innate responsibility to his birthright.

Having offered a regional map of Woodstock and explored the significance of each of the sub-locales, I will now consider Scott's nesting of locales within locales. Woodstock as a site clearly functions, at one level of representation, as a microcosm of England, and the Royalist/Roundhead occupation of the Lodge mirrors the Civil Wars, just as Sir Henry's 'restoration' to Woodstock foreshadows Charles' Restoration. Similarly, Woodstock as locale facilitates Scott's thematic exploration of monarchical legitimacy and the corrupting potential inherence in court culture that is ultimately positioned with the context of all Britain. I want, however, to analyse the significance of Scott's nesting

---

25   Tara Ghoshal Wallace also posits a well-considered argument about the significance of Charles II's conflicts between his natural body and his body politic in both *Woodstock* and *Peveril of the Peak* (Tara Ghoshal Wallace, 'Monarchy and the Middle-Period Novels,' *The Edinburgh Companion to Sir Walter Scott*, ed. Fiona Robertson. (Edinburgh: Edinburgh University Press, 2012), 106–7, see especially 115–7).

26   Hart, *Scott's Novels*, 101.

of sub-locales within the main locale of Woodstock. Malpas' argument that "a nested, place-based system of location […] make[s] sense of the interconnected and so unitary character of some spatially extended region" has specific relevance to Woodstock, when one considers the embedding of Woodstock Lodge within Woodstock Chase and Park, and the nesting of Woodstock itself within the broader landscape of England encompassing Eversly Chase and Rochester.[27]

I have already discussed the significance of Dr Rochecliffe's study and Victor Lee's apartments being so deeply and inaccessibly situated within Woodstock Lodge. Scott's placement of Woodstock Lodge within Woodstock Park and Woodstock Chase allows him to assess the risk to common law of the monarch's abusing his public status in order to realize his private whims, and the impact of court culture on society. Hart suggests that Woodstock has dual roles: "both as setting and as symbolic prize in an historic struggle [which] makes unnecessary the customary strategy of connecting the forces and events of public history and private natures and destinies".[28] Sroka notes a different duality of purpose:

> Woodstock Palace with its Lodge and Park functions as external and internal place. Throughout the novel it works as setting, the literal scene of the conflict between Cavaliers and Roundheads. Symbolically, it functions as the valuable repository of national power, tradition, and the large place of one's country.[29]

I argue rather that Woodstock, as a unitary locale, has three roles. First, it illustrates the impact and effect of various forms of law and their associated injustices perpetrated under Cromwellian jurisdiction during the Interregnum. Second, it demonstrates the superiority of Charles' own attempts to restore social order and natural justice, indicating his potential as monarch should he assume his legitimate sovereignty. Finally, it is ultimately positioned as a site that enables potential to be realized. For example, it is sufficient to enable Charles to rise above his personal desire and assume his sovereign responsibilities with regard to effecting Everard and Alice's reconciliation and marriage. Woodstock is also where both Everard and Alice grew up, they being the morally superior characters in the novel and the symbols of reconciliation

---

27   Malpas, *Place and Experience*, 105.
28   Hart, *Scott's Novels*, 104.
29   Kenneth M. Sroka, 'Fairy Castles and Character in *Woodstock*,' *Essays in Literature*, 14 (Fall 1987), 190.

for the future. The nesting of locales in *Woodstock* enables Charles to effect one instance of reconciliation and social order, which readers are to interpret as of wider significance: as McMaster suggests, "the palace of Woodstock, in which almost all of the action takes place, becomes something like a symbol of England".[30]

There is considerable movement between locales in the final chapter of Woodstock, signalling preparation and increasing readiness for Charles' restoration, and heralding a new form of sovereignty. The Lees have removed from Woodstock to Eversly Chase—there is literally no place for the obdurate Royalist position or for the old monarchical edifices, for Woodstock no longer exists. The significance of the location of the final scene, is, of course, its position outside the physical confines of Woodstock. The restoration of Charles' legitimate and recognized sovereignty means that his authority is no longer confined to a nested locale. Charles is both literally and metaphorically on the road from Brussels—that locale of exile—via Rochester to England's metropolis, in the process of his transformation from outcast to triumphantly reinstated monarch. He will assume his legal and judicial responsibilities in the nation's powerbase, from which he will henceforth reign.

The Centrality of Martindale

The centrality of Woodstock as a symbol of national reconciliation, restored sovereignty and counter-revolution in that novel is thus realized through Scott's embedding of sub-locales with the wider, but still confined, setting of the novel. As Hart explains:

> [Woodstock] links public and private destinies, embodies political and ideological relations in domestic ones, focused the problem of the vital continuity of civilized values on the problem of the survival of an ancient house. Spatial concentration is uniquely possible because the struggle for Woodstock serves so well as microcosm for the larger struggle.[31]

In *Peveril of the Peak*, on the other hand, it is through the protagonist's experience of several locales that the thematic importance of Martindale is foregrounded. Malpas argues that "[t]he concept of place is essentially the concept of a *bounded*, but open region *within which* a set of interconnected elements

---

30   McMaster, *Scott and Society*, 128.
31   Hart, *Scott's Novels*, 104.

can be located".[32] In *Peveril of the Peak*, Scott employs Julian Peveril's travels between Martindale, the Isle of Man, London, and Newgate to meld the significance of specific places and their respective laws and forms of justice in the context of a "bounded" England. He focuses primarily on three things: the ambiguous physical and legal relationship existing between England and the Isle of Man; the centrality of London in the creation of law, and of Newgate in the execution of law; and Martindale as the locale on which these laws are imposed and in which Charles' natural justice is embedded. Ultimately, just as "there is no geographically located base of virtue to sustain the hero's identity," neither is there a site where natural law, and hence natural justice, can function effectively without the intervention of a superior form of legal and judicial sovereignty.[33] As such, Scott positions Charles II as the only entity able to construct this locale through the creation of Martindale-Moultrassie. By juxtaposing Martindale—which bears in microcosm England's societal scars from both the Civil Wars and the Popish Plot, but which is also the site of Charles' demonstrating his capacity to effect true justice—with other, inferior locales riven with injustice, Scott establishes his counter-revolutionary argument supporting Charles' restoration.

Martindale's roles are therefore threefold, just as Woodstock's are in the novel of that name. The locale acts as an example of a site where the impact is felt of various forms of law and the injustices they perpetrate, thereby enabling their later contrast with Charles' superior natural law and justice. At the same time, Martindale demonstrates its worthiness to receive this natural law and justice. Finally, it functions as the site where Charles effects an instance of natural justice that can be read as a symbol of the greater good he could achieve if he chose. Thus, like Woodstock, Martindale operates as the figurative and thematic centre of the novel. *Peveril of the Peak* opens at Martindale, moves to the arcane Isle of Man, returns to (a decayed and politically vulnerable) Martindale, proceeds to London where Charles II is to be found, and closes at Martindale, its potential fully and ultimately restored by Charles' intervention in the operation of law and of justice.

Scott sets the first ten chapters of *Peveril of the Peak* at Martindale. These chapters introduce the co-existing justice systems and laws, the history of the locale in the context of the Civil Wars, and the conflicting ideologies residing there. In these chapters Scott shows the tentatively successful operation of natural and common law through the relationship of the Peverils with Major Bridgenorth. Their precariously balanced friendship is based on instinctive

---

32   Malpas, *Place and Experience*, 170.
33   McMaster, *Scott and Society*, 138.

human kindness and a deliberate ignoring of political and religious differences, unlike the relationship between the Lees and Markham Everard in
Woodstock, which has been fractured by these differences. Throughout both
Woodstock and *Peveril of the Peak* Scott twins religion and politics; as McMaster
points out, "theology [is] always a 'substitute' for politics with Scott".[34] At Martindale Scott explores several aspects of divine law (the supreme form of law
in the seventeenth century), addressing the issues of the differing hermeneutic
interpretations of divine law in Restoration England and the frequent disparity
between divine law and the actions taken in its name.

However, Scott's primary task in these early chapters is to establish Martindale as a locale where compromise can potentially be achieved despite the
resident "opposing fanaticisms".[35] Moreover, Martindale is shown to have the
potential to operate as a locale of successful governance and sovereignty. Scott
then seeks to contrast it with a site of failed anachronistic feudalism. First, the
Countess of Derby's descent on Martindale heralds the arrival of feudal laws
and justice from the Isle of Man into the uneasily contrived peace of Martindale, thus destroying the natural law operating there. Second, Julian departs
from Martindale in the Countess' wake to take up his residence on the archaic
Isle of Man. In each instance, feudal law—an extreme form of positive law—is
contrasted with the natural law operating at Martindale.

The Isle of Man is an important locale in Scott's analysis of the multiplicity
of laws and justice systems present in Restoration England, and therefore in
the appraisal of his success in defending Charles II and his restoration. Hart
says of the Isle: "As setting it has dual significance: as the dark place of fanatic
and vengeful conflict; as the 'old world' of little cultural change, withdrawn
from the mainland of intrigue and new disorder".[36] Yet I would argue that its
significance extends well beyond that simple duality. The Isle also acts as a
link between the initial themes and issues of law and justice resulting from
Charles' restoration established in the introductory chapters of the novel, and
the concerns and conflicts that have developed since Julian's leaving Martindale. Furthermore, it functions in the full glory of its negativity—as the site of
a failed legal, judicial and social system, and an active contrast to Scott's ultimate presentation of the natural justice effected by Charles.

The Isle's primitive, unsophisticated landscape is marked by irrevocable division. The Derby's oppressive and dogmatic governance and sovereignty have
failed to respond effectively to the legal, judicial and social changes emanating

---

34   Ibid., 128.
35   Hart, *Scott's Novels*, 105.
36   Ibid., 106–7.

from England. Similarly, rigid adherence to the strict hierarchy of feudalism has not healed the social fracturing that has resulted from the changing social and political ideologies of the Isle. Indeed, this arcane sovereignty has created and fomented dissension across Manx society, necessitated Julian's departure, and initiated his quest for justice. Thus, just as in *The Heart of Mid-Lothian* Jeanie Deans must quit Edinburgh to effect natural justice, Julian has to leave the Isle of Man to obtain a justice that transcends the myriad forms of justice being manipulated and abused on the Isle. His doing so demonstrates the need for a monarchical authority able to achieve social reconciliation and public benefit through natural justice, not social fragmentation through feudal law and private vendetta. This natural justice is, ultimately, achieved only by Charles—Scott implicitly argues this throughout his detailed analysis of the complex issues of monarchy, responsibility, law and justice on the Isle of Man.

Following Julian's remove from the Isle of Man, his journey to London in search of natural justice involves a brief but essential return to Martindale, upon which an inferior form of law and consequent injustice have been visited. Scott uses the locale to consider the movement towards justice: the transition from a definitely failed and mediaeval political system where true justice cannot function, to a flawed but superior alternative where natural justice, although not currently present, can still be achieved. In these few chapters, he foregrounds his concerns about positive law by tracing its imposition and the injustice to which it gives rise at Martindale. Martindale was initially depicted as a site where natural law resided, albeit uneasily. It was not able to withstand the effects of feudal law; nor can it operate in the face of positive laws created solely in response to the perceived threat of the Popish Plot. Scott's concern centres on what is, in this case, the reactionary nature of positive law, and its potential for manipulation by those given extraordinary powers because of a perceived crisis. This was, of course, a situation he had explored some years earlier when writing *The Heart of Mid-Lothian* in which he traced Jeanie Deans' sojourn to London in search of justice to ameliorate injustice wrought by positive law. In *Peveril of the Peak*, Julian in returning to Martindale finds his parents and himself embroiled in an overt failure of justice, with individuals denied any form of impartial legal recourse. Even though Martindale continues to exist as a place where natural law could once again operate successfully (however much this locale's potential has been reduced), at this stage of the novel there is no room for such law at this beleaguered locale.

Scott creates the device of the Peveril Pole-star, located at Martindale, to track symbolically Julian's progress in his search for justice. The Pole-star has several attributed histories, each significant. It is a "signal of general hospitality, which in ancient times, guided the wandering knight or weary pilgrim";

initially it was a "love-lighted watchfire" lit by a "former lady of Martindale" to guide her husband home through a storm; and later ascribed as being an assertion of the Peverils' "*suzeraineté* over the whole country" (*Peveril*, 235). But the Pole-star's significance extends beyond all these. Scott recounts how it "continued to beam more or less brightly" throughout the Civil Wars (ibid.), and continues to do so during all the trials experienced since then. However, it has obviously been (temporarily) extinguished as a result of the imposition of positive law on the estate. Guidance is the essential principle of each story applied to the Pole-star, guidance offered by the inhabitants of Martindale Castle itself. Yet the change in circumstances now places Martindale itself in need of guidance. Misdirected positive law has the power to quench a star that has been kindled for generations, so voracious is that law's power and so vulnerable, at this point, is Martindale. When the Pole-star is prematurely lit, it is in anticipation of the wrongs of Martindale being rectified, and demonstrates the villagers' active loyalty to the Peverils. For the star to be permanently rekindled, guidance, in whatever form, must be provided by an external figure of unquestionable authority and ability.

Julian is aware that the Peveril Pole-star will not, and indeed cannot, return to its former permanency, or fulfil its promise to provide guidance, constancy, love and hope, if he accepts Major Bridgenorth's offer of escape from England. In none of his encounters with the law has he found any vestige of the justice he sought, initially for the Countess of Derby, but now on behalf of his own family and hereditary social dependants. Freed by another display of village loyalty, Julian is able to continue his journey, the success of which will be acknowledged by the Pole-star ultimately shining out as a beacon of natural justice.

From the decayed and (temporarily) subjugated locale of Martindale, Julian proceeds to London, "the grand central point of intrigues of every description," the most complex and convoluted locale in *Peveril of the Peak* (*Peveril*, 310). Scott's references to both London and Newgate emphasize their labyrinthine and weblike natures; moreover, a bewildering array of political and personal plots and counterplots exists (or attempts to exist) at court. London is where Julian finds the natural justice for which he has been searching. However, Scott does not position the metropolis as a place where true justice exists inherently.

Scott's analysis of the Isle of Man and of Martindale centred on the operation of established feudal and natural laws, respectively, and on the implementation of (and reaction to) laws and justice systems formulated in and emanating from London, as a result of belief in the Popish Plot. On the Isle of Man and at Martindale, law and justice, although often misguidedly or inappropriately applied, were used to achieve or maintain goals that had a significant ideological basis, or to avenge perceived wrongdoing. In London, however, law and its presumed resultant justice are shown to be little more than tools used to achieve various political and personal ambitions and goals. Scott therefore uses London to contrast the corruption and self-interest involved in the creation or maintenance of various laws, laws produced or applied only for political or personal benefit, with Charles' ultimately disinterested creation of natural law. For all that, Scott also contrasts London, that sophisticated metropolis, with both the Isle of Man and Martindale, ensuring his argument encompasses both the rural and urban environments of Charles' "bounded" England.

One might first consider Buckingham's "ruinous arena" and then Newgate as examples of vested interests and the degradation of justice (*Peveril*, 381). The former, in addition to being a physical representation of Buckingham's character, is emblematic of London's political anarchy, and of the social effects of the current laws and justice systems. All is disorder and caprice—there is none of the stability and adherence to principle necessary to the law and justice Julian seeks. Natural law and justice are not to be found here: there is no interest in the concept of true justice, and a more formal and appropriate institution must provide it.

Newgate, despite it being recognized as a formal and legal institution of justice, exemplifies frighteningly the potential evil of so-called legal justice when its only point of reference is positive law, and functions also as an illustration of the dire need for an institution of true justice. It is a fitting complement to Buckingham's abode, and is equally incapable of, and uninterested in, the provision of true justice. If Buckingham's hotel reflects the social and political instability of London, Newgate is the representation of the worst aspects of the laws and justice systems operating during the time of the Popish Plot. It is at Newgate that Scott develops his critique of positive law to encompass its logical counterpart—legal justice. The inherent limitations of legal justice are shown to result from its reliance on positive law and the consequent potential for legal justice to be abused and perverted. If positive law, unable to be fettered by any other form of law that Scott has yet presented, can be manipulated by those given extraordinary legal powers but unendowed with other necessary merits, legal justice must, by association, have this same vulnerability. The locale of Newgate fails to provide a judicial buffer against the social hysteria and reaction of positive law; rather it is defined by those devastating effects of positive law. Newgate is the negation of justice. The manipulation and misconstruing of language within Newgate are a reflection of the maltreatment of justice itself. The turnkey at Newgate explains this to Julian: "I cannot say that guiltiness or not guiltiness argufies much, saving they be words in the verdict" (*Peveril*, 375). Scott uses the misinterpretation and misuse of language as a tool of disorientation—suddenly there is no acknowledged consistency of meaning. None of the concepts and ideals on which Julian has based his anticipation of his journey's successful outcome—constancy, actual and surrogate filial duty, steadiness of purpose and principle, commitment to morals and beliefs—has any recognized place or significance in Newgate.

The issues of public and private roles are of great importance in the London chapters. It is here that Scott justifies his continued emphasis on, and examination of, the intertwining of public and private ideologies and ambitions. Scott has demonstrated the potential of each locale through the management of conflict between private and public issues and ideologies. Division and disorder are the only result of the complex relationship between personal and political issues on the Isle of Man; similarly, the bewildering combination of private and public concerns in London appears to be purely negative and destructive. However, Charles, at an individual level, is able to construct a public and private justice that, although it is shown decisively to be incapable of operating in London, can function successfully at Martindale. Julian must leave London to experience the permanence of Charles' natural law and justice at Martindale, where public and private issues have already existed as potentially complementary forces, rather than mutually antagonistic ones, which they are on the Isle of Man and in London.

Throughout *Peveril of the Peak*, as Julian traverses different locales and experiences a variety of laws and forms of justice, Scott establishes very definite criteria for the justice required to restore the locale of Martindale. Thus the thematic importance of Martindale lies in its interconnectivity with, and contrast to, the Isle of Man, London, and Newgate. As Julian's journey towards justice continues, Scott's depiction of various failed sites of governance and sovereignty builds a compelling argument that culminates in Charles' creation of Martindale-Moultrassie through his application of the principles of natural law and justice to the locale of Martindale. By tracing Martindale's fortunes in the context of the Isle of Man, London and Newgate, Scott considers the failings of the many laws and forms of justice present in Restoration England, and in response posits a powerful defence of Charles II and his restoration. The Isle of Man functions as a point of reference to initiate, and to construct the basis of, many elements of the argument Scott continues to develop throughout the novel. Scott's achievement in the Isle of Man chapters is not merely to explore the inadequacies and failures of feudal law and justice by analysing the roles and obligations inherent in monarchy and the potentially contradictory nature of public and private justice. It is in the context of his presentation and appraisal of a failed political system that he establishes the need for a form of justice that transcends the essentially flawed forms functioning (or attempting to function) on the Isle.

Thus, Scott's argument supporting the restoration of Charles II requires the depiction of the Isle of Man as the site of a failed political system. Scott then implicitly compares and contrasts the vulnerable and reduced Martindale both with its initial portrait in the introductory section of the novel and with the failed feudal system of the Isle of Man, simultaneously indicating Martindale's current deterioration and its ongoing potential. The movement between Martindale and London is illuminating in that Julian moves between and among so many institutions of public and private justice. As McMaster points out, on his arrival in London, "Julian soon leaves the relative safety of the suburbs to experience in quick order the Park, Chiffinch's, Newgate, the Tower, the Court of King's Bench, the court".[37] Central to Scott's argument is the fact that Julian finds no aspect of natural law or justice residing in any of these sub-locales of London. Indeed it would impede his argument for Charles' restoration if London was itself positioned to provide the natural justice Julian seeks so desperately. Similarly, the Newgate Julian enters is nightmarish and grotesque in its ironic depiction of a judicial institution that supposedly ensure the fair and impartial administration of law, but in fact subjects its inmates to injustice and petty tyranny. The conflict between the assumed and actual qualities of the gaol enables us to consider further the role of established meaning and interpretation in Julian's search for natural law and justice. In addition, it illuminates the need to create additional criteria for the natural law and justice Charles is to effect. Scott has already discussed, in relation to the Isle of Man and Martindale, the extent to which the definition and concept of justice can be manipulated and mutilated by self-interest and ideological position, to the point where justice fails to have a generally recognizable—and recognized—meaning. The natural justice Charles is to effect must have none of this flexibility of meaning, or the vulnerability to misinterpretation, misrepresentation and inappropriate application that other forms of Restoration justice are shown to have.

Charles' initial achievement of justice—the outcome of the Peverils' trial—is accomplished by an individual who is the monarch rather than by the public exertion of his office of kingship. This distinction is emphasized by Charles' choosing to set in train the Peverils' release at a meeting at the apartments ("where Charles often held his private parties") of Chiffinch, "prime minister of his master's pleasures," rather than in a formal institution of justice (*Peveril*, 322). This instance of justice being effected privately is covertly contrasted with Scott's portrayal of the injustice achieved in Newgate, formal and public institution of justice that it is. However, although this situation of natural justice supports Scott's defence of Charles' restoration, another, more substantial

---

37   Ibid., 139.

and permanent creation of natural justice is required. The ultimate success of Scott's presentation of Charles' restoration as a positive chapter in England's history is broadly established by the creation of Martindale-Moultrassie. Scott's argument culminates in the scene in which Charles forcibly constructs this stable environment where natural law provides natural justice for the individual, and, in microcosm, for society.

Placing Legal and Judicial Sovereignty in *Woodstock* and *Peveril of the Peak*

Central to Scott's analysis of the various agencies of legal and judicial sovereignty in *Woodstock* and *Peveril of the Peak* are the notions of disinterest and nobility. Scott uses these qualities to establish Markham Everard and Julian Peveril as the heroes of the two novels, deserving of the monarch's involvement in the restoration of justice and social order they both so ardently desire. Scott also assesses the worth of various characters engaged in the creation or execution of law and justice according to these attributes. Ultimately, while many characters in *Woodstock* and *Peveril of the Peak* can be considered to be the embodiments of specific types of law, only Charles is positioned as the embodiment of natural justice, which Scott effects by having him consciously choose to act with disinterest and nobility.

Caroline McCracken-Flesher and Alexander Welsh both comment on "the phenomenon of the inadequate hero" in the Waverley canon who "seem[s] passive to the point of weakness," swept up in events and choices he does not fully understand.[38] Julian Peveril and Markham Everard are very different heroes from that protagonist. Indeed, it can be argued that *Peveril of the Peak* chronicles "the misadventures of a good-natured but inexperienced young man in the face of courtly intrigue and Machiavellian plots".[39] However, Julian displays a constancy of purpose and a moral rectitude that set him apart from Scott's archetypal heroes in the Waverley canon. Similarly, Markham Everard

---

38   Caroline McCracken-Flesher's 'Scott's Jacobitical Plots,' *The Edinburgh Companion to Sir Walter Scott,* ed. Fiona Robertson (Edinburgh: Edinburgh University Press, 2012), 50. McCracken-Flesher considers the Jacobite novels to be the novels in which this hero is primarily to be found, however Nigel, for example, in *The Fortunes of Nigel* is another of this ilk. Welsh discusses the various heroes to be found in the Waverley Novels, including the rationale for the archetypal Waverley hero and the 'exceptions' in *The Hero of the Waverley Novels: With New Essays on Scott* (Princeton: Princeton University Press, 2014), 21–39.

39   Kelly, *English Fiction,* 161.

is not the typical young, idealistic and innocent hero of Scott's earlier novels, such as *Waverley* and *Old Mortality*, swept by romantic fervour, an almost adolescent zeal and circumstance into a historical conflict he does not fully comprehend. Everard is no political *ingénu* but an experienced soldier who knows his political choices have cost him his love, but whose concerns remain socially focused: "If I have sacrificed my private happiness, it is that my country may enjoy liberty of conscience, and personal freedom" (*Woodstock*, 72).

Both men are engaged in the pursuit of justice on behalf of others, thus manifesting disinterestedness and nobility. Julian leaves the Isle of Man and commences his quest for justice in the capacity of surrogate son to both the Countess of Derby and Major Bridgenorth. His decision to go to Martindale involves the assumption of responsibility as the actual son of the house, in response to recognition of the danger to which his own family is unwittingly exposed. Nonetheless Scott shows that, as the son of the house, Julian's obligations extend beyond his immediate family concerns to others whose welfare remains dependent on the house of Peveril. Julian now has the opportunity to realize his ambitions of fulfilling his social role—not as he once naively hoped, living "like my fathers, among my own people, car[ing] for their comforts, decid[ing] their differences"—but by actively seeking the creation of a justice that provides for all (*Peveril*, 138). Similarly, Everard's support of Cromwell in *Woodstock* has no basis in personal benefit, as his cogitations and hesitations demonstrate:

> "Yet, it must be so," he said at last, with a deep sigh. "Among the contending parties, [Cromwell] is the strongest—the wisest and most moderate—and ambitious though he be, perhaps not the most dangerous. Some one must be trusted with power to preserve and enforce general order, and who can possess or wield such power like him that is head of the victorious armies of England? Come what will in future, peace and the restoration of law ought to be our first and most pressing object."
>
> WOODSTOCK, 73

He derives no benefit from requesting that Cromwell remove the Commissioners from Woodstock and allow the return of the Lees. For both Julian Peveril and Markham Everard, their focus is on the restoration of social order and justice for those around them, not on personal profit.

Having established these two heroes as embodying both disinterest and nobility in their respective pursuits of justice, Scott then considers various individuals charged with some form of governance or sovereignty in *Woodstock* and *Peveril of the Peak*. The Commissioners, having already demonstrated their grossly inappropriate application of positive and martial laws, are also shown to be manifestations of self-interest. When Everard informs them of Cromwell's orders that they depart Woodstock, their reluctance is palpable. Harrison retorts:

> I looked, amongst the three of us, that we might honestly, and piously, and with advantage to the Commonwealth, have gained out of this commission three, and it may be five thousand pounds. And does Cromwell imagine I will part with it for a rough word? No man goeth a warfare on his own charges.
>
> WOODSTOCK, 176

The Commissioners, having voiced their intent to use Parliament's military resources to ensure their financial gain from their continued sequestration of Woodstock, are, however, happy to accord with Cromwell's commands upon being informed they are to be engaged

> in a much greater matter, namely, the disposing of the royal property, and disparking of the King's forest at Windsor. [...]
>
> Colonel Desborough acquitted his right honourable and excellent cousin and kinsman of all species of unkindness; Master Bletson discovered, that the interest of the state was trebly concerned in the good administration of Windsor, than it was in that of Woodstock. As for Harrison, he exclaimed, without disguise or hesitation, that the gleaning of the grapes of Windsor was better than the vintage of Woodstock.
>
> WOODSTOCK, 177

Even so, all three remain "determined at least to keep sight of Woodstock, until they were well assured of some better and more profitable commission" (*Woodstock*, 178). The Commissioners' focus on personal gain as a result of their engagement in the execution of law in Woodstock is mirrored by the Duke of Buckingham's involvement in the creation of law in *Peveril of the Peak*. Buckingham is overtly presented as the embodiment of self-interest. His political machinations are directed towards the creation and execution of laws that will result in his having the autonomy to make "laws of [his] own" in his "little kingdom" of the Isle (*Peveril*, 296). For Buckingham, the law is shown to be little more than a mechanism to be (ab)used for the achievement of various political and personal ambitions and goals. For him and his ilk, the widespread social and individual effects of the Popish Plot are incidental to the political benefits to be gained from the 'horrid plot' and the associated court manoeuvrings and duplicity. Buckingham's mansion, in addition to being a representation of courtly intrigue and London's political instability is "the true emblem of an understanding and talents run to waste, and become more dangerous than advantageous to society, by the want of steady principle, and the improvidence of the possessor" (*Peveril*, 381). It is also emblematic of Buckingham's character and innate self-interest, housing his myriad conspiracies and intrigues:

> His gardens were destroyed—his pavilions levelled—his splendid stables demolished—the whole pomp of his suburban demesne laid waste, cumbered with ruins [...]—much was demolished, very little, in comparison, was reared up in its stead, and nothing was completed.
>
> *PEVERIL*, 380–1

Its very anarchy is the direct result of his inherent opportunism; in this instance an attempt at property development, in others political gain.

Oliver Cromwell and the Countess of Derby, in their capacities as sovereigns—Cromwell of England during the Interregnum and the Countess of the Isle of Man—are also assessed in terms of their disinterest and nobility. Both are found wanting. Despite the fact that Scott's representation of Cromwell incorporates both the latter's positive and negative characteristics, throughout *Woodstock* Scott draws frequent attention to Cromwell's political ambition, generated as much by his personal hunger for kingship as by any disinterested assumption of leadership. He is, in many ways, as driven by self-interest as are his generals, as is made clear by Markham Everard—Scott's moral barometer in the novel—and his ongoing concerns regarding Cromwell's suitability as sovereign:

> "There is no help for it," he said; "it must be Cromwell or anarchy. And probably the sense that his title, as head of the Executive Government, is derived merely from popular consent, may check the too natural proneness of power to render itself arbitrary. If he govern by Parliaments, and with regard to the privileges of the subject, wherefore not Oliver as well as Charles?"
>
> *WOODSTOCK*, 71

Scott is less diffident in his appraisal of the Countess of Derby; the Isle of Man is shown, through her character and ambiguous political as well as moral position, to be a political and social anomaly, existing apart from, but not immune to, English law. Scott considers the issue of monarchy very carefully in the

chapters detailing life on the Isle of Man, contrasting and comparing, by implication, the principles of sovereignty embodied in the Derby family with those
of Charles. The suggestion is that Charles may be a licentious and, at times,
irresponsible king, yet he takes his responsibilities as monarch far more seri-
ously than the Earl does his own, and portrays none of the arrogance that the
Countess constantly displays in her sweeping unconcern for her own subjects.
In addition, Charles, although notionally king by divine right, does not rely on
antiquated concepts of absolute rule and royal decree as the Countess does.
In none of the situations created by or resulting from the Countess of Derby's
vengeful beheading of Christian is true or natural justice applied. The concept
and interpretation of justice are distorted to the extent that the very definition
of justice is determined by the Countess' self-interest.

In both *Woodstock* and *Peveril of the Peak*, Scott's analysis of Cromwell
and the Countess (and Earl) of Derby is ultimately directed towards contrast
with Charles. By contrasting Charles' character with that of Cromwell and
the Countess of Derby, and by contrasting the nature of the justice he effects
with that achieved by each of those characters, Scott presents Charles as the
embodiment of natural justice. However, Scott makes no attempt to present
a whitewashed image of Charles in either novel, focusing on Charles' sexual
desires and proclivities, and on the potential and actual damage to his sovereignty as a result. Yet, having used the qualities of disinterest and nobility to
assess the various embodiments of the laws in Cromwellian and Restoration
England throughout *Woodstock* and *Peveril of the Peak*, Scott directs attention
not to Charles' constitutional or legal authority, but to his "personal authority
and power over the regulation of civil affairs".[40] Charles' personal concepts of
justice may indeed be belated and require some external inspiration, but his
interventions in both novels are the only instances of undeniable justice that
need no interpretation, and are invulnerable to either manipulation or abuse.
The "ultimate counter-revolutionary figure of Charles II" is the only person, in
his time, who is able to institute natural justice and societal reconciliation in
both *Woodstock* and *Peveril of the Peak*, by effecting the marriages of Alice Lee
and Markham Everard, and of Alice Bridgenorth and Julian Peveril.[41]

---

40   Daniel Cottom, 'Violence and Law in the Waverley Novels,' *Studies in Romanticism*,
      20 (Spring 1981), 78.
41   Fiona Robertson, *Legitimate Histories: Scott, Gothic, and the Authorities of Fiction* (Oxford:
      Clarendon Press, 1994), 267.

CHAPTER 3

Oppression, Justice and Monarchy in *Peveril of the Peak* and *The Heart of Mid-Lothian*

> No oppression is so heavy or lasting as that which is inflicted by the per-
> version and exorbitance of legal authority.
>
> JOHNSON[1]

∴

At one point in her *Bardic Nationalism*, Katie Trumpener highlights Scott's redefinition of how place is used as a signifier in the national and the historical
novel:

> The national tale before *Waverley* presents late-eighteenth-century cul-
> turalist assumptions, the influence of geography on character, setting
> and events, in particularly concentrated and politicized forms, upholding
> the distinctiveness and autonomy of place. And from *Waverley* onward,
> the historical novel shows the collapse and transfiguration of place, as
> an annalistic accretion of time within the stability of place gives way to
> the phenomenological development of places. The national tale before
> *Waverley* maps developmental stages topographically, as adjacent worlds
> in which characters move and then choose between; the movement of
> these novels is geographical rather than historical. In contrast, the his-
> torical novel [...] finds its focus in the way one developmental stage col-
> lapses to make room for the next and cultures are transformed under the
> pressure of historical events.[2]

Although elements of Trumpener's astute analysis of the destruction and
recreation of sites may be discerned in *Peveril of the Peak* and *The Heart of*

---

1 Samuel Johnson, 'Essay 148,' *The Rambler*, vol 3, ed. Alex Chalmers (Philadelphia: J.J. Woodwards, 1827), 232.
2 Katie Trumpener, *Bardic Nationalism: The Romantic Novel and the British Empire* (Princeton:
   Princeton University Press, 1997), 141.

Mid-Lothian, I suggest that, in fact, a more constructive blending of place occurs: one imbued with the monarchy's rejuvenation of social order through the successful conflation of disparate cultures and politics. Therein lies Scott's counter-revolutionary argument, set in the context of the violence and social destruction generated by the Popish Plot and the Porteous Riots, which are respectively depicted in *Peveril of the Peak* and *The Heart of Mid-Lothian*. In clarifying that argument's design, I shall make particular use of Casey's conceptualizing of how built sites can be successfully embedded in the formal construction of place.[3]

Of the six novels focused on in this study in which I argue Scott effects a continuous rehabilitation of the Stuart and Hanoverian dynasties, *Peveril of the Peak* and *The Heart of Mid-Lothian* have special significance. As I have remarked above, those two novels are by no means the only novels in the Waverley canon to chart a heroic protagonist's quest that culminates in a monarch's effecting the justice that is wanting—*The Fortunes of Nigel* has already been considered in this light, while *Woodstock* explores the role of the unrecognized and yet-to-be-restored Charles II.[4] But they are of particular interest because, viewed together and in order of the historical periods with which they deal, they demonstrate how Scott's counter-revolutionary perspective, and his use of place to communicate it, transcend the specifics of dynastic sovereignty. Written at and about different times—*Peveril of the Peak* in 1823 about the Popish Plot of 1678 and *The Heart of Mid-Lothian* in 1818 about the Porteous Riots of 1736—they excited very different critical appraisals, both at the time of their publication and subsequently.[5] Further differences are that *Peveril of the Peak* charts the pursuit of justice in England by an English male aristocrat, while *The Heart of Mid-Lothian* focuses on the travails of a Scottish female peasant in her attempt to bring about British justice in Scotland. Lumsden outlines a number of similarities between the two novels—these being the only Waverley Novels in four volumes; both following the same narrative pattern; and both novels being a means of demonstrating historical progression.[6] I suggest a further,

---

3   See Edward S. Casey's *Getting Back into Place: Toward a Renewed Understanding of the Place-World* (Bloomington: Indiana University Press, 1993), specifically Chapters 5 and 6.

4   Other Waverley novels with a plot in which the monarch is personally engaged in effecting a form of justice include *The Abbot* and *Ivanhoe*.

5   *Peveril of the Peak* has been generally regarded as one of Scott's less successful novels, with even Scott having "no very great opinion of *Peveril*; yet he thought the third volume 'much superior to the two first'" (Graham McMaster, *Scott and Society* (Cambridge: Cambridge University Press, 1981), 129). *The Heart of Mid-Lothian* has enjoyed constant critical acclaim and is considered one of the best novels in the Waverley corpus.

6   See Alison Lumsden, *Walter Scott and the Limits of Language*, (Edinburgh: Edinburgh University Press, 2010), 150–2 for a detailed discussion of these and other similarities between the

and critical, similarity: in both novels, Scott creates an argument supporting the notion of the monarchy even while portraying the respective flaws and limitations of the sovereign of the day. Moreover, Scott signals in each the reconciliation of fundamentally divisive societal issues in these novels through the creation of new built environments, which he implies herald respective futures of greater peace and prosperity.

Place is thus an intrinsic and sophisticated signifier of Scott's counter-revolutionism in each novel. He uses place in both novels to explore the effectiveness of various individuals, forms of governance and institutions in effecting natural justice, and the propensity for them to abuse the legal authority vested in them. He then uses this same mechanism to consider the capability of the monarch (and of monarchy as an institution) to effect societal justice and cohesion. This is not to suggest that in either novel Scott is a wholesale apologist for the monarchy. Rather, in both he seeks initially to demonstrate the corrosive and disruptive effects on society of unresolved conflict in the aftermath of a major social and political upheaval. In *Peveril of the Peak* this event is Charles' restoration to the English throne in 1660 after the Interregnum. In *The Heart of Mid-Lothian* it is the Union of Scotland and England in 1707. Each monarch's reign is therefore riven with social discord and uncertainty that give rise to events such as the Popish Plot and the Porteous Riots. In both novels, Scott seeks at once to define the role of the monarch in the midst of such events, and to establish who is responsible for the individual and social injustices resulting from these events. Scott traces the journey of each of his protagonists in such a way as to demonstrate that both a monarch's failure to prevent injustice and the abuse of legal authority by various other individuals and institutions are to blame for the social disorder and injustice resulting from the Popish Plot and the Porteous Riots. Having shown that those institutions are unable and disinclined to effect justice, Scott then depicts how each monarch (or his representative) eventually redresses the injustice inflicted on the protagonist's family, arrests the discord rending society and achieves social harmony—or at least an emblem of it. No other legal or judicial institution is capable of, or committed to, securing such natural justice as the monarchy exercises for the protagonist's benefit. Therefore, in both *Peveril of the Peak* and *The Heart of Mid-Lothian* Scott ultimately demonstrates that only the institution of monarchy can achieve true justice and lasting social order, a central tenet of his overarching counter-revolutionary argument in these novels. In terms of cultural and social geography, the presence of oppression in a society

---

two novels. Another important similarity exists in that both protagonists are involved in historic moments, but neither the Popish Plot or the Porteous Riots are on a scale comparable to those informing, say, *Waverley* or bookending the events of *Woodstock*.

functions as one of the most overt indicators of social injustice. As such, a useful means of exploring how Scott achieves the rehabilitation of Charles II and
Caroline is through the motif of oppression, which is intrinsic to each novel.

In her conceptual framework of oppression, Iris Marion Young outlines five
aspects or "faces" of oppression—namely, cultural imperialism, marginalization, exploitation, powerlessness and violence—which provide a productive
model for analysing Scott's fictional representations of oppressive forces.[7] To
consider the various faces of oppression and their representations in *Peveril of
the Peak* and *The Heart of Mid-Lothian* enables an assessment of Scott's portrayal of the weaknesses and failures of the respective monarchs, of the legal
abuses practised by various entities, and of the justice ultimately exercised by
the monarch which overcomes some instance of social oppression. That is to
say, doing so foregrounds Scott's counter-revolutionary argument.

In both *Peveril of the Peak* and *The Heart of Mid-Lothian* Scott depicts oppression primarily as the result of legal authority's being exceeded, exploited
or abused. Thus, in *Peveril of the Peak*, he makes it clear that Charles II's attempts to address the religious and political issues dividing England upon his
restoration are unsuccessful, so that legalized marginalization continues to
divide the kingdom. It is self-serving courtiers and legal administrators, Scott
asserts, who embed marginalization—the primary face of oppression in the
novel—in the law. Similarly, cultural imperialism dominates *The Heart of Mid-
Lothian*. As a result of George II and Caroline's failure to resolve issues arising
from the Union of Scotland and England in 1707, cultural imperialism becomes
enshrined in England's legal authority over Scotland. Despite the Acts of Union
preserving the authority of Scottish law, *The Heart of Mid-Lothian* explores two
instances where the English representative of the monarchy overrides Scottish
justice, thus demonstrating the cultural imperial forces in play. The Porteous
Riots are incited by a legal authority, John Porteous, exceeding and abusing his
power, and then being granted a reprieve by his queen. Effie Deans' death sentence is the result of a Scottish law premised on the assumption of guilt without positive proof—an instance of the law itself transgressing the principles of
natural justice—and which Jeanie Deans recognizes can only be overturned
by that same English monarchical figure.

To combat the oppression embedded in legal authority requires the protagonists in both novels to engage personally with the monarch. Both Julian
Peveril and Jeanie Deans embark on their respective journeys knowing that
success is only to be achieved by personal royal intervention. The meetings

---

7   Iris Marion Young. *Justice and the Politics of Difference* (Princeton: Princeton University Press,
     1990), 5.

between monarch and subject are efficacious primarily because, as Young suggests, the "model of politics [...] founded in face-to-face relations poses as the alternative to the impersonality, alienation, commodification, and bureaucratization of governance".[8] These meetings, therefore, make clear that the monarch must transcend the legal authority that fails so spectacularly to effect true justice, and that only the monarch has the facility and (at least, in ideal terms) the imperative to ensure that injustice inflicted by legal authority is redressed and remediated.

Young's framework of oppression and "conceptualizations of spatio-temporal relations" therefore illuminate Scott's counter-revolutionary argument supporting the notion of monarchy in both novels.[9] In *Peveril of the Peak* Scott assigns primary responsibility for the various oppressions being experienced by society to the court, to administrators or institutions of (supposed) justice, or to the revolutionary elements of society. In *The Heart of Mid-Lothian*, while he shows Caroline to be complicit in the legalized cultural imperialism being imposed on Scotland, Scott also shows the monarchy's representative to have an active role in remediating injustice and creating social order in microcosm, free from cultural imperialism. He also assigns primary responsibility for another face of oppression—violence—to the excessive zeal of various legal entities, and to the revolutionary elements and lower classes of society. In these ways he adroitly constructs a rehabilitation of both monarchies, Stuart and Hanoverian.

Marginalization, Exploitation and Powerlessness in *Peveril of the Peak*

In tracing the focus of Scott's writing from *Waverley* on, Lumsden comments that "[b]y 1820 Scott was clearly weary of subjects dealing with Scotland's relatively recent history".[10] In the 'Essay on the Text' in the Edinburgh Edition of *Peveril of the Peak* she points out that it seems "almost inevitable that, having shifted his attention away from Scotland in the 1820s, Scott would eventually turn to this period in an English context".[11] To that point, a significant feature of *Peveril of the Peak* is that it spans the tumultuous years in England

---

8   Ibid., 5.
9   Felicity Callard, 'Iris Marion Young,' *Key Thinkers on Space and Place* 2nd edn, ed. Phil Hubbard, Rob Kitchin and Gill Valentine (London: Sage, 2011), 485.
10 Lumsden, *Walter Scott and the Limits of Language*, 135.
11 Lumsden. 'Essay on the Text,' *Peveril of the Peak*, 498.

(and the Isle of Man) leading up to Charles' Restoration in 1660 and the events surrounding the Popish Plot of 1678. Scott devotes the first ten chapters of the novel to the period immediately following Charles' Restoration. The events of these chapters cast long shadows over later developments in the novel. In my previous chapter, I considered the attempts made in *Woodstock* by both the Royalists and the Independents (as well as the Presbyterians) to engage in marginalization so as to dominate the political-religious landscape. I argued that Charles' bringing about the marriage of Alice Lee and Markham Everard indicated that he, when once restored to the English throne, might be able to facilitate reconciliation between warring social parties. If *Peveril of the Peak* is considered alongside *Woodstock*, Scott's early focus in the former on the depth of the politico-religious chasms still existing in the kingdom is all the more marked. The societal divisions explored in these early chapters, and the ease with which longstanding political loyalties sweep aside attempts at reconcili-ation, demonstrate the difficulty of moving society beyond the political and religious marginalization inherent in the Civil Wars and the Interregnum.

This unresolved marginalization, coupled with the desire for social domina-tion, allows a widespread belief in the (supposed) Popish Plot to flourish, and enables the law to be abused as a means of suppressing it. This leads in turn to other forms of oppression—exploitation and powerlessness. While Scott concedes that Charles fails to address these faces of oppression at key points of the novel, he is primarily concerned with various parties' use of the law to visit oppression on others, whether for their own personal benefit or political advantage. He overtly dissociates Charles from visiting oppression on his sub-jects, and links violence specifically with rebellion, zealotry and extremism. Thereafter he contrasts Charles with various perpetrators of marginalization, exploitation, powerlessness and violence whose sole purpose is social domina-tion. Ultimately, Scott uses Julian's face-to-face meetings with his monarch to position Charles as both the only source of natural justice and the only entity able—when he so wishes—to effect lasting social reconciliation and harmony.

When Scott initially presents the locale of Martindale, he gives us a synopsis of the history of the characters and their conflicting ideologies. He also shows how complex are the issues dividing the Peverils and Major Bridgenorth—and society generally. Commencing with the involvement of both Sir Geoffrey and Major Bridgenorth in the Civil Wars, the opening chapters of the novel trace the waxing or waning public and private fortunes of both individuals over several years. Thereby Scott depicts the political and religious divisions that continue to fray the social fabric of the Restoration and to undermine tenta-tive attempts at reconciliation. The Countess of Derby's trespass into the wary co-existence of the Royalist Peverils and the Presbyterian Bridgenorth destroys the precarious balance achieved as both parties attempt to transcend their political and religious differences. It quickly becomes apparent that Charles' efforts to reach social reconciliation through legal avenues—by the passing of the Indemnity and Oblivion Act in 1660 (to which both Bridgenorth and the Countess make reference)—have done little to foster greater political tolerance.[12] The intrusion of the Countess of Derby and her rabid Royalism into Martindale inflames the smouldering "opposing fanaticisms" that continue to divide Britain.[13] With this resurrection of political and religious enmity comes the abandonment of tolerance, as each antagonist tries to marginalize and dominate the other, primarily by assuming legal authority.

Bridgenorth, on hearing that the Countess of Derby has executed his brother-in-law William Christian, discards his role as family friend and adopts his public legal persona to pursue vengeance on his relative's behalf:

> "Pardon me, madam," said the Major "[…];—to yourself I have nothing to say but what is respectful; but to this woman I must speak as a magistrate. She has confessed a murder in my presence—the murder too of my brother-in-law—as a man, and as a magistrate, I cannot permit her to pass from hence, excepting under such custody as may prevent her further flight. […] Charlotte, Countess of Derby, I attach thee of the crime of which thou hast but now made thy boast."
>
> "I shall not obey your arrest," said the Countess composedly; "I was born to give, but not to receive such orders. What have your English laws to do with my acts of justice and of government, within my son's hereditary kingdom? […] What right can you assert over me?"
>
> PEVERIL, 59

Lady Peveril also questions Bridgenorth's magistracy, again demonstrating the legalized nature of marginalization occurring in the wake of Charles' Restoration:

> "I know not that," said Lady Peveril. "That you were a magistrate, Master Bridgenorth, under the late usurping powers, I know well—but till I hear of your having a commission in the name of the King, I now hesitate to obey you as such."
>
> PEVERIL, 60

---

12   The Indemnity and Oblivion Act 1660 (also known as An Act of Free and General Pardon, Indemnity, and Oblivion) limited the reprisals against those previously involved in establishing and maintaining the Interregnum to those engaged in the regicide of Charles I.

13   Francis R. Hart, *Scott's Novels: The Plotting of Historic Survival* (Charlottesville: University Press of Virginia, 1966), 105.

Bridgenorth retreats, thwarted, and the following day is again unsuccessful in enforcing his legal authority to marginalize the Countess and Sir Geoffrey, with Sir Geoffrey tearing up the notionally official warrant of arrest. However, Sir Geoffrey then celebrates his own acquisition of legal authority as a newly appointed Justice of the Peace. He engages in what is another act of marginalization by removing Nehemiah Solsgrace from his position as Presbyterian parson and reinstating his own Episcopalian minister. Thus, at Martindale Scott demonstrates that although Charles II as established a precedent in moderation and forgiveness by having the Act of Indemnity and Oblivion passed, this tolerance has not been embraced by his subjects. The Countess of Derby is especially scathing in her rejection of such magnanimity:

> Charles Stuart may, if he pleases—and it doth seem to please him—consort with those whose hands have been red with the blood, and blackened with the plunder, of his father and of his loyal subjects. He may forgive them if he will, and count their deeds good service. What has that to do with this Christian's offence against me and mine?
>
> *PEVERIL*, 60

Scott also foregrounds how this recourse to legal force is used by Royalists and Presbyterians alike to effect political and religious marginalization of individuals. However, this legalized marginalization occurs at an institutional level during the latter years of Julian Peveril's residence on the Isle of Man. The fabrication of the Popish Plot is, of course, premised on effecting the marginalization of Catholics throughout England. Therefore, the various laws initiated in direct response to the Plot are focused on marginalizing a vulnerable segment of society, and not on the achievement of justice. Scott makes it clear that Charles, fearful of his father's fate at Whitehall, is derelict in failing to stand against the oppression being visited on Catholics. However, he also makes it apparent that Charles' courtiers and their tools are the ones who engineer the delirium surrounding the Plot, for their political and personal benefit, ironically through the words of the Earl of Derby:

> I read one program on the subject, by a fellow called Oates, and thought it the most absurd foolery I ever perused. But that cunning fellow Shaftesbury, and some others amongst the great ones, have taken it up, and are driving on at such a rate as makes harness crack, and horses smoke for it. The King, who has sworn never to kiss the pillow his father went to sleep on, temporises, and gives way to the current.
>
> *PEVERIL*, 157

In addition, the marginalization inherent in the laws relating to the Popish Plot gives rise to another face of oppression across society—that of exploitation. Young defines exploitation as being "under the control, according to the purposes, and for the benefits of other people".[14] Scott shows how marginalization allows exploitation to flourish—again, at both an individual and a social level. The increasingly extremist Bridgenorth, still consumed by wreaking vengeance on the Countess of Derby, seeks to exploit the laws surrounding the Popish Plot for this purpose. The Countess, a staunch Catholic, is now herself the target, rather than the executor, of legalized marginalization.

It is the marginalization following on from the Popish Plot that gives Bridgenorth and the Countess of Derby the opportunity to exploit their private relationships with Julian Peveril. Bridgenorth entices Julian to consider undertaking a subversive political activity in exchange for Alice Bridgenorth's hand in marriage. This proposed exploitation of Julian as son-in-law is superseded, however, by the Countess of Derby's actual exploitation of him as her surrogate son. She conscripts him in lieu of her own son, the Earl of Derby, to journey to London and secure the House of Derby's safety. Both of these stratagems demonstrate the abuse of private, domestic relationships to achieve public ambitions, and mirror the greater social exploitation occurring as a result of the marginalization intrinsic to the fabricated Popish Plot. The Plot itself is a devious attempt to exploit the hysterical public fear of supposed Catholic influence, and is generated to further the private ambitions of courtiers such as the Duke of Buckingham. Should the Countess and Earl of Derby be found guilty of participation in the Plot, the Isle of Man would become forfeit to the heir—Buckingham, as Fairfax's son-in-law.

Through these two instances of exploitation, Scott demonstrates the intertwined nature of the public and the private, the domestic and the social, in the various attempts to marginalize aspects of society and thereby dominate Britain's politico-religious agenda. This occurs at all levels of society; Charles is himself the victim of attempted exploitation. His failure to master his sexual appetites makes him vulnerable to political abuse. Throughout the novel, affairs of state revolve around the exploitation of personal desires, as is demonstrated by the novel's subplot in which Christian and Buckingham conspire to effect Charles' enslavement by Alice's charms:

> [T]he scene prepared was no longer the intrigue of a court-pander, and a villainous relation for the ruin of an innocent girl, but became a state

---

14   Young, *Justice and Difference*, 49.

intrigue, for the removal of an obnoxious favourite, and the subsequent
change of the King's sentiments upon various material points.
PEVERIL, 307

But this brings us back to the characterization of Charles. Scott demonstrates
that while Charles' weaknesses as a monarch diminish his sovereignty, his
courtiers are more actively evil in seeking to exploit their king for their own
advantages.

Exploitation at an individual and a social level is not the only evil to follow
hard on the heels of marginalization. The rendering of powerlessness—
another of Young's faces of oppression—can easily result when marginalization is embedded in the law. From the minute Julian arrives in England from
the Isle of Man, Scott shows how individuals can be made powerless when
faced with the abuse of legal authority. He uses the activities of Charles
Topham, the personification of abusive legal officialdom, to demonstrate how
easily government can legalize the mistreatment of individuals in the notional
service of the commonwealth:

> The man, with an air of extreme dignity, pulled from his pocket, and
> thrust into Peveril's hand, a warrant, subscribed by the Speaker of the
> House of Commons, empowering Charles Topham, their officer of the
> Black Rod, to pursue and seize upon the persons of certain individuals
> named in the warrant; and of all other persons who are, or should be, ac-
> cused by competent witnesses, of being accessory to, or favourers of, the
> hellish and damnable Popish Plot, at present carried on within the bow-
> els of the kingdom; and charging all men, as they loved their allegiance,
> to render the said Charles Topham their readiest and most effective as-
> sistance, in execution of the duty entrusted to his care.
> *PEVERIL*, 206–7

Scott also explores what happens when an institution, rather than an individual, is engaged in the abuse of law. Julian's incarceration at Newgate, that formal
institution of legal authority, represents the worst aspects of the marginalization and powerlessness obtaining at the time of the Popish Plot. In the Newgate
scenes, Scott expands his critique of abusive forms of legal authority to include
legal justice, showing how law can be manipulated by people who have little
judgment but easy access to extraordinary legal powers, and who maintain an
excessive attachment to their authority. Just as Topham and his subordinates
show how positive law can be misused, Newgate and its gaolers indicate the

depths to which the administration of legal justice can sink. Charged with the impartial administration of law and the alleviation of oppression, instead it subjects its inmates to further marginalization and powerlessness.

When Julian eventually finds himself in the presence of his monarch, Charles himself disingenuously makes reference to his own powerlessness in the face of the legal authority surrounding the Popish Plot. He attempts to excuse his failure to pursue justice:

> "Look you there," said the King; "I knew [Sir Geoffrey Peveril] was in trouble; and yet how to help the stout old Knight, I can hardly tell. I can scarce escape suspicion of the Plot myself, though the principal object of it is to take away my own life—were I to stir to save a plotter, I should certainly be brought in as an accessory."
>
> *PEVERIL*, 328

Here Scott positions Charles as weak but not wicked. He ascribes wickedness to those officials and institutions entrusted with legal and judicial authority, and it is their abuses of this trust that causes oppression throughout the novel. I have argued thus far that Scott's exploration of oppression in *Peveril of the Peak* enables him to deflect responsibility for the marginalization and exploitation of, and the visiting of powerlessness on, various individuals and entities. Charles does indeed fail to fulfil the role of the monarchy in preventing injustice—but his inadequacies are those of omission, not commission. Responsibility for the rampant injustice emanating from the Popish Plot, Scott argues, lies with those courtiers eager to realize political and personal advantage from the oppression of others, and those officials and institutions with extraordinary legal powers but little regard for justice.

Having considered powerlessness, I want now to consider Scott's representation of another face of oppression—violence—for doing so introduces another aspect of the counter-revolutionary argument that permeates this novel. Through his recounting of violent incidents, Scott considers the role of extremism and rebellion in dividing society in two ways. First, he charts Major Bridgenorth's journey from tolerance to zealotry, and back again. Second, he explicitly sets up for comparison the two forms of government seeking to replace the monarchy, represented by the Fifth Monarchists and the Duke of Buckingham respectively.

Scott traces Ralph Bridgenorth's escalating fanaticism in the context of his increasing disapproval of Charles as restored monarch and his (Bridgenorth's) own movement toward illegality. Positioned early in *Peveril of the Peak* as an

inherently moral and upright individual, Major Bridgenorth originally supported Charles' Restoration as a means of ending the oppression inherent in
the Interregnum. We are told:

> Upon considering the crisis in which the country was placed, it appeared
> to Major Bridgenorth, as it had done to Fairfax, and other leaders of the
> Presbyterian party, that their frank embracing of the royal interest was
> the wisest and most patriotic measure which they could adopt in the cir-
> cumstances, when all ranks and classes of men were seeking refuge from
> the uncertainty and varied oppression attending the repeated contests
> between the factions of Westminster Hall and of Wallingford House.
>
> PEVERIL, 22–3

Yet his increasing discontent with Charles' monarchy mirrors his descent into
extremism and illegality. As the novel progresses, so too do Bridgenorth's ten-
dencies towards religious—and therefore political—fanaticism. Once a mag-
istrate using legal authority to effect a private vendetta, he becomes an avowed
rebel planning public revolution by "commencing hostilities against the state"
(*Peveril*, 441). Bridgenorth's initial involvement in the Popish Plot was moti-
vated by a private ambition to avenge his brother-in-law's death at the hand of
the Countess of Derby. But his alliance with Christian and his engagement in
Fifth Monarchy extremism is in response to his religious aversion to Charles,
his Catholic sympathies and his licentious way of life. His judgment, especially
if one considers his choice of companions (Christian and Buckingham), becomes increasingly suspect as his appetite for violence and rebellion burgeons.
Bridgenorth's all-consuming obsession is to replace Charles with an alternative government. To this end he contemplates—and justifies—the unleashing
of violence. In his lengthy conversations with Julian Peveril, he articulates his
concept of a superior form of government. In the final volume of the novel,
Scott juxtaposes Bridgenorth's theorizing of government with the reality of
the alternatives. Both the Fifth Monarchists, represented by Christian, and the
Duke of Buckingham have been intimately, and intricately, involved in bringing various other faces of oppression to bear throughout the novel—marginalization, exploitation and powerlessness. Christian and Buckingham are astute
politicians revelling in Machiavellian intrigue. Not content to manipulate the
legal authority surrounding the Popish Plot, they engage actively in illegality
and rebellion, utilizing yet another face of oppression—violence—to pursue
their personal agendas of power and domination. Against this alternative form
of sovereignty Scott positions the figure of Charles, newly invigorated to assume his monarchical responsibilities and clearly focused on securing social

order. It is in this environment of rejuvenation that Charles' achievement of justice and of social harmony occurs, as a direct result of his meetings with Julian Peveril.

In his journey towards justice, Julian Peveril travels from the Isle of Man to Martindale, and thence to the outer suburbs of London. Only then does Scott allow him into the presence of his monarch. Julian has two significant meetings with Charles, following on a brief, introductory meeting engineered by Fenella/Zarah. Their first meeting of importance takes place, not as the intended private audience between sovereign and subject, but as an almost farcical encounter where the public and the private collide "at the apartments of Chiffinch, the centre of all affairs, whether of gallantry or business" (*Peveril*, 416). As part of Buckingham and Christian's plot to gain political ascendancy at Court, Alice Bridgenorth has been unwittingly cast to replace the Duchess of Portsmouth as the King's mistress. She begs for her sovereign's protection from the wayward Buckingham, who is also in attendance and intent on seducing her. In the midst of this mayhem, Julian requests Charles' help to obtain justice on behalf of his family. Charles directs him to the Council, and promises, "your father will not want an intercessor in his King, so far as the laws will permit my interference in his behalf" (*Peveril*, 329). Charles and Julian's second meeting, some eighteen chapters later, occurs after Julian's confinement within Newgate and the Tower, and after the Peveril trial. The Peverils have been found innocent of involvement in the Popish Plot, as a result of Charles' secretive intervention in the processes of justice. This second—and final—meeting takes place at Whitehall at the express command of Charles, who seeks to unravel the intricacies of the Buckingham–Christian plot to remove him from the English throne. It closes with Charles facilitating the marriage of Julian Peveril and Alice Bridgenorth.

These two meetings between monarch and subject make clear the need for the monarch to transcend the legal authority operating during the Popish Plot if true justice is to be achieved and social order established. They also demonstrate that only the monarch has the facility and the imperative to ensure that the injustice consequent upon the misappropriation or abuse of legal authority is remediated. I suggest that the achievement of a just outcome is a direct result of the immediacy inherent in these meetings, for, as Young contends, face-to-face relations remove the disadvantages of "temporal and spatial distancing" that normally separate the monarch from his subjects.[15] Thus, Charles is presented with a situation from which myriad distancing mechanisms have been removed, enabling his clear-sighted appraisal of the injustice being

---

15   Ibid., 234.

perpetrated, and his granting of justice in its stead. Scott pointedly refers to the need for Charles to be confronted by the propinquity of rampant injustice: "Charles, who generally felt deeply so long as an impressive object was before his eyes, indulged for a moment the old man's rapture.—'My good Sir Geoffrey,' he said, 'you have had some hard measure; we owe you amends, and will find time to pay our debt'" (*Peveril*, 485).

Daniel Cottom astutely suggests that "it is because of the value which Scott places upon personal contact that the image of law in his novels is so torn by contradictions".[16] There is, evidently, deep irony in the fact that the monarch charged with overseeing the English legal processes and institutions of justice is required to transcend them so as to effect natural justice. However, this need for Charles II to rise above the abuse of the law aimed at societal marginalization underpins Scott's counter-revolutionary support of sovereignty in *Peveril of the Peak*. Charles is galvanized into effecting justice by his meeting with Julian and a subsequent meeting with the outspoken—and out of favour—Duke of Ormond. Ormond reiterates the need to sweep aside the various blinds and distractions that obscure from his monarch a clear view of injustice. He urges Charles to witness first-hand the suffering of his subjects: "For God's sake, then, sire," said the Duke of Ormond, "turn your eyes, which have just rested on the corpse of one old friend, upon the distresses of others" (*Peveril*, 413). Only when confronted by this immediacy does Charles move to restrict the abusive legal authority overseeing the Popish Plot trials generally and the Peverils' trial in particular. By doing so, Charles arrests the pendulum swinging disastrously between political expediency and popular hysteria in the governing of the nation. His behind-the-scenes involvement "produce[s] a marked effect on the conduct of the Crown Counsel, and even the Judges" (*Peveril*, 417).

Nevertheless, the singularity of such justice is not sustainable, for it does not enable a social reconciliation free from the threat of oppression—whether marginalization, exploitation, powerlessness or violence—that has pervaded the novel. Ultimately, Scott depicts positive individual and social consequences when the monarch does engage fully in his sovereign responsibilities. Charles' personal concepts of justice may well be belated and inspired only by his proximity to individual subjects and their suffering, but his intervention in the Peveril trial achieves the only undeniable instance of natural justice that occurs in the novel. Charles is thereby shown to be the only entity with the power to wield the natural justice necessary to absolve the Peverils of any

---

16   Daniel Cottom, 'Violence and Law in the Waverley Novels.' *Studies in Romanticism*, 1 (Spring 1981), 72.

involvement in the Popish Plot, and to create a social environment premised on reconciliation. Scott emphasizes the symbolic significance of Charles' act of social unification: "the bells of Martindale-Moultrassie were ringing for the union of the families, from whose estates it takes its compound name" (*Peveril*, 495). Scott places the creation of this emblem of social order in the final two sentences of the novel; some might argue that we cannot know, then, that societal reconciliation will ensue. This would be to ignore the myriad instances throughout *Peveril of the Peak* where Scott shows justice and clemency operating at both Martindale and Moultrassie, even in their most divisive moments. Of all the locales in the novel, Martindale is the only one where it is possible for Charles to establish a microcosm of social and political order, free from all of the faces of oppression depicted in other locales. Ultimately, this is how *Peveril of the Peak* demonstrates that "[f]or Scott the monarch is, in effect, the spirit of the laws—the inspiring presence which is supposed to settle all disputes over the interpretation of the laws".[17]

Cultural Imperialism, Violence and Distance in *The Heart of Mid-Lothian*

In *Peveril of the Peak* Scott depicts the effects of the unresolved societal divisions resulting from the Civil Wars and the Interregnum. In *The Heart of Mid-Lothian*—"undoubtedly one of the most powerfully written and intellectually fascinating of all the Waverley texts," as Lumsden and Hewitt emphasize—focuses again upon politico-social issues unsolved, this time those arising from the Union of Scotland and England in 1707.[18] Of course, *The Heart of Mid-Lothian* is not the only Waverley novel to do so, and Scott's focus on cultural imperialism across his Scottish novels has been an area of recent critical interest. David Hewitt, for example, points out that *Rob Roy* also considers the issues of cultural imperialism, marginalization and oppression in the context of Hanoverian rule, questioning the morality of imperialism and the associated disadvantage of those affected by trade and "turned into victims by the laws that enforce the rule and the mercantile ideology of the Hanoverian state".[19] In

---

17   Ibid., 79.
18   Alison Lumsden and David Hewitt, 'Essay on the Text' in Walter Scott's *The Heart of Mid-Lothian*, ed. Alison Lumsden and David Hewitt (Edinburgh: Edinburgh University Press, 2004), 524.
19   David Hewitt, '*Rob Roy*: Trade, Improvement and the Destruction of 'Native' Culture,' *Literary Tourism, the Trossachs, and Walter Scott*, ed. Ian Brown (Glasgow: Scottish Literature International, 2012), 95–7.

a similar vein, as Miriam L. Wallace suggests and James Kerr concurs, *The Heart of Mid-Lothian* uses the political Act of Union between England and Scotland of 1707 as a vehicle for mediating the relationship and reconciling differences between London and Edinburgh.[20] Indeed, Kerr considers Jeanie's "journey [to be] a key structural element of Scott's belated protest on behalf of his homeland against English cultural imperialism, a cautious and deferential form of national self-assertion".[21] Cognately, Fernando Todo considers the use of dialect across Scotland and its inability to be understood uniformly across the unified Britain to be politically significant in both *Rob Roy* and *The Heart of Mid-Lothian*:

> Writing about his country after the Treaty of Union of 1707, Scott depicts Scotland as a multilingual, multidialectal nation, now part of a larger state, the United Kingdom. This kingdom has as its citizens people, who, like some of the Highlanders in *Rob Roy* 'have no English' and speak only Gaelic, and others who use Lowland Scots, not always understood in England, as in the case of Jeanie Deans in *The Heart of Mid-Lothian*.[22]

I suggest this use of dialect is a further representation of cultural imperialism in *The Heart of Mid-Lothian*, as well as in *Rob Roy* and other Scottish novels focused on issues of cultural difference and potential loss in the Waverley canon.[23]

It is therefore hardly contentious to suggest that cultural imperialism is the central facet of oppression in *The Heart of Mid-Lothian*, given that much of the conflict and disharmony existing between Scotland and England arises from

---

20   See: Miriam L. Wallace, 'Nationalism and the Scottish Subject: The Uneasy Marriage of London and Edinburgh in Sir Walter Scott's *The Heart of Mid-Lothian,' History of European Ideas*, 16 (1993), 41 and James Kerr, *Fiction Against History: Scott as Storyteller* (Cambridge: Cambridge University Press, 1989), 75.

21   Kerr, *Fiction Against History*, 69.

22   Fernando Todo, 'The Function of Linguistic Variety in Walter Scott's *The Heart of Mid-Lothian,' The Edinburgh Companion to Scottish Romanticism*, ed. Murray Pittock (Edinburgh: Edinburgh University Press, 2011), 190–1.

23   Penny Fielding takes the point further, arguing that the instability of Scotland's position within the national discourses of Great Britain—including but not confined to political, social, legal, and religious—fundamentally shaped and informed the concept and nature of Scotland-as-geographical-place in Scott's (and other Scottish Romanticists') prose and poetry. See Penny Fielding, *Scotland and the Fictions of Geography: North Britain, 1760–1830* (Cambridge: Cambridge University Press, 2008). See 83, 84–5 for specific reference to *The Heart of Mid-Lothian*.

experiences of unequal national power. In fact, Young's definition of cultural imperialism in *Justice and the Politics of Difference* captures much of the Scottish experience of this face of oppression throughout *The Heart of Mid-Lothian*:

> Those living under cultural imperialism find themselves defined from the outside, positioned, placed, by a network of dominant meanings they experience as arising from elsewhere, from those with whom they do not identify and who do not identify with them.[24]

The novel is explicit in depicting English cultural imperialism over Scotland, and of the use of legal authority to subordinate Scotland. Scott's exploration of cultural imperialism and the law through, principally, the Porteous Riots and Effie Deans' trial for infanticide enables his use of both instances as mechanisms for considering the role of the monarch in instigating cultural imperialism, and for juxtaposing the revolutionary and conservative attempts to resist that imposition of cultural dominance.

The Porteous Riots and Effie Deans' trial are, of course, the principal events by which Scott alerts us to the systemic cultural imperialism infecting the legal frameworks operating in the two countries notionally forming a single nation. The Porteous Riots are a public rebuttal of the dominance of English law over Scottish law. Similarly, Jeanie Deans seeks a reprieve for Effie from a law found in Scotland but not in England, that law's continued existence being the result of "the prejudice in government against the [Scottish] nation at large" (*Mid-Lothian*, 320). Thus, Scott establishes cultural imperialism as both a public and a private experience of legality in Scotland under the Hanoverian monarchy. Gary Kelly points out that "[i]f the Tolbooth is the dominating social and historical symbol in *The Heart of Mid-Lothian*, the centre of the action is a woman who represents not the public, the legal, and the historical, but the domestic, the personal, the immediately affective—Jeanie Deans".[25] Ian Duncan agrees, suggesting that "[t]he problem of the law—the relation between legality and justice, letter and spirit—in the absence of the divine presence of the sovereign—turns from public to private and domestic life".[26]

The nexus between the law, the public and the private serves several purposes in *The Heart of Mid-Lothian*. Lumsden suggests the multiplicity of

---

24   Ibid., 59.

25   Gary Kelly, *English Fiction of the Romantic Period, 1789–1830*, Longman Literature in English Series (Harlow: Longman, 1989), 153.

26   Ian Duncan, *Modern Romance and Transformations of the Novel: The Gothic, Scott, Dickens* (Cambridge: Cambridge University Press, 1992), 155.

discourses—"those of the law, religion and national identity—drive the Anglo-Scottish narrative of the novel,"[27] while Kerr claims that by intertwining the public and private legal situations throughout *The Heart of Mid-Lothian* and "directly linking Jeanie's pleas for her sister's life with the actions of the Porteous mob, Scott claims for his heroine a range of influence which takes in the whole political establishment of Britain".[28] It also allows Scott to show the British monarchy to be initially active in promoting various forms of cultural imperialism imposed on Scotland, but also to be the legal mechanism that can remediate the effects of cultural imperialism under Hanoverian rule. The duality of the monarchy's position is made explicit when the Duke of Argyle suggests that Caroline might view Jeanie's private plea for justice as an opportunity to address the social unrest resulting from the Porteous Riots. Granting Jeanie's petition, he says circumspectly, "may be highly useful in conciliating the unfortunate irritation which at present subsists among his Majesty's good subjects in Scotland" (*Mid-Lothian*, 335). Scott, however, has a further purpose. His forcible welding of these two situations of injustice together—both of them the result of cultural imperialism—allows him to contrast the methods used by various parties to counter injustice. He draws specific and sustained attention to the rebellious, and indeed revolutionary, attempts of George Staunton and the Porteous rioters to effect justice in defiance of the monarchy, contrasting them with Jeanie Deans' endeavour to gain a reprieve for Effie from her monarch. In doing so, "Scott's foundation of a national fiction aligns itself with the counter-revolutionary containment of radical populist ideology in the period".[29] Duncan draws attention to one commonality between the two crimes being punished in the novel:

> 'The horrid delict of bringing forth children in secret' shares with smuggling the distinction of being a murder made by the law, that is, a capital penalty imposed from Westminster for reasons of state: Effie is to die under a 'William and Mary Act' for the discipline of a refractory Scotch capital.[30]

However, it is also important to note another commonality, namely, how central George Staunton is to these two situations of inherent injustice and cultural imperialism. His involvement in smuggling in Scotland ignites the English

---

27   Lumsden, *Walter Scott and the Limits of Language*, 107.
28   Kerr, *Fiction Against History*, 71.
29   Duncan, *Modern Romance*, 14–5.
30   Ibid., 155.

cultural imperialism inherent in Porteous being granted a reprieve which then results in the Porteous Riots; equally, it is his seduction of Effie Deans which creates the situation of her being charged with infanticide. It is ironic that the actions of Staunton, an Englishman, cause legalized cultural imperialism to be visited upon Scotland. Scott sets Staunton up as the epitome of the Porteous Rioters' revolutionary spirit early in the novel. It is no accident that he leads the storming of the Tolbooth, intent on overturning the English pardon of John Porteous in favour of the original Scottish sentence to hang, by literally taking the law into their own hands.

As Fiona Robertson notes, he is a "satire on the masquerading revolutionary, as perfect a combination as any anti-Jacobin could desire of indulgent bourgeois upbringing (spoilt by his mother), adolescent rebellion, promiscuity, and sentimental attachments posing as egalitarian principles".[31] James P. Carson similarly draws attention to Staunton's representation of the crowd intent and of the Gothic, suggesting these are "conjoined in the figure of Robertson/Staunton, who leads a riot in women's clothes, who speaks in the inflated rhetoric of the Gothic hero/villain, and who ends his career as a gloomy, awe-inspiring, and self-tortured Roman Catholic".[32] Staunton's disregard for the law enables him to use the illegal activities of storming of the Tolbooth and executing John Porteous to accomplish another unlawful act, the physical removal of Effie Deans from the arms of the law. As he says:

> I was at first uncertain what measures I ought to adopt for your sister's liberation, when the general rage excited among the citizens of Edinburgh on account of the reprieve of Porteous, suggested to me the daring idea of forcing the jail, and at once carrying off your sister from the clutches of Danger, and bringing to condign punishment a miscreant.
>
> *MID-LOTHIAN*, 304

While Jeanie Deans functions as a moral contrast to her sister Effie throughout *The Heart of Mid-Lothian*, with Scott using the criteria of fecundity, contentment and social stability to demonstrate Jeanie's ethical superiority and resultant happiness, Jeanie is also juxtaposed against Staunton in several ways. Using the criteria of legality and unlawfulness, Scott seeks to validate and reward the conservative and show the negative social and individual effects of

---

31   Fiona Robertson, *Legitimate Histories: Scott, Gothic, and the Authorities of Fiction* (Oxford: Clarendon Press, 1994), 209.

32   James P. Carson, *Populism, Gender, and Sympathy in the Romantic Novel* (Basingstoke: New York: Palgrave Macmillan, 2010), 46.

the radical and the rebellious. Thus, unlike Staunton, Jeanie Deans plays no part in either the Porteous Riots or Effie's situation. Indeed, she cannot even contemplate impeding the spirit of the law by lying to save her sister, as George Staunton (characteristically) urges her to do. Rather, she bows to the processes of the law, seeking to operate wholly within them. When Effie is found guilty of infanticide and sentenced to hang, Jeanie sets out for London to seek her sister's reprieve, again ensuring that her actions fall within the constraints of the law. As she tells the Duke of Argyle, "I am given to understand there is law for reprieving [Effie], if it is in the king's pleasure" (*Mid-Lothian*, 320).

By contrast, George Staunton, having previously planned to remove Effie illegally from jail during the Porteous Riots, now has the ill-founded but typically dramatic, and again illegal, intent of appealing to Queen Caroline's taste for revenge. His grandiose plan is to gain Effie's freedom by "surrendering [...] in the person of the heir of the family of Willingham, the notorious George Robertson, the accomplice of Wilson, the breaker of the Tolbooth prison, and the well-known leader of the Porteous mob" (*Mid-Lothian*, 305). Yet again, Staunton functions as a revolutionary with absolute disregard for the illegality of his scheme. It is interesting to note how Scott depicts the two characters' departures for London. Jeanie prosaically sets out on foot, her intention to make a long, wearisome journey in order to appeal to her monarch's notions of natural justice and compassion; Staunton, by contrast, leaps dramatically into the saddle, and his enthusiasm and impulsive recklessness literally cripple his endeavour to free Effie by illegal barter. Yet again, his volatile zeal fails, while Jeanie's steadfast commitment to her purpose is ultimately successful. It is not insignificant that Jeanie frames her response to Caroline's attempt to draw together the Porteous Riots and Effie's plight by distancing herself from the rioters, referencing her lawful status and avowing the Deans family's support for the monarchy:

> I would hae gaen to the end of the earth to save the life of John Porteous, or of ony other unhappy man in his condition; but I might lawfully doubt how far I am called upon to be the avenger of his blood [...]. But my sister—my puir sister Effie, still lives, though her days and hours are numbered!—She still lives, and a word of the King's mouth might restore her to a broken-hearted auld man, that never, in his daily and nightly exercise, forgot to pray that his Majesty might be blessed with a long and a prosperous reign, and that his throne, and the throne of his posterity, might be established in righteousness.
>
> MID-LOTHIAN, 340

Thus, by connecting the Porteous Riots and Effie's death sentence—two instances of legalized cultural imperialism—Scott juxtaposes the failure of the
revolutionary Porteous Riots because of their opposing the monarchy, and
Jeanie's success, achieved through her support of, and appeal to, the monarchical status quo. Kerr makes a similar point: "[i]n arguing for mercy, Jeanie is at
once violating and reinforcing the given order of the Kingdom. She is a reactionary rebel, whose momentary disruption of the status quo serves to evoke
from its highest authorities the justice and mercy of which they are capable".[33]

Cultural imperialism is not the only face of oppression Scott employs in assessing revolution and moderation in *The Heart of Mid-Lothian*, for he extends
his analysis to incorporate another face of oppression—violence—to bring
into focus the respective moral rectitudes of the rebellious and the moderate
elements of society. Violence is a constant feature throughout the novel, and
Scott uses violent events to assert the moral superiority of the moderate and
the conservative. Two specific instances of violence premised on notions of
cultural imperialism are especially apposite: the Porteous Riots themselves and
the crowd's attack on Madge Wildfire in Carlisle. Scott's ambivalence towards
violence has been noted by several critics.[34] Robertson, for example, considers "[s]ome of the ideological tensions in *The Heart of Mid-Lothian* [...] are
especially appropriate to a period in which Scott clearly feared mob violence
but also saw the difficulties caused by trying to deal with it in courts of law".[35]
Cottom argues that "the reign of law may be thought to increase the confusion
and injustice among men instead of ordering the commonweal more fairly
and efficiently," and points out that "the attempt to govern a society by controlling violence may actually be an incitement to greater violence".[36] While
these suggestions are pertinent when considering instances of violence in the
novel, it is also important to note the overt connections Scott makes between
revolution and violence. When George Staunton and his cohorts embark on
their rampage, they aim, by their overt aggression against the established order, to overturn, rather than to overcome, the perceived injustice inflicted on

---

33   Kerr, *Fiction Against History*, 77.
34   See, for example, C.M. Jackson-Houlston, *Gendering Walter Scott: Sex, Violence and Ro-
      mantic Period Writing* (New York and Oxon: Routledge, 2017), especially 22–40 and 88–106;
      Bruce Beiderwell, *Power and Punishment in Scott's Novels* (Athens: University of Georgia,
      1992), 62–80; Robertson, *Legitimate Histories*, 205–14; and Cottom, 'Violence and Law,'
      65–84.
35   Robertson, *Legitimate Histories*, 214.
36   Cottom, 'Violence and Law,' 67, 68.

Scotland.[37] By contrast, Reuben Butler, another figure of moderation, is an unwilling spectator of this violence, as is Jeanie of the mob violence in Carlisle upon her return from London.

Scott never allows his heroes and heroines to inflict actual violence on others; this both demonstrates their moderation and preserves their innocence.[38] In *The Fortunes of Nigel*, Nigel shoots an unknown intruder who is attempting to kill Martha Trapbois. Not only is the intruder nameless, but Nigel is positioned as rescuing a threatened woman—a true, romantic hero. In *Peveril of the Peak* Julian Peveril only fires upon Bridgenorth in self-defence—and his gun misfires, doing no damage. In *Waverley* Edward Waverley takes no life but instead saves the life of his political enemy, Colonel Talbot. Similarly, Jeanie Deans and her fiancé witness, but are not actively engaged in, the violence in *The Heart of Mid-Lothian*; only revolutionaries or the urban lower classes resort to such acts. While the purpose of this violence may be to draw attention to legal injustice and perhaps to effect political change, often it is a mindless expression of xenophobia and cultural imperialism, as Scott makes clear when Madge Wildfire is attacked in Carlisle after the hanging of Meg Murdockson. "Shame the country should be harried wi' Scotch witches and Scotch bitches this gate—but I say hang and drown" succinctly suggests one of the Carlisle mob (*Mid-Lothian*, 361).

Scott does not paint a flattering picture of this urban, lower class mob:

> There came up, however, a parcel of savage looking fellows, butchers and graziers chiefly, among whose cattle there had been of late a very general and fatal distemper, which their wisdom imputed to witchcraft. They laid violent hands on Madge, and tore her from the carriage, [and the] rest of her entreaties were drowned in the shouts of the rabble. [...] As they drove off, they heard the hoarse roar with the mob preface acts of riot or cruelty, yet even above that deep and dire note, they could discern the screams of the unfortunate victim.
>
> *MID-LOTHIAN*, 363

---

37   Baker argues that "Scott's treatment of illegitimate violence in *The Heart of Mid-Lothian* is only one example of his more general fascination with the subject. While mercenaries, irregular forces and outlaws figure significantly as early as his initial trilogy of Scotch novels, the problem of what constitutes a proper martial relationship to the state becomes a particular theme with, as Andrew Lincoln argues, *Rob Roy*, *A Legend of the Wars of Montrose*, and, I would add, *Ivanhoe*" (Samuel Baker, 'Scott's Worlds of War,' *The Edinburgh Companion to Sir Walter Scott*, ed. Fiona Robertson (Edinburgh: Edinburgh University Press, 2012), 78–9).

38   I am grateful to A.D. Cousins for his insights regarding the representation of innocence in the Scott canon.

As Jane Millgate contends, "[i]t is hard for Jeanie or the reader to feel completely comforted by the apparent restoration of the laws of natural justice in the pardoning of Effie, when that pardon is undercut by [the death of Madge Wildfire]".[39] Indeed, Scott makes it clear that the violent English antipathy towards the Scots has not been lessened by Jeanie's journey to the pinnacle of British justice. He depicts no magical transformation in the relationship between the English and their Scottish neighbours. Scott's focus is directed, not to a reconciliation between the two nations, but to a way by which Scotland can reside effectively under English rule without being oppressed by the cultural imperialism and violence that suffuse the first three volumes of the novel.

This, then, is why Jeanie is whisked away to Knocktarlitie, "an idyllic promised land where justice is poetic—[...] a West Highland Arcadia rather than [a] quotidian and unruly city".[40] I am not suggesting Knocktarlitie exists as an ideal place, free from any vice or wrongdoing. Smuggling, fornication and witchcraft take place in this locale, the same activities that resulted in legalized cultural marginalization and mob violence earlier in the novel. What is different is the response to those unlawful activities. Millgate points out that for Scott, "the law was to be read and interpreted not as an atemporal system but as an historical construct," and it is this interpretation of the law that is in evidence at Knocktarlitie.[41] Wrongdoing in Knocktarlitie results in punishment but not oppression. Smuggling and illicit sexual liaisons, although not approved of, do not attract harsh legalistic or inherently unjust repercussions. A woman convicted of witchcraft is censured in private rather than in public, specifically to prevent any "risk of ill usage which the poor woman might undergo at the hands of the rabble" (*Mid-Lothian*, 422). Madge Wildfire should have been so fortunate in Carlisle. Carolyn F. Austin notes that "[t]hese threats to social stability need not be so harshly repressed given the region's inhabitants' unfailing loyalty to the duke of Argyle".[42] It is indeed true that Knocktarlitie society's commitment to the Duke of Argyle allows the law to be a less restrictive presence. However, it is important to note that the Duke is also positioned by Scott not only as a Scottish nobleman but as the Hanoverian monarchy's (idealized) representative in Scotland, committed to negotiating the difficulties of unification between the two countries and cultures.

---

39   Jane Millgate, 'Scott and the Law: *The Heart of Mid-Lothian,' Rough Justice: Essays on Crime in Literature*, ed. M.L. Friedland (Toronto: University of Toronto, 1991), 105.

40   Duncan, *Modern Romance*, 150.

41   Millgate, 'Scott and the Law,' 100.

42   Carolyn F. Austin, 'Home and Nation in *The Heart of Mid-Lothian,'* SEL: *Studies in English Literature, 1500–1900*, 40, (Autumn 2000), 630–1.

This aligns with the notion that it was through the Scottish aristocracy that advocacy of the Union was generated amongst the Scots. As Gottlieb points out "cultural leadership north of the Tweed fell to men with visible positions of power and prestige in the national institutions still remaining in Scotland".[43] Through Argyle, Scott positions his counter-revolutionary argument of Scotland's residing harmoniously within, and as part of, Great Britain, while maintaining its Scottish identity: the Duke's presence is critical for the achievement of this. Argyle's authority in Scotland is unquestionable. He has been instrumental in quelling Highland resistance to the Hanoverians, and the Jacobite cause has made frequent overtures to him. In the context of the "political disequilibrium of Scotland's relationship with England," it is therefore Argyle who constructs the Deans' future at Knocktarlitie, thereby demonstrating how Scotland can function optimally within the wider geographical, political and cultural environs of English–Scottish unification.[44] However, this situation is far removed—and deliberately distanced physically and culturally—from the locales where Jeanie experienced and witnessed both cultural imperialism and violence in her journey towards justice.

It is in that broader context of cultural imperialism and violence that Young's concept of "community privileg[ing] face-to-face relations" functions as a useful lens through which to view Scott's use of the notion of distance in the novel.[45] Throughout *The Heart of Mid-Lothian* Scott uses degrees of distance and propinquity to distinguish further the wayward from the dutiful, the rebel from the moderate, the failures from the successful. The ardent Effie Deans is eager to move from her father's home. Her seduction occurs after she leaves home, mirroring Staunton's distance from his own family residence as he engages in smuggling in Scotland. Both return home fleetingly after their illicit activities, only to break away and place themselves permanently at a significant distance from their familial and societal roots—whether St Leonard's Crags or Willingham. Their living in London signals their continued isolation from their respective families and societies. Ultimately, Effie returns to her family, now situated at Knocktarlitie, but in disguise—yet another indicator of her disconnection from her origins. From there, upon George Staunton's death, she leaves Great Britain altogether, entering a Roman Catholic convent; now she is distanced in physical, social and religious terms. As Kerr suggests, "[t]heir adherence to the laws of passion isolates Effie and Staunton from Jeanie's world,

---

43   Gottlieb, *Feeling British*, 19.
44   Kerr, *Fiction Against History*, 77.
45   Young, *Justice and Difference*, 223.

from the benign and stable social order asserted in the Roseneath episodes".[46] By contrast, Jeanie Deans, "who seldom stirred half a mile from home," only does so to gain a reprieve for Effie from the Queen (*Mid-Lothian*, 244). This achieved, she is transported to her new abode—where her father and future husband await her—and she does not again venture from her domestic environs. Thus, Scott suggests, the rebel moves away from his or her familial and societal place in the world—as do Flora in *Waverley* and Redgauntlet in that eponymous novel—while the moderate remains both connected and loyal to her origins and obligations.

Concepts of geographical distance and closeness have additional significance in *The Heart of Mid-Lothian*, especially when used in connection with the monarchy's role in remediating justice and ensuring social order. Distance and proximity—physical, social and cultural—are critical to Scott's depiction of the monarchy as initially fomenting, and then assuaging, the effects of cultural imperialism. Fundamental to this analysis, therefore, is the role of George ii's regent, Queen Caroline, in the processes of justice that further inflame societal discontents, as are the actions of both Caroline and the Duke of Argyle in then healing those societal rifts. As in *Peveril of the Peak*, face-to-face meetings in this novel are critical to alleviating injustice and to constructing an example of social order that in microcosm asserts Scotland's harmonious residence within the parameters of the Union with England.

In the early chapters, Scott emphasizes what happens when the monarch is absent from the lands he or she governs: because the rightful sovereign is absent, John Porteous acts in excess of his legal authority. Moreover, Caroline's own complicity in English cultural imperialism in Scotland, and her conscious and sustained animosity towards her Scottish subjects, exist at least partly because she is at such a physical and cultural remove from them. Conversely, Scott insists that proximity between sovereign and subject will ultimately generate just outcomes and, indeed, social order. Formal institutions of law cannot replicate this intimacy, as is demonstrated by Caroline and Jeanie's "oral interview [being] explicitly opposed to the written word which characterizes the regular administration of the law".[47] Jeanie's journey, therefore, brings to the fore not only the spatial distance between Edinburgh and London, but also the political distance between Scotland and England. Just as Julian Peveril, in *Peveril of the Peak*, must meet his sovereign face to face to restore justice and social order, so too must Jeanie Deans. But Julian, as an English aristocrat, need only overcome "temporal and spatial distancing" to put himself in the royal

---

presence.[48] Jeanie Deans, a Scottish peasant, is distanced from the Hanoverian monarchy not only by time and geography, but also by nationality, culture and class. Scott shows clearly how hard it is for her to overcome these different forms of distance. When Jeanie prepares to leave Scotland, Reuben Butler points out the many obstacles standing between sovereign and subject—and then propounds a solution:

> "Yes, Jeanie," said Butler; "but [the king and queen's] magnificence—their retinue—the difficulty of getting audience?" [...] "the kings now-a-days do not sit in the gate to administer justice, as in patriarchal times. I know as little of courts as you do, Jeanie, by experience; but by reading and report I know that the King of Britain does every thing by means of his ministers." [...] "O, Jeanie, this is entirely a wild dream. You can never see [the king and queen] but through some great lord's intercession."
> MID-LOTHIAN, 245–6

It may well be, as the Duke of Argyle says, that "God has the hearts of kings in his own hand" but it is Argyle who facilitates Jeanie's meeting with her monarch (*Mid-Lothian*, 324). He bridges the distance between them by adhering to his origins and obligations as a Scot, as a nobleman, and—most importantly—as a representative of the monarchy, for as Jeanie tells him (and us):

> [A'] the world kens that the Duke of Argyle is the country's friend and the poor man's friend; and that ye fight for the right, and speak for the right, and that there is nae name like yours in our present Israel, and so they that think themselves wranged draw to refuge under your shadow; and if ye winna stir to save the bluid of an innocent country-woman of your ain, what should we expect frae southerns and strangers?
> MID-LOTHIAN, 321–2

When Jeanie, by the Duke's grace, is finally admitted to the royal presence, considerable distance still divides her from the Queen. This is evident from the Queen's unsuccessful attempts to 'place' Jeanie during their interview, in turn as the Duke's (unlikely) mistress, his distant cousin, a Campbell, or a Scot hailing from Inverary or Argyleshire. Again, the duke is instrumental in lowering the barriers separating monarch and subject, as he helps Jeanie navigate the shoals of the interview. This is not to diminish the significance of Caroline's remediating the injustice inflicted on Effie, especially as "it is the personal

---

48   Young, *Justice and Difference*, 233.

presence of the ruler and the possibility of royal intervention into judicial proceedings [...] which is accorded approval".[49] Rather, I am suggesting that Jeanie's experience of sovereignty face to face in *The Heart of Mid-Lothian* extends beyond her interview with Caroline. For there are limited outcomes from this meeting. Caroline, as representative of George II and of the Hanoverian monarchy, does indeed effect an instance of justice. However, it is her Scottish counterpart who creates a locale of social order and harmony. Scott deliberately uses the broader notion of personal interaction with the institution of sovereignty to create a more nuanced argument by which to reconcile "Scotland and England within the received form of the Union".[50]

As such, Scott does not limit Jeanie's contact to one representative of the monarchy, and neither does he confine that contact to a single—and singular—instance of engagement. He carefully establishes the benefits of ongoing face-to-face encounters between the institution of monarchy and its subjects through the many meetings, over many years, between Jeanie and the Duke of Argyle. Not only does the duke facilitate Jeanie's interview with the Queen and thus help effect a symbol of lasting societal (albeit utopian) reconciliation in the novel. In his dual capacity of Hanoverian courtier and Scottish nobleman, he builds and maintains harmonious societal relations premised on the tenets of natural justice. Ultimately, therefore, Scott's yoking together of the outcomes of Jeanie Deans' face-to-face meetings with both representatives of the monarchy demonstrates the creation of justice and social order at the hands of the Hanoverians, resulting in what is generally deemed to be a counter-revolutionary idyll within Scotland. Millgate suggests that "it is remarkable how often in his novels legal right endings coincide with narrative right endings".[51] I suggest that this is not remarkable at all, but intentional in its alignment of judicial and narrative rectitude. Scott's counter-revolutionary argument purposefully amalgamates the monarchical remediation of injustice and the creation of social order with the traditional narrative devices of marriage and individual happiness. As Karl Kroeber suggests, "Jeanie's success symbolizes the unification of individual righteousness and social lawfulness, which unification is the theme not only of *The Heart of Mid-Lothian*, but of all the Waverley Novels".[52]

---

49   Cottom, 'Violence and Law,' 72.

50   Kerr, *Fiction Against History*, 75.

51   Millgate, 'Scott and the Law,' 95.

52   Karl Kroeber. *Romantic Narrative Art* (Madison: University of Wisconsin Press, 1960), 187.

CHAPTER 4

Landscaping Justice, Rebellion and Dynastic Failure in *The Heart of Mid-Lothian, Waverley* and *Redgauntlet*

> Our environment, conceived as landscape scenery, is fundamentally
> linked to our political landscape.
>
> KENNETH R. OLWIG[1]

∴

There is no shortage of critical appraisal focused on Scott's use of landscape to explore his thematic concerns in the Waverley Novels.[2] As Jenni Calder points out, much of Scott's popularity was the direct result of "his conjuring of a mythic history out of mountains, lochs and ruins".[3] Of course, Scott uses Highland

---

1   Kenneth R. Olwig, *Landscape, Nature, and the Body Politic: From Britain's Renaissance to America's New World* (Madison: University of Wisconsin Press, 2002), xxxii.

2   See, for example, James Buzard's *Disorienting Fiction: The Autoethnographic Work of Nineteenth-Century British Novels* (Princeton: Princeton University Press, 2005); Penny Fielding's 'Curated Regions of the North: Art and Literature in the "Scottish Border" and the "Transpennine Corridor,"' *Visual Culture in Britain*, 15 (2014), 159–72, and *Scotland and the Fictions of Geography: North Britain, 1760–1830* (Cambridge: Cambridge University Press, 2008); and Yoon Sun Lee's chapter on Scott in *Nationalism and Irony: Burke, Scott, Carlyle* (Oxford: Oxford University Press, 2004), 74–104. See also the following recent commentary on Scott and his use of landscape: Chris Ewers. 'Roads as Regions, Networks and Flows: *Waverley* and the "Periphery" of Romance,' *Journal for Eighteenth-Century Studies*, 37 (2014), 97–112; E. García Díaz. 'An Overview of Justice in Sir Walter Scott's Waverley Novels: *The Heart of Mid-Lothian*.' *Oñati Socio-legal Series* [online], 4 (2014), 1167–72; Anna Faktorovich. *Rebellion as Genre in the Novels of Scott, Dickens and Stevenson* (Jefferson, NC: McFarland, 2013); Caroline McCracken-Flesher's 'Scott's Jacobitical Plots,' *The Edinburgh Companion to Sir Walter Scott*, ed. Fiona Robertson (Edinburgh: Edinburgh University Press, 2012), 47–58 and 'Walter Scott's Romanticism: A Theory of Performance,' *The Edinburgh Companion to Scottish Romanticism*, ed. Murray Pittock (Edinburgh: Edinburgh University Press, 2011), 139–49.

3   Jenni Calder. 'Figures in a Landscape: Scott, Stevenson and Routes to the Past,' *Robert Louis Stevenson: Writer of Boundaries*, ed. Richard Ambrosini and Richard Dury (Madison: University of Wisconsin Press, 2006), 121.

© KONINKLIJKE BRILL NV, LEIDEN, 2018 | DOI 10.1163/9789004352780_006

and Border landscapes for such purposes as to represent the Jacobite cause as anachronistic in relation to a united and prosperous future Britain. However, with Sharpe's notions of monarchical representation in view, I wish to explore how Scott uses landscape to represent the sovereign body politic—whether actual or aspiring—in such a way as to construct the counter-revolutionary, "unifying national narrative" with which *The Heart of Mid-Lothian*, *Waverley* and *Redgauntlet* each close.[4] I want, therefore, to consider these three novels in relation to Sharpe's iconographic work but also in the context of Kenneth R. Olwig's *Landscape, Nature, and the Body Politic.* A landscape theorist, Olwig examines interrelated notions of landscape, country, nature, nationality and sovereignty. His analysis commences with the ascension of James VI and the Stuart dynasty to the English throne. Among other things, he considers James' use of landscape in the theatre to position the sovereign body politic as a geo-political ideal in connection with the Stuart ambition to unite Scotland and England. Olwig's primary point of reference is Jonson's *Masque of Blackness* of 1605, a copy of which Scott held in his library at Abbotsford.[5]

Like Olwig, Scott has a fascination with the nexus of landscape, politics and sovereignty. Both are intrigued by the idea of geography being represen-tative of political and social institutions. Particularly relevant to *The Heart of Mid-Lothian*, *Waverley*, and *Redgauntlet* is what Olwig terms the "body geo-graphical," that is, the use of landscape to represent the sovereign body poli-tic.[6] With this in mind, I want first to consider how Scott uses landscape in *The Heart of Mid-Lothian* to create what Olwig might call a unified geopolitical vision of post-Union Britain; for the locales of Richmond and Knocktarlitie are constructed to function—at one level, at least—as positive representations of the sovereign body politic, and as sites of natural justice premised on Tory notions of landscape. I then want to explore how Scott constructs the failed and degenerative nature of rebellion and the Jacobite cause as he presents individual, dynastic, political and geographical landscapes in *Waverley* and *Redgauntlet*. It thus becomes clear that Scott's twinning of various characters and their families with the associated landscapes enables the positioning of rebellion as an inherently futile and barren endeavour. Conversely, counter-revolutionary support of the Hanoverian monarchy is represented as innately

---

4   Olwig, *Landscape, Nature, and the Body Politic*, xxix.

5   *Jonson's (Ben) Works; with notes, &c. and a Biographical Memoir*, by William Gifford. 9 vols (L.P. Lond, 1816) is included in the *Catalogue of the Library at Abbotsford* (at page 209). *The Masque of Blackness* is included in the third of the nine volumes comprising this work, spe-cifically Vol 3, 2–9.

6   Olwig, *Landscape, Nature, and the Body Politic*, 67.

regenerative. Furthermore, Scott uses the "body geographical" concept to depict the fading relevance of the Stuart dynasty in the face of the Hanoverian monarchy's social and political dominance throughout Britain. In both *Waverley* and *Redgauntlet*, therefore, notions of place, space and landscape are fundamental to Scott's depicting the dwindling importance of the Stuart sovereign body politic, and thus the Hanoverian monarchy's consolidation of its political stature and stability. Ultimately, it can be seen that the theatrical representation of landscape to construct a counter-revolutionary social idyll, such as Olwig traces in *Landscape, Nature, and the Body Politic*, is mirrored by Scott's own narrative representation of landscape in *The Heart of Mid-Lothian*, *Waverley* and *Redgauntlet*.

A Just Landscape in *The Heart of Mid-Lothian*

Olwig asserts that "[t]he meaning of landscape is closely tied [...] to questions concerning representation, both artistic and political".[7] Scott seems to be of a similar opinion, if one considers his representations of Richmond and Knocktarlitie in *The Heart of Mid-Lothian*. Each of these locales is portrayed in both artistic and political terms, and each illuminates critical aspects of Scott's interpretations of justice and law in post-Union Great Britain. Indeed, Duncan similarly observes that in *The Heart of Mid-Lothian*, "Scott directs the reader to a total representation [...] at once *panoramic*, like a view of the city, and *historical*, occupied with a sequence of events".[8] Yet I would further suggest that Scott positions his attempted reconciliation of post-Union England and Scotland by embedding various concepts of law and justice in both landscape *and* characterization. In *The Heart of Mid-Lothian*, as I discuss in the penultimate chapter of this book, the positive representation of the sovereign body politic as natural body is split between two characters in the absence of George II: Caroline and the Duke of Argyle. I contend that, in the same way, Scott splits his positive representation of the sovereign body politic as landscape between two locales, Richmond and Knocktarlitie. Moreover, Scott positions both places—unlike, for example, Edinburgh—as sites of natural justice premised on Tory notions of landscape.

With this in mind, it is useful to consider Nigel Everett's succinct exposition of those notions:

---

7   Ibid., xxv.
8   Ian Duncan, *Modern Romance and Transformations of the Novel: The Gothic, Scott, Dickens* (Cambridge: Cambridge University Press, 1992), 147.

Government most accords with the nature of things when it has clearly marked all the boundaries and distinctions, connections and dependencies, which at once diversify and harmonize the order of nature. Society is most natural when due authority has been given to its "leading, guiding, and governing part [so as to create] a grand chorus of national harmony [and] a beautiful array of truth and Nature".[9]

Ultimately, the difference between Richmond and Knocktarlitie—those two geographical representations of the Hanoverian sovereign body politic—lies in the types of law underpinning their respective landscapes. By setting up the two locales in this way, Scott can reconcile the tensive political relationship between England and Scotland, which is presented at one level as a conflict between natural and customary law.[10] As Olwig likewise argues, "[j]ust as place and space require each other for definition, the same might be said of the ideals of natural and customary law and their associated landscape ideals".[11] Thus, when considering Scott's representations of the sovereign body politic in *The Heart of Mid-Lothian*, three locales are of particular interest: Edinburgh, Richmond and Knocktarlitie. Fielding's notion of 'regions' is a pertinent one to introduce at this point, for she argues that:

> [a]mid the abstract philosophy of the interrelations of and distinctions between 'space' and 'place,' 'region' has taken root in […] more material discourses […]. But the discourse of regions is also infused with a debate about their spatial ontology: how they come into being as identifiable geographical spaces, and come to define what a region is. At the heart of this debate is a tension between two different structures that bring the region into being. The first assumes that a region can be determined by the larger structure of which it is a part. It is this usage that feeds into the idea of the region as economic structure, and reminds us of the Latin etymology of the word, taking us back to the idea of 'regiment': the rule of the king. […] The second way regions are imagined is much more centripetal, in contrast to the external identification of regional extents and limits.

---

9   Nigel Everett, *The Tory View of Landscape* (New Haven and London: Yale University Press, 1994), 100.

10 "Yi-Fu Tuan describes the relationship between the sense of landscape and country as place and polity […] and that of landscape as scenery as being 'tensive'" (Olwig, *Landscape, Nature, and the Body Politic*, 221). I extend this meaning to apply to the relationship between the laws existing in England and Scotland.

11 Ibid., 225.

According to this model, a region gathers itself organically, growing out
from something autochthonous that precedes the naming of the region.[12]

In this context, it can be seen that Edinburgh, Richmond and Knocktarlitie,
each viewed simultaneously as regions defined by the dominant political, legal
and governance structures of England, and as geographic constructs premised
on local socio-political traditions and culturally specific institutions, laws, mores and justices, are integral to Scott's carefully nuanced representations of the
sovereign body politic in the novel.

The Edinburgh that Scott depicts in *The Heart of Mid-Lothian* functions as a
means by which to show that law dissociated from natural justice gives rise to
social division and discord, despite its careful application. Indeed, Scott takes
pains to demonstrate that the law in Edinburgh, as it relates to the trials of both
John Porteous and Effie Deans, is scrupulous in its administration. However,
Edinburgh, with the Tolbooth physically and metaphorically situated at its
heart, is the site of rebellion and of perceived injustice, where English natural law dominates both Scottish customary law and notions of natural justice.
Indeed, Scott draws attention to the way those engaged in John Porteous' execution construe of their actions as "an act of justice" and "impos[e] upon their
cruel and revengeful action a shew of justice and moderation" (*Mid-Lothian*,
58). This conflict between the two types of law expresses the wider discontent
resulting from the Union of 1707, reflecting the failure of what Olwig deems essential for a legal system premised on common law—agreement on the nexus
between local custom and formalized law. Injustice is perceived to exist when
the law fails to express a "reasonably shared system of values".[13] This experience of disparate cultural values, and the failure of the law to effect justice in
John Porteous and Effie Deans' respective situations, result in Porteous' execution and in Jeanie's journey to London. Yet this is not to suggest that Scott positions the customary law of Scotland as uniformly superior in effecting natural
justice. Effie's incarceration and trial are quite legitimate under Scottish law;
Jeanie's expedition is premised on the Queen's power to override that Scottish law with natural justice. Despite—or perhaps because of—Edinburgh's
plethora of legal expertise and institutions of justice, it is not the seat of natural justice, and social order cannot be (re)constructed there. This metropolis of
Scots law is constructed by Scott as a location of artifice, detachment and util-
ity. It is important to note that Jeanie Deans does not ultimately return to the

---

12   Penny Fielding, 'Curated Regions of the North: Art and Literature in the "Scottish Border"
      and the "Transpennine Corridor,"' *Visual Culture in Britain*, 15 (2014), 159–60.

13   Olwig, *Landscape, Nature, and the Body Politic*, 58.

geopolitical construct that is Edinburgh, although that is her naïve intent. The Duke of Argyle insists on her being spirited away to a landscape far removed from that city where Scott depicts the operation of law to be mechanical, universal and impersonal—essentially a Whig construct that effects legality but not justice.

In the Edinburgh chapters John Porteous is shown to exacerbate the ill-feeling between Scotland and England. Critical to the focus on law, legality and justice in these chapters is the significance of Porteous acting so poorly as a representative of the sovereign body politic. As Duncan argues:

> Captain Porteous enforces the absent sovereignty of which he is a delegate by illegal violence, firing on an unruly crowd; that absent sovereignty asserts itself, in turn, by a breach of statute pardoning Porteous of murder; the mob rises up, breaks upon the Edinburgh gaol, and lynches Porteous, in the name of an abrogated justice.[14]

This negative representation of the Hanoverian sovereign body politic is central to Scott's depiction of the issues leading up to the Porteous Riots. In the absence of the monarch, he implies, legal mechanisms are exceeded and illegal acts take place in the name of the law. The sovereign's physical and metaphorical distance from Edinburgh results in English law overriding Scots law, leading to the Porteous Riots. Similarly, in Effie Deans' case, the absence of the monarch means that there is no recourse in Scotland against a callous law that is inherently unjust.

Thus, Jeanie Deans sets out to procure a justice that can, and does, transcend the mechanics of legality, one that is natural, organic and particular—one that accords, in fact, with Tory notions of landscape and of politics.[15] She locates, not one, but two representatives of the Hanoverian sovereign body politic: Caroline, the English representative of the sovereign body politic, remediates an instance of injustice; the Duke of Argyle, the complementary Scottish representative, effects lasting and harmonious social order. Similarly, Richmond is where Jeanie's plea for justice on Effie's behalf is successful, but Knocktarlitie is where her aspirations to an orderly, peaceful and fruitful life in a clement society are realized. There is value, then, in exploring how differently Scott

---

14   Duncan, *Modern Romance*, 155.

15   C.M. Jackson-Houlston's *Gendering Walter Scott: Sex, Violence and Romantic Period Writing* (New York and Oxon: Routledge, 2017), 88–106 considers the ethics residing in and between English and Scottish law.

landscapes his positive representations of the sovereign body politic in Richmond and in Knocktarlitie.

As Jeanie accompanies the Duke of Argyle to meet Queen Caroline, Scott represents the environs of Richmond as the embodiment of Tory notions of beauty, in terms of a veritable counter-revolutionary idyll:

> The carriage rolled rapidly onwards through fertile meadows, ornamented with splendid old oaks, and catching occasionally a glance of the majestic mirror of a broad and placid river. After passing through a pleasant village, the equipage stopped on a commanding eminence, where the beauty of English landscape was displayed in its utmost luxuriance. Here the Duke alighted, and desired Jeanie to follow him. They paused for a moment on the brow of a hill, to gaze on the unrivalled landscape which it presented. A huge sea of verdure, with crossing and intersecting promontories of massive and tufted groves, was tenanted by numberless flocks and herds, which seemed to wander unrestrained and unbounded through the richest pastures. The Thames, here turreted with villas, and there garlanded with forests, moved on slowly and placidly, like the mighty monarch of the scene, to whom all its other beauties were but accessories, and bore on his bosom an hundred barks and skiffs, whose white sails and gaily fluttering pennons gave life to the whole.
>
> MID-LOTHIAN, 329

Through the eyes of the Duke, Scott shows us the beauty of "this inimitable landscape, with the feeling of delight which it must give to the bosom of every admirer of nature" (*Mid-Lothian*, 329). Only once this landscape has been noted—together with the Duke and Jeanie's very different comparisons of it with their native Scotland—do they progress "through several complicated mazes" to the gardens of Richmond, "carpeted with the most verdant and close shaven turf, which felt like velvet under their feet, and screened from the sun by the branches of the lofty elms which united over the path" (*Mid-Lothian*, 330). Significantly, though, having depicted the luxury and privacy of the immediate surrounds of the gardens in which Jeanie Deans has her audience with the Queen, Scott makes no further reference to the landscape and does not describe "the precincts of the royal demesne" (*Mid-Lothian*, 343). The landscape need represent nothing here, in the actual presence of the sovereign's natural body.

Within this locale Scott positions two worthy representatives of the sovereign body politic, Queen Caroline and the Duke of Argyle. Both are unquestionably loyal to the notion of sovereignty and to the Hanoverian monarchy itself. Indeed, Caroline's loyalty to both concepts is the source of her ire at "the gross insult and outrage done in [the Duke's] capital city to the royal authority, at the very time when it was vested in [her] unworthy person" (*Mid-Lothian*, 336). However, crucial differences exist between the Queen and the Duke, and at one level these relate to the questions of law and justice that separate Scotland from England. The Duke values customary law; the Queen's preference, not surprisingly, is for natural law. Olwig makes a clear distinction between the two:

> Custom and customary law are based on historical precedent and are constantly undergoing a process of revision, whereas the justice of natural law is […] timeless. […] The former ideal lends itself to governance by a representative body because the fundamental purpose of such a body is to lay down common principles of law based upon the customs and practice of the populace. The latter ideal is more appropriate to the rule of an elevated regent seeking to bring uniform justice to a broad variety of polities.[16]

These contrasting approaches to justice divide the Queen and the Duke. This appears in the Queen's initial response at Richmond to the Duke's request for her intercession with George II on Effie Deans' behalf.

> "It appears to me, my Lord," she replied, "that this is a severe law. But still it is adopted upon good grounds, I am bound to suppose, as the law of the country, and the girl has been convicted under it. The very presumptions which the law construes into a positive proof of guilt exist in her case; and all that your Grace has said concerning the possibility of her innocence may be a very good argument for annulling the Act of Parliament, but cannot, while it stands good, be admitted in favour of any individual convicted upon the statute."
>
> MID-LOTHIAN, 337

As Scott invested the landscape at Richmond with the qualities of the sovereign body politic, so he invests the natural bodies of the Queen and the Duke of Argyle with the conflict between the natural law invested in the monarch and the customary law of Scotland.

Only when these two monarchical representatives transcend this conflict can natural justice be achieved for Effie. Therefore, it is Jeanie Deans'

---

16   Olwig, *Landscape, Nature, and the Body Politic*, 223.

navigation of the relationship between the Queen and the Duke of Argyle that is important in this locale, not her experience of its physical geography. Her penetrating these conflicting laws to reach the Queen's heart is what effects natural justice; that justice is premised on compassion and righteousness, rather than relying on the law as it stands. The Duke also sees natural justice as a matter of the heart rather than of legal definitions and rulings: "I would advise his Majesty to be guided by his own feelings and those of his royal consort; and thus, I am sure, punishment will only attach itself to guilt, and even then with cautious reluctance" (*Mid-Lothian*, 340). Jeanie's final view of the political landscape of Richmond is one of unity and conscious reconciliation between the representatives of the sovereign body politic, between customary and natural law, and between Scotland and England. "Our business is, I think, ended for the present, my Lord Duke," said the Queen, "and, I trust, to your satisfaction. Hereafter I hope to see your Grace more frequently, both at Richmond and Saint James's" (*Mid-Lothian*, 341).

It is only when Jeanie is removed from the presence of the Queen and from "Richmond Park, so long the favourite residence of Queen Caroline," that Scott recommences describing the various landscapes through which his heroine travels on her way to her new home, Knocktarlitie (*Mid-Lothian*, 343). His presentation of the latter differs markedly from that of Richmond, and has a different purpose. He identifies it as yet another Tory landscape, showing the sovereign body politic in an admirable light; yet customary law prevails here, enabling the maintenance of a Scottish identity as well as a harmonious existence under British natural law. Olwig recounts how carefully James VI and I sought to represent to his court the narrative of a unified England and Scotland under his sovereignty as the King of Great Britain through masques.[17] In a similar way, as Kerr and Julian Meldon D'Arcy each suggest, Scott aimed to reconcile conflicting visions of Britain in *The Heart of Mid-Lothian* by subsuming the past and present of British politics within an ahistorical transitioning towards a harmonious and prosperous national community.[18] However, in that context Scott is not merely, as Avrom Fleischman argues, constructing "Roseneath [a]s a symbolic landscape of modern Scotland".[19] Scott is also seeking to create an

---

17   Ibid., xxix.
18   See specifically: James Kerr, *Fiction Against History: Scott as Storyteller* (Cambridge: Cambridge University Press, 1989), 64 and Julian Meldon D'Arcy, 'Roseneath: Scotland or "Scott-Land"? A Reappraisal of *The Heart of Midlothian*,' *Studies in Scottish Literature*, 32 (2001), 27.
19   Avrom Fleishman. *The English Historical Novel: Walter Scott to Virginia Woolf* (Baltimore and London: Johns Hopkins Press, 1971), 93.

example of how Scotland could amicably reside within the broader political landscape of Great Britain.

Scott constructs Knocktarlitie as particularly Scottish while nonetheless operating successfully within its identity as part of Great Britain. It is at Knocktarlitie that "[t]he Heart of Mid-Lothian is restored, in the facetious terms of the novel's epilogue, on the right side of the body [of Scotland]," that is, in this pastoral idyll rather than in Edinburgh.[20] The creation of this ideal locale is premised on Tory concepts of landscape, notions of customary law and the embodiment of the sovereign body politic. Scott's notions of landscape, as represented by Knocktarlitie, align with inherently Tory notions of landscape, as did Richmond. Knocktarlitie represents those "[t]raditional social relations [which], in Tory terms, emphasized a hierarchical view of society in which wealth was supposed to be accompanied by obligations and rank by duties".[21] Thus Knocktarlitie—an "idyll of the counter-revolution, an image of the benevolent forces of community"—is a political and social ideal manifesting Tory notions of benevolence, harmony, and customary law.[22] This ideal is integral to Scott's notion that social reconciliation and harmony can be achieved with the acceptance of cultural difference and diversity. Knocktarlitie, which Kerr says "can be best described as an improver's pastoral," demonstrates how Scott imagines a Scotland unified with Britain.[23] Customary law—which countenances a degree of lawlessness—continues to operate here, within defined boundaries. Millgate astutely notes that the law is the "product of cultural and social circumstance, and its effective administration and reform require a full understanding both of the principles of justice and the workings of the society within which that justice is in practice to be applied".[24] Thus, Scott's construction of Knocktarlitie is vested with dense symbolism exploring the relationship between England and Scotland, law and justice, unification and cultural difference.

Scott makes a similar point in the early chapters of *The Heart of Mid-Lothian*:

> Contraband trade, though it strikes at the root of legitimate government, by encroaching on its revenues,—though it injures the fair trader, and

---

20   Duncan, *Modern Romance*, 150.

21   Everett, *The Tory View of Landscape*, 4.

22   Fiona Robertson, *Legitimate Histories: Scott, Gothic, and the Authorities of Fiction* (Oxford: Clarendon Press, 1994), 210.

23   Kerr, *Fiction Against History*, 66.

24   Millgate, Jane. 'Scott and the Law: *The Heart of Midlothian*,' *Rough Justice: Essays on Crime in Literature*, ed. M.L. Friedland (Toronto: University of Toronto, 1991), 108.

debauches the mind of those engaged with it,—is not usually looked upon, either by the vulgar or by their betters, in a very heinous point of view. [...] Smuggling was almost universal in Scotland in the reigns of George I. and II.; for the people, unaccustomed to imposts, and regarding them as an unjust aggression upon their ancient liberties, made no scruple to elude them wherever it was possible to do so.

                        MID-LOTHIAN, 22

He shows this blend of customary and natural law operating successfully in Knocktarlitie under the Duke's careful and watchful eye. Duncan appears disconsolate that "the grace that intervenes at the climax of Jeanie Deans' quest turns out to be the idealized return of an absconded feudal chief".[25] But to view the Duke of Argyle solely as a feudal anachronism is to ignore his simultaneous significance as the representative of the sovereign body politic and the embodiment of traditional Tory concepts of governance and benevolence. It is important to recognize, as Everett does, the centrality of "proper chieftains" to the social harmony envisaged in Tory landscaping and in Scott's representation of Knocktarlitie.[26]

Everett suggests that "[m]any later Tories—notably Sir Walter Scott—were attracted by the idea of 'chieftains,' but imagined that such men live in proximity to their 'people,' not, in Scott's words, 'isolated' and 'detached' from connections and relationship".[27] Scott depicts the Duke of Argyle as this ideal chieftain. Knocktarlitie is governed by notions of natural justice, as evidenced by the Duke's frequent presence—simultaneously the royal representative and the "chieftain" of his people. Customary law, Scott implies, can operate successfully in a wider context of natural law when the guiding principles of the sovereign body politic are those of natural justice. Duncan suggests that Scott effects an encasing of a Whig romance within a Tory one, while Kerr emphasizes the restoration of the ideal relationship between sovereign and subject.[28] While both are correct, ultimately Knocktarlitie is the lived experience of customary law residing under English natural law, the novel closing with Scott's conservative vision of the ideal society that incorporates prosperity and harmony for all that exist in this constructed social order. Thus, it is not, as D'Arcy argues, that "the superficially idyllic setting of Roseneath is constantly undermined by a

---

25   Duncan, *Modern Romance*, 154.

26   Everett, *The Tory View of Landscape*, 100.

27   Ibid., 100.

28   See: Duncan, *Modern Romance*, 154, 167–8 and Kerr, *Fiction Against History*, 77.

series of ironic parallels and comments embedded in the text".[29] Knocktarlitie, able to encompass sufficient flexibility in its legal system to accommodate local customs and environmental conditions, demonstrates how Scotland can operate within Britain's rule successfully. By embracing rather than forsaking its Scottishness, Knocktarlitie operates within an agreed context of harmonization between political landscapes that is represented in the depiction of its geography.

Scott depicts Roseneath in great detail, making specific reference to both its geographic and its cultural landscapes, which are successfully maintained by the Duke of Argyle. Our first glimpse of it is as follows:

> They landed in this Highland Arcadia, at the mouth of the small stream which watered the delightful and peaceable valley. Inhabitants of several descriptions came to pay their respects to the Captain of Knockdunder [...].
>
> Besides these, there were a wilder set of parishioners, mountaineers from the upper glen and adjacent hills, who spoke Gaelic, went about armed, and wore the Highland dress. But the strict commands of the Duke had established such good order in this part of his territories, that the Gael and Saxons lived upon the best possible terms of good neighbourhood.
>
> *MID-LOTHIAN*, 398

In the context of these dual landscapes—geographic and cultural—Scott realizes his beliefs regarding the successful functioning of law and justice: "It is only in its natural soil, where it has long been planted, that the tree can be expected to flourish".[30] In this way he attempts to reconcile the divisions between England and Scotland.

Place and Rebellion in *Waverley*

Being a rebel is no easy career choice in Scott's novels. Nor is it the choice of the rational, principled and clear-sighted moderate. Rather, rebellion is represented as delusional fanaticism operating in a maelstrom of sectarianism and fantasy. This is especially true in *Waverley* and *Redgauntlet*: at no time does

---

29   D'Arcy, 'Roseneath,' 34–5.

30   Walter Scott (*Edinburgh Annual Register*, 1808, 345–54) quoted in Millgate, 'Scott and the Law,' 100.

Scott confer on his rebellious characters the future of prosperity, social inclusion and domestic harmony that his counter-revolutionary characters ultimately enjoy. He does, however, explore the fates of both the revolutionary and the conservative characters through the same three narrative lenses in both novels. Scott considers the significance of key characters' fates in terms of personal, socio-political and geographic landscapes: that is to say, in the context of its individual ramifications, its dynastic consequences and the impacts on the locale to which he or she is linked.

It is valuable to consider the relationship between landscape and political discourse, given that Scott like many others at the time—Whig and Tory— "tended to identify with the country as the natural source of political legitimacy. [As such, the] landscape of the country provided the site for a social and political discourse concerned with the naturalization of power".[31] Scott's use of various personal, political and geographical landscapes in both novels allows consideration of the 'social and political discourse' between the adherents to the Stuart monarchy and those loyal to the Hanoverian sovereign body politic. Welsh argues that

> [t]he face of the land as well as the features of heroes and heroines physically represent the dualism of law and nature, reason and passion, sobriety and romance. Physiognomy and topography together supply the primary symbols for the thematic structure of the Waverley Novels.[32]

Rather—in *Waverley* and *Redgauntlet*, at least—it is through both the landscape and the fates—individual and dynastic—of various characters that Scott seeks to represent the dualism of political past and future.

In the context of this duality, the characters of Sir Everard and Rachel Waverley, Richard Waverley, Fergus and Flora Mac-Ivor, and the Baron of Bradwardine, and their respective locales of Waverley-Honour, Glennaquoich and Tully-Veolan are especially significant in *Waverley*.[33] Hugh Redgauntlet, Lilias and Darsie Redgauntlet and Alan Fairford are similarly important

---

31   Ibid., 102.

32   Alexander Welsh. *The Hero of the Waverley Novels: With New Essays on Scott* (Princeton: Princeton University Press, 2014), 56.

33   P.D. Garside suggests that in *Waverley* "relevant characters can be divided into three categories: actual historical figures, those who appears to be mostly fictitious though representative of the period, and generic characters who combine attributes relating to a number of persons Scott knew about" with Baron Cosmo Comyn Bradwardine and Fergus Mac-Ivor being examples of that last category (P.D. Garside's 'Historical Note' in Walter Scott, *Waverley*, ed. P.D. Garside (Edinburgh: Edinburgh University Press, 2007), 514).

in *Redgauntlet*, as are the locations of Brockenburn Glen and Cumberland. Through these characters and locales, using the notions of past and future, degeneration and renewal, Scott demonstrates the waning significance of the Stuart cause in the face of the Hanoverian dynasty's domination.

The early chapters of *Waverley* introduce the reader to the history and intricacies of the Waverley dynasty. Sir Everard Waverley and his sister, Rachel, are securely ensconced at Waverley-Honour, the ancestral domicile of the Waverley family. Two aspects of these characters' lives are emphasized—their traditional politics and their single status. The ardency of their Jacobite sympathies has resulted in estrangement from their Whig brother, Richard. Sir Everard has long since embraced bachelorhood; Rachel Waverley is a confirmed spinster. By depicting familial regeneration being effected by their alienated brother whose politics, and indeed livelihood, are premised on his Hanoverian sympathies, Scott implicitly aligns Jacobitism with infertility. Yet Scott makes no attempt to portray Richard Waverley as in any way morally superior to Sir Everard. Indeed, he stresses the entirely self-serving reasons for Richard's turning Whig. That regeneration is possible at Waverley-Honour, despite its current barrenness, is demonstrated by Scott's establishing Richard Waverley's son, Edward, as the *de facto* son of the house: a simultaneous emblem of familial reconciliation and rejuvenation. Edward's upbringing—positive and negative—is linked overtly with this locale: his love of romance, history and adventure is kindled and nurtured; his lack of discipline, naivety and social isolation continue unchecked. His quixotic journey into the Highlands and into Jacobitism is founded, therefore, in his upbringing at Waverley-Honour, a representation of a dynastic tradition of nostalgic attachment to a cause—the time of which has past. It is no accident that Chapter II is titled 'Waverley-Honour—a Retrospect.'

This locale is brought from the past to the future through the regeneration ultimately effected by Edward Waverley, as he dissociates himself from his individual and dynastic Jacobite loyalties and re-establishes his allegiance to the Hanoverian monarchy. Towards the end of the novel, Scott positions his return from Scotland to Waverley-Honour in terms of superiority of landscape, dynastic restoration and improvement in Edward's own character:

> [Edward] then, for the time since leaving Edinburgh, began to experience that pleasure which almost all feel who return to a verdant, populous, and highly-cultivated country, from scenes of waste desolation, or of solitary and melancholy grandeur. But how were those feelings enhanced when he entered on the domain so long possessed by his fore-fathers [...]
>
> The appearance of Waverley, embrowned by exercise, and dignified by the habits of military discipline, had acquired an athletic and hardy

character, which [...] surprised and delighted all the inhabitants of
Waverley-Honour.

WAVERLEY, 352

Edward Waverley's excursion into the political and geographic landscapes
of Scotland is defined primarily by another august Jacobite dynasty—the
Mac-Ivors. While Waverley's family is "inclined in principles to the Stuart race,"
Fergus and Flora Mac-Ivor are far more zealous in their Jacobitism and their
fates are similarly harsh (*Waverley*, 144). Regeneration in any form is not an
option for either sibling. Flora Mac-Ivor's affections are divided between a
long-dead Royalist hero, Captain Wogan, and her "enthusiastic zeal" which allows her no ambition save "the restoration of [her] royal benefactors to their
rightful throne" (*Waverley*, 143). Both are fruitless passions, historical and current failed endeavours. While in *The Heart of Mid-Lothian*, Scott depicts Effie
Deans' barrenness and her ultimate residence in a convent on the Continent as
moral punishment for her rebellion against familial and societal norms, Flora
Mac-Ivor's chosen sterility in *Waverley* is constructed as her political enthusiasm denying her a fulfilled life. What Hart refers to as "Flora's tragically limited
vision" and her resultant fanatical attachment to the Jacobite cause ultimately
result in a wasted existence, whether consumed by futile rebellion or clois-
tered in a convent.[34] Her physical deterioration, resulting from her anguish at
the Chevalier's defeat and Fergus' death sentence, represents a more comprehensive wastage, that of a life and a dynasty wholly committed to a desperate,
delusional and ultimately failed cause.[35]

    If Flora—and her fate—represent feminine Jacobite enthusiasm, Fergus
is the equivalent depiction of masculine zealotry. Fergus Mac-Ivor—both "a
diagnosis and a commemoration of Jacobitism"—is permanently exiled from
life itself.[36] *Waverley* traces Fergus' decline from a gallant Chief fulfilling his

---

34   Francis R. Hart, *Scott's Novels: The Plotting of Historic Survival* (Charlottesville: University
      Press of Virginia, 1966), 20.
35   Douglas S. Mack makes a similar point that aligns with the notion of the appropriate-
      ness of Flora McIvor's barrenness. He argues that "the fierce enthusiastic Flora McIvor,
      an unreconstructed, and unreconstructable, Jacobite deeply in sympathy with the French
      and Catholic culture of the exiled Jacobite court [...] will never be able to find a secure
      place in the sober realities of the Protestant British Empire—the Empire, that in Scott's
      eyes, embodies the future. Flora is a powerful and attractive figure, but in Scott's novel
      she embodies aspects of the Scottish past that must be left behind if the British future
      is to be embraced" (Douglas S. Mack, *Scottish Fiction and the British Empire* (Edinburgh:
      Edinburgh University Press, 2006) 54–5).
36   Hart, *Scott's Novels*, 24.

hereditary role over the Glennaquoich clan and landscape to a confined traitor condemned to a tortuous death:

> "Is it of Fergus Mac-Ivor they speak thus," thought Waverley, "or do I dream? Of Fergus, the bold, the chivalrous, the free-minded, the lofty chieftain of a tribe devoted to him? Is it he, that I have seen lead the chase and head the attack,—the brave, the active, the young, the noble, the love of ladies, and the theme of song,—is it he who is ironed like a malefactor, who is to be dragged on a hurdle to the common gallows to die a lingering and cruel death, and to be mangled by the hand of the most outcast of wretches?"
>
> *WAVERLEY*, 343

Just as Waverley-Honour traces the capacity of the Waverley family to forgo the futility of the Jacobite cause and embrace the potential for stability, prosperity and regeneration embodied by the Hanoverian monarchy, Glennaquoich— the Mac-Ivor estate—is an apt landscape representation of the infertility and barrenness of the Jacobite movement. Glennaquoich embodies the desperation and paucity of the Jacobite cause and the narrow existence of the Mac-Ivor family. Ultimately it has no ongoing relevance, no potential for the rehabilitation that infuses both Waverley-Honour and Tully-Veolan, both sites of regeneration under the stewardship of Edward Waverley. Increasingly, Glennaquoich functions merely as an identifier: the appellations 'Glennaquoich' and 'Mac-Ivor' become virtually interchangeable. Both terms signal the degeneration of a noble clan with no future and no place in a unified Britain post-1745.

By contrast with the assumed forfeiture of Glennaquoich and the absence of the Mac-Ivor dynasty, Scott's closing chapters of *Waverley* depict at length the restoration and capacity for regeneration of Tully-Veolan and its ties with Waverley-Honour. By doing so, he implies reconciliation between England and the Scottish Lowlands. Within one of those emblems of rejuvenation—Tully Veolan—Scott neatly conflates the Highland landscape and the characters of Fergus Mac-Ivor and Edward Waverley into a pictorial representation of their ill-fated and anachronistic endeavour. The Jacobite cause is masterfully represented as frozen in time and consigned to the status of treasured historical memorabilia:

> a large and animated painting, representing Fergus Mac-Ivor and Waverley in their Highland dress, the scene a wild, rocky, and mountainous pass, down which the clan were descending in the back-ground. [...] [T]he ardent, fiery, and impetuous character of the unfortunate Chief

of Glennaquoich was finely contrasted with the contemplative, fanciful, and enthusiastic expression of his happier friend.

WAVERLEY, 361

This painting has occasioned considerable critical commentary: responses range from a general dissatisfaction at a deficient attempt at conclusion or a clumsy transformation of the dynamic to the static, to a perceived reduction, through visual representation, of the "lived experience" of the second Jacobite Rebellion of 1745 to a confined 'place' of decorative artwork.[37] McCracken-Flesher notes that frequently "[t]he tartan-clad Englishman who looms from [this] in the novel's last chapter is held to figure Scott's British-oriented nostalgia and prefigure a Scotland locked in the romance of the past through England's cultural and economic dominance,"[38] while Lumsden argues that

> what most critics overlook is that the painting [...] may well be *intended* to be an inadequate conclusion to what has gone before [and what] is being offered here is an ironic comment on the inability of graphic art to adequately convey the complexities of experience and the ongoing tensions which persist in society in spite of the progress of history.[39]

Lumsden's argument focuses on the unsatisfactory nature of the painting and its demonstration that "graphic art cannot keep the past alive [...] and that role may lie, instead, with the far more 'debatable' and lively form of the printed word".[40] Elsewhere, writing of *Redgauntlet*, she contends that "Jacobitism is thus positioned within [*Redgauntlet*'s] construction of identity not as a defeated cause, but rather, as an excess or residue which like the painting of Fergus and Edward, disrupts any final or absolute construction of self; an emotional force which cannot be easily silenced, but which must be given space in any

---

37   See, as examples: Georg Lukács, *The Historical Novel* (London: Merlin Press, 1989); Lamont's 'Introduction' to *Waverley*, ed. Claire Lamont (Oxford: Oxford University Press, 1986); Ian Duncan, 'Scott and the Historical Novel: A Scottish Rise of the Novel,' *The Cambridge Companion to Scottish Literature*, ed. Gerard Carruthers and Liam McIlvanney (Cambridge: Cambridge University Press, 2012), 103–16; Cairns Craig, *Out of History: Narrative Paradigms in Scottish and English Culture* (Edinburgh: Polygon, 1996), specifically 39.

38   McCracken-Flesher, *Possible Scotlands*, 17.

39   Alison Lumsden, *Walter Scott and the Limits of Language* (Edinburgh: Edinburgh University Press, 2010), 81.

40   Ibid., 81.

future construction of identity".[41] Scott may have sought to represent, through the confinement and reduction of place and the associated 'lived experience,' both the individual experience (that conveniently erases the horror of later events, most notably Waverley and Mac-Ivor's last meeting, and Mac-Ivor's gruesome death) while passing comment on the status of the Jacobite cause. Ultimately, Charles Edward's cause has no physical presence beyond a romanticized and static geographic representation of his failed sovereign body politic with Scott, having confined the Jacobite cause and its adherents to a rosy-hued, nostalgic moment of past glory. Duncan makes the insightful point that:

> the alert reader recognises the painting's sentimental purification of Waverley's adventure, at odds with Scott's persistently ironical narration of it in the preceding volumes. The painting mirrors the story we have been reading—published in Edinburgh and London—even as the story invites us to reflect on that representation and its historical conditions, including the conditions of our reading.[42]

In this context, Scott redirects attention to the Waverley dynasty, newly reinvigorated, with Edward's marriage to Rose Bradwardine signalling social stability, prosperity, and fertility in the unified Great Britain under Hanoverian rule.

It is important to note the changes wrought in the Waverley family, which extend beyond Edward Waverley's somewhat chastened return to his allegiance to the Hanoverian sovereignty. Most *Waverley* critics, preoccupied with the significance of Fergus Mac-Ivor and Evan Dhu Maccombich's deaths, overlook that of Richard Waverley. His passing intimates the breadth of Scott's counter-revolutionary argument throughout *Waverley*. Earlier passages made clear Scott's contempt for Richard's reasons for embracing Whiggery and for his subsequent duplicity and disloyalty to his monarch. It is also imperative to register that Richard dies (as does Fergus Mac-Ivor) as the result of his own actions and choices against his monarch. Fergus dies at the hands of the law; Richard of "a lingering disorder, augmented by the unpleasant predicament of suspicion in which he stood, having been obliged to find bail, to a high amount,

---

41   Alison Lumsden, "'Beyond the Dusky Barrier:' Perceptions of the Highlands in the Waverley Novels,' *Mìorun mòr nan Gall, 'The great ill-will of the Lowlander'?: Lowland perceptions of the Highlands, medieval and modern*, ed. Dauvit Broun and Martin MacGregor (Glasgow: University of Glasgow, Centre for Scottish and Celtic Studies, 2007), 181.

42   Ian Duncan, 'Scott and the Historical Novel: A Scottish Rise of the Novel.' *The Cambridge Companion to Scottish Literature*, ed. Gerard Carruthers and Liam McIlvanney (Cambridge: Cambridge University Press, 2012), 108–9.

to meet an impending accusation of high treason" (*Waverley*, 302). Nonetheless, the death of each is the direct result of their actions against, and disloyalty to, the Hanoverian monarchy. It is not inconsequential that Richard's disingenuous interpretation of his downfall being due to "[a]n unjust monarch and an ungrateful country" is overtly associated with concepts of both sovereignty and landscape (*Waverley*, 130).

It is valuable to contrast here the selfish interests of an avowed Whig with the innate integrity of a Jacobite sympathiser—each a descendant of an honourable lineage. While Richard Waverley besmirches his family's name by his actions against the Hanoverian monarchy, the Baron of Bradwardine is assimilated into the future, unified Britain due to his nobility and through his coalition with the Waverley dynasty—themselves reclaimed from their Jacobite leanings, and hence resurrected. Through the union of Edward Waverley and Rose Bradwardine, Scott employs his typical metaphor of romance and marriage as a means of establishing individual happiness, ensuring dynastic continuance and signalling social unification. Both the Waverley and Bradwardine dynasties are therefore shown to be deservingly fruitful, prosperous and secure, and thus, in *Waverley*, "we can see how Scott rewards with wealth and power those who he considers to be on the right side in the historical struggle".[43]

Locale and Dynastic Failure in *Redgauntlet*

Scott employs the narrative mechanisms of personal, familial and geographic landscapes in *Redgauntlet* as well as in *Waverley*. Through both the landscape and the fates of specific individuals and dynasties, rabid Jacobitism is positioned—indeed, physically located—as an inherently marginalized enthusiasm, anachronistic to the point of absurdity in the (fictitious) events of 1765. Scott's creation of this fictitious rebellion heralds a fascinating departure from his weaving fiction around a significant historical event. Tara Ghoshal Wallace and Gottlieb each note the anomaly of *Redgauntlet* within the Waverley canon of a figmental incident existing at its heart, while G.A.M. Wood and David Hewitt draw attention to the actuality of Jacobite activity and Prince Charles' presence in Britain post 1745 being documented.[44] Regardless, there exists a certain ephemerality throughout *Redgauntlet* as a result of its

---

43   Kerr, *Fiction Against History*, 83.
44   See: Tara Ghoshal Wallace's 'Historical *Redgauntlet*: Jacobite Delusions and Hanoverian Fantasies,' *Romanticism*, 21 (2015), 145–59; Evan Gottlieb's *Walter Scott and Contemporary Theory* (London: Bloomsbury Academic, 2013), 47–8; and G.A.M. Wood and David

self-reflexive fictionality that pervades both locale and characterisation. Intrinsic to analysis of the geographic landscape as a representation of the Jacobite cause throughout the novel—that "ambiguous, haunting late masterpiece," as Stuart Kelly frames it—is the notion of transience.[45]

In *Redgauntlet* Scott depicts the overwhelming futility of the Stuart cause in a political landscape dominated by the Hanoverian monarchy through the characters of Hugh Redgauntlet, Lilias and Darsie Redgauntlet and Alan Fairford, and the locales of Brockenburn Glen and Cumberland.[46] Through this multiplicity of perspectives, as well as through those sites, *Redgauntlet* focuses (among other motifs and themes) on the notion of diminishment of causes over time, the need for continuing national as well as personal relevance for a cause to have lasting social resonance, and the realization that there is indeed (at times) significant loss and cost at those nationalist and personal levels when sovereignty is embedded so deeply across two (and more) nations. Wallace suggests that in *Redgauntlet* Scott paints a convincing replica of a flawed legal system, a depiction of Charles Edward's diminished character, and a careful assessment of the Hanoverian dynasty as accepted but not beloved by the populace.[47] It is by doing so that Scott's deeply 'pragmatic nationalism' enabled him to uphold his counter-revolutionism while remaining conscious of societal dissatisfactions leading to uprisings of the time and representing those through both character and locale.

Hugh Redgauntlet, that "fanatical unreconstructed Jacobite," is, not unnaturally, pivotal to any exploration of Scott's use of characters and their associated landscapes to represent the fates of the Stuart sovereign body politic.[48] He is the predominant presence throughout the eponymous novel, entirely dedicated to supplanting the Hanoverian sovereign body politic with the resurrected Stuart monarchy. Donning numerous aliases—"a self-denying hermit at one time—at another, the apparent associate of outlaws and desperadoes—at another, the subordinate agent of men whom I felt in every way my inferiors"—he strides restlessly between the various locales comprising his world, aiming to ignite a sustained passion for the Stuart cause to match his

---

Hewitt's 'Historical Note' in Walter Scott, *Redgauntlet*, ed. G.A.M Wood and David Hewitt (Edinburgh: Edinburgh University Press, 1997), 442.

45   Stuart Kelly, *Scott-Land: The Man Who Invented a Nation* (Edinburgh: Polygon, 2010), 185.

46   Julian Meldon D'Arcy, *Subversive Scott: The Waverley Novels and Scottish Nationalism* (Reykjavík: Stofnun Vigdísar Finnbogadóttur í erlendum tungumálum: Háskólaútgáfan, 2005), 192–3.

47   Wallace, 'Historical *Redgauntlet*,' 146.

48   Ibid., 146.

own fierce zealotry (*Redgauntlet*, 320). That world, however, is as anachronistic as his own endeavours, being inherently "feudal in character, attached to the ideals of the past: in actuality it is hardly a 'world' at all, for it exists only in the imaginations and memories of a few people".[49] He is a fitting representative of the Jacobite movement in 1765, for he is as reduced a figure as it is.

Given Scott's use of property as a means of determining political legitimacy, it is important to recognize the significance of Redgauntlet's lack of estate. He does not preside over substantial property, as did Mac-Ivor over Glennaquoich, Edward Waverley over Waverley-Honour or the Baron of Bradwardine over Tully Veolan in *Waverley*. The Redgauntlet property and the dynastic name has already been forfeited for the Jacobite cause, a symbol of political illegitimacy. While known as the Laird by impoverished peasants and various outlaws, Redgauntlet in his many guises oversees little more than the hovel in Brockenburn Glen and the small house in Cumberland. His constant movement between these and other locales emphasizes his transient potency and political illegitimacy: he is as much a wanderer as Wandering Willie and, indeed, the "Royal Wanderer" himself (*Redgauntlet*, 353).

The peripheral nature of Charles Edward's cause means that Redgauntlet, the fanatic, is not destined to play the role he craves nor have the impact on the political landscape he so ardently desires. Unlike Mac-Ivor twenty years earlier, Redgauntlet faces neither death nor enforced exile upon discovery of his political activities. To his mortification, the threat he poses to the Hanoverian sovereignty is so insignificant that it warrants no punishment, no call to arms. The cause to which he has devoted his life is simply deemed unworthy of military attention: Colonel Campbell refuses to waste military resources on this endeavour. As Anne Frey and Bruce Beiderwell each demonstrate, "Campbell's amnesty solidifies Hanoverian rule more strongly than fighting a civil war would have done".[50] Faced with the inconsequentiality of himself and the cause that defines him, denied the political martyr's role visited upon Mac-Ivor in *Waverley*, Redgauntlet removes voluntarily from Great Britain—where there is no longer any 'place' for the Stuart monarchy. Interestingly, his departure from the political and geographical landscape mirrors Flora Mac-Ivor's: he ultimately removes to the physically confined space of a cloister where

---

49   Mary Cullinan, 'History and Language in Scott's *Redgauntlet*,' SEL: *Studies in English Literature, 1500–1900*, 18 (Autumn 1978), 662–3.

50   Anne Frey, *British State Romanticism: Authorship, Agency, and Bureaucratic Nationalism* (Stanford: Stanford University Press, 2009), 100. See also: Bruce Beiderwell, *Power and Punishment in Scott's Novels*, 1992 and 'Scott's *Redgauntlet* as a Romance of Power,' *Studies in Romanticism*, 28 (Summer 1989), 273–89.

regeneration—dynastic or political—is impossible. As with Flora's fate in *Waverley*, Scott in *Redgauntlet* portrays irreclaimable revolutionary enthusiasm as redirecting only into religious zealotry.

Such is the (in)significance of Redgauntlet as an individual, traced upon his personal landscape and fleetingly upon the wider political geography. However, as a representative of the Redgauntlet dynasty he has additional relevance in Scott's counter-revolutionary argument in the novel. He is, indeed, the last of his family, despite the existence of his dead brother's children—Darsie and Lilias. Just as Scott emphasized in *Waverley* that Sir Everard and Rachel Waverley had no offspring, he makes the point that Redgauntlet also has no immediate descendants.[51] While Edward Waverley becomes the *de facto* son of the House of Waverley and the means by which that line is regenerated, neither Lilias nor Darsie align themselves with the Redgauntlet dynasty, despite their hereditary loyalties and sacrifices.

Nonetheless, issues of identity, loyalty and dynastic fate are also intrinsic to Darsie Latimer. Darsie is defined early in the novel by his lack of identity—his "want of ancestry [and] connections, [his being] a lone thing in this world" (*Redgauntlet*, 3). His meandering on the Solway—so close to and yet so removed from his native England—depicts the aimless wandering of one in search of family, heritage, and hence identity. His kidnapping at the hands of his uncle and his subsequent voyaging uncovers the truth. Far from lacking family and heritage, Darsie discovers he is the head of the ancient Redgauntlet dynasty, its fortunes irrevocably tied to various losing causes throughout the centuries. Darsie's identity—his personal landscape—is merely confirmed by his adventures; it is not created by them. Despite his family's traditional politico-religious loyalties, despite his father dying for the Jacobite cause in 1745, Darsie is a Protestant and a staunch Hanoverian, his sympathies defined more by his upbringing in the Fairford household than by his dynastic heritage. It is important to note that Darsie is not, as Edward Waverley was in *Waverley*, a *de facto* son of the dynastic house in which he has resided. Indeed, Saunders Fairford states that he stands in the position of *"factor loco tutoris"*

---

51   In *Redgauntlet*, however, Scott does not use this as a means of rewarding or punishing political or religious choices as he implicitly does in *Waverley* with regard to Sir Everard and Rachel Waverley. The Quaker brother and sister, Joshua and Rachel Geddes, also have no descendants, but this is never sheeted home to their being political or religious anachronisms. Cullinan points out that their significance—especially Joshua's—is opaque, with markedly different interpretations being made about their thematic importance in the novel. "Some critics find [Joshua] admirable, while others find him hypocritical and unpleasant" (Cullinan, 'History and Language,' 672).

(in place of a tutor) and not *factor loco parentis* (in place of a parent) to Darsie
(*Redgauntlet*, 73). As Scott emphasizes throughout the novel, Darsie Latimer
is Alan Fairford's brother in all but blood. The marriage between Alan Fairford and Lilias Redgauntlet has, therefore, multiple significances, more than is
usual with the marriages with which Scott often closes his novels. Frequently
the marriage in a Waverley novel signals a reconciliation of opposing politico-
religious conflicts between two families, thereby signifying a wider restoration
of social order and an ongoing familial lineage.

Naturally, Alan and Lilias' marriage signals a form of dynastic continuance, as it often does in the Waverley canon. However, the motif of familial
regeneration in *Redgauntlet* differs markedly from that in either *The Heart of
Mid-Lothian* or *Waverley*. The barrenness of Effie and George Staunton's marriage is positioned as a judgment on their self-centred rejection of societal
norms and family connections, while Jeanie Deans' fecundity is testament to
her righteousness and her marrying within her station in *The Heart of Mid-
Lothian*. Fergus Mac-Ivor and Flora Mac-Ivor in *Waverley* each endure fates
that preclude procreation, while Edward Waverley marries Rose Bradwardine,
signalling the regeneration of that dynasty and the subordination of Jacobite
sympathies to Hanoverian loyalties. By contrast, Scott's representation of the
House of Redgauntlet is "of a family once numerous, wealthy, and powerful, but
now in decline partly because of its support for Jacobitism".[52] While the marriage between Alan and Lilias signals a form of dynastic continuation, it also
represents the outcome Redgauntlet both feared and predicted—"if Scotland
and my father's House cannot stand and flourish together, then perish the very
name of Redgauntlet! perish the son of my brother, with every recollection
of the glories of my family, of the affections of my youth" (*Redgauntlet*, 320).
Darsie, at the close of the novel, remains single and "[t]here is no indication
that the Redgauntlet line will continue; in fact, it would seem that without a
cause the family has no reason to exist".[53] Just as Hugh Redgauntlet's politics
have no place in Great Britain, neither, it would appear, does the fated House
of Redgauntlet.

On another note, earlier in the novel, the Chevalier has responded disparag-
ingly to Alan Fairford's referencing his bourgeois origins—"I have no hereditary
claim to distinction of any kind" (*Redgauntlet*, 277). However, Lilias Redgauntlet's marriage to Alan Fairford implies the generation of a new family and a
new social order whereby merit trumps nobility of birth. Subsumed within

52   Joanne Wilkes, 'Scott's Use of Scottish Family History in *Redgauntlet*,' *The Review of English Studies*, 41 (May 1990), 201.
53   Cullinan, "History and Language," 674.

the Fairford family, the Redgauntlets are transposed from an anachronism to an emblem of progress and prosperity. In this way Scott depicts what Douglas S. Mack describes as "the Jacobite conspiracy dissolv[ing] before the unshakable power of the Hanoverian regime—a power that is unshakable precisely because it is founded on the freely given consent of men of property like the Fairfords".[54] In this context, it is important to recognize the absence of locale with regards to the marriage between Alan Fairford and Lilias Redgauntlet. So firmly established is the Hanoverian sovereign body politic and so marginalized the Stuart dynasty, Scott has no need to signal the reconciliation of two families, the restoration of political order and social unification through the merging of property ownership. A new dynasty is being built on very different grounds from those of earlier novels: Alan's roots are not in some country estate, but in Edinburgh as a man of letters whose ability will determine his future in a world of political stability and prosperity. Further, Lilias and Alan's marriage reinforces that Darsie, having always been their ideological brother, is now officially part of the progressive Fairford family, firmly committed to the stability and prosperity of the Hanoverian regime.

Redgauntlet opened with Darsie Latimer having no known identity, cast adrift within society as a result, confined to Scotland, and vulnerable to the political zealotry of the Jacobite cause. *Redgauntlet* closes with Arthur Redgauntlet conscious of his identity, restored to his family and rightful position in society, able to move between Scotland and England as he pleases, and free to follow his own political preferences. It is not inconsequential, I believe, that "the last we hear of Sir Arthur Darsie Redgauntlet is that he was presented to George III by Lieutenant-General Campbell".[55]

Marginalized Sovereignty in *Waverley* and *Redgauntlet*

Having explored Scott's combined use of character, space and place in order to demonstrate the fate of rebellion, we turn to his application of those same inter-relationships to represent the failed Stuart monarchical dynasty itself in *Waverley* and *Redgauntlet*. Olwig draws attention to the representation of the sovereign body politic as "a means of symbolizing the embodiment of the state in a new and abstract way as a relationship in geographic space".[56]

---

54   Mack, 'Culloden and After: 101.
55   Wilkes, 'Scott's Use of Scottish Family History in *Redgauntlet*,' 209.
56   Ibid., 89.

The portrayal of the Hanoverian sovereignty's dominance through the 'body geographical' can be traced easily enough in both *Waverley* and *Redgauntlet*. There is greater interest in exploring how Scott uses 'place' and 'space' to explore Charles Edward's attempts to dominate the topographic and political landscapes of Great Britain.[57]

Olwig explains that in the early seventeenth century "[s]cenes of [an] imagined British landscape were created to provide the setting for [...] narratives legitimating the British hegemony of the [...] new Scottish-English Stuart dynasty".[58] In *Waverley* and *Redgauntlet* Scott constructs an imagined British landscape that illustrates the marginalized status of the Stuart monarchy and thus legitimates the sovereignty of the Hanoverian dynasty. Within that conservatively imagined landscape, Scott explores the Jacobite cause, and its attempts to reinstate the Stuart sovereign body politic, through the notion of the 'body geographical'—where the body of the state becomes one with the landscape. The authority of the monarch "now transcends his physical body and is made tangible in the landscape".[59] In this way the diminishment of the Chevalier and his cause becomes apparent by means of the geography through which he passes and the dwellings in which he resides.

Of course, the significance of movement between locales in a number of Waverley Novels has evinced commentary. Welsh, for example, suggests that the differences between the locales of England and Scotland, Lowlands and Highlands mark sociological rather than political variance. However, Garside notes that Highland sites tend to be fictional in the early chapters of Scott's Scottish novels and more historically recognizable and significant in the latter ones, as does Blair.[60] There is another, equally important relevance of those differences between Scott's depictions of the Highlands, the Scottish Lowlands and England in *Waverley*, which become clear as Charles Edward moves from Holyrood to St Leonard's Hill and then journeys towards England through the Lowlands. Each locale functions as a geographical representation

---

57 In tracing the historical chronology and locations of Charles Edward's activities during the 1745 landing, Garside notes insightfully that "Waverley's early experiences in Scotland are closely connected with [these] events, though Waverley himself and to some extent the reader also are often oblivious to this" (Garside, 'Historical Note,' *Waverley*, 499–500, 501).

58 Olwig, *Landscape, Nature, and the Body Politic*, xxix.

59 Ibid., 90.

60 See specifically: Welsh, *The Hero of the Waverley Novels*, 56; Garside, 'Historical Note,' *Waverley*, 512; and David Blair, 'Scott, Cartography, and the Appropriation of Scottish Place,' *Literature and Place, 1800–2000*, ed. Peter Brown and Michael Irwin (Bern: Peter Lang, 2006), 94–5.

of the limitations and failed nature of his cause; each marks a critical point in Scott's mapping of the journey from idealistic dreaming to the ultimate futility of the Jacobite cause. The specifics of the 'body geographical' in each locale illuminate the diminishment of Charles Edward as potential sovereign body politic.

It is no accident that Edward Waverley is taken to Holyrood, that "palace of [Charles Edward's] ancestors" for the specific purpose of meeting his 'sovereign' (*Waverley*, 204). Scott thus represents the initial presence and the aspirations of the Stuart sovereign body politic through this hallowed geographical space, simultaneously redolent of Scottish and Stuart history, and emblematic of a superseded monarchy. As Kerr astutely observes in almost Sharpian terms, Scott consciously depicts the artificial construction of monarchical legitimacy through the dubious authenticity of the various portraits of the Stuart dynasty in Holyrood.[61] Of greater significance is the depiction of Holyrood as a striking representation of the Stuart monarchy's historic power now definitively made obsolete. The Stuart interest has receded from England to a remnant of its pre-Jamesian Scottish roots and sovereign power in Britain now resides across the Border with the Hanoverian dynasty. Scott introduces Charles Edward, both as a character and in geographic terms, as inherently anachronistic: a spent historical force surrounded by the outmoded political structures of the Scottish clans.

This depiction of the Stuart sovereign body politic is reinforced at St Leonard's Hill, as the various clans comprising the Highland army prepare for battle. Charles Edward's army is literally the physical body of the Jacobite cause. As such, it contains a number of prescient representations of a movement that is about to reach its zenith at the victory soon to be achieved at Prestonpans. It is at St Leonard's Hill that Edward first sees the Chevalier's army in its entirety, and witnesses the factionalism simultaneously underpinning and debilitating the Jacobite cause. While the standard of the Chevalier is positioned at the front of the column, behind it are myriad chieftain and clan standards—"rather too many in respect of their numbers" (*Waverley*, 227). As Edward Waverley gazes about him, the deficiencies of the army (and thus the cause) become apparent. The leading men of each clan are well armed, appropriately garbed, hardy, and disciplined. The lower ranks, however, are "indifferently accoutred, and worse armed, half naked, stinted in growth, and miserable in aspect [... and] forced into the field by the arbitrary authority of the chieftains" (*Waverley*, 228). The rear of the army comprises actual brigands and outlaws, equipped with, at best, pole-axes, swords without scabbards,

---

61   Kerr, *Fiction Against History*, 35–6.

scythes and stakes. Waverley's disbelief mirrors the reader's: "a body not then exceeding four thousand men, and of those not above half the number, at the utmost, were armed, [aimed] to change the fate, and alter the dynasty, of the British kingdoms" (*Waverley*, 229).

Similarly, Scott draws ongoing attention to the factionalism that constantly undermines the unity of Charles Edward's cause, again demonstrated through the body of the army. Cairns Craig notes that it "is of the very nature of [Scotland], as Scott conceives it, that its apparently bounded space is riddled with connections, visible or concealed, with other places, and that its apparently unified territory is full of concealed spaces and places where apparently historically redundant forms of society live on".[62] Through an army defined by the chieftains' individual clan loyalties, purposes and ambitions, Scott demonstrates the lack of a unified national identity across Scotland—a major factor leading to the failure of Charles Edward's ambitions.

The descent of Charles Edward's army from the Highlands to the Lowlands of Scotland and into England is nuanced with geographical implications. Blair considers that "[t]he Jacobite incursion from that space into 'mapped' Scotland is shown to be [...] a disruption of history, property, ideology, and of place itself".[63] However, the 'disruption' depicted by Scott is conspicuously muted. The Chevalier's progress through various Scottish towns towards England, as commentated by Edward Waverley, demonstrates a significant diminishment of support for the Jacobites. In these locales the limited appeal of the Chevalier's cause becomes apparent. Attention is drawn to the yawning disparity between the keenly anticipated cumulation of joyful Stuart supporters and the wary, suspicious reception actually experienced: the Jacobite cause is no longer the calling card for the influential, the wealthy or the politically astute. It attracts the marginalized, the politically rabid and those with little to lose: "every one that was in distress, and every one that was in debt, and every one that was discontented" (*Waverley*, 281). Scott depicts no groundswell of support for Charles Edward in any of these locales, but rather a deliberate absence of those expected to engage in the conflict. The Chevalier's body geographical fails to increase in the face of sustained support for the Hanoverian monarchy.

Consequently, the Jacobite army—but not its head, Charles Edward— retreats into Scotland, attempting to avoid the retribution of the Hanoverian sovereign body politic. Thus, the geographical space occupied by the Stuart monarchy is reduced, commensurate with its diminishing chances of success. Soon after, Edward Waverley is separated from the Chevalier's army and

---

62   Cairns Craig, 'Scott's Staging of the Nation,' *Studies in Romanticism*, 40 (2001), 21.

63   Blair, 'Scott, Cartography,' 106–7.

Charles Edward quite literally disappears—from both the narrative and the political landscape. In the context of the body geographical representing the status of the sovereign body politic, Charles Edward's withdrawal from Great Britain and its inconsequentiality for Edward Waverley, specifically, signifies the comprehensive failure of the Chevalier's aspirations and his impact on Great Britain as a whole.

If *Waverley* closes with the confirmed absence—and thus political insignificance—of the Stuart monarchy, *Redgauntlet* depicts a mere shadow of the Jacobite cause that invigorated parts of Great Britain in *Waverley*, with Scott again tracing its demise through landmark and landscape. Early on, Darsie Latimer comments to Alan Fairford that even the memory of Charles Edward is dead: "The Pretender is no more remembered in the Highlands, than if the poor gentleman were gathered to his hundred and eight fathers, whose portraits adorn the ancient walls of Holyrood" (*Redgauntlet*, 16). No longer does the cause divide and disrupt society; those 'out' in 1745 live harmoniously beside their once deadly enemies. If Edward Waverley and the Baron of Bradwardine were concerned about the quality and nature of those joining the Chevalier's army in 1745, those engaged in an "enterprize directed against a dynasty now established for three reigns" would cause them far greater disquiet (*Redgauntlet*, 317).

Redgauntlet's endless wandering, inveterate transience and unswerving loyalty to the Chevalier's cause achieves only "encouragement from some, because they want a spell of money from him; and from others, because they fought for the cause once, and are ashamed to go back; and others, because they have nothing to lose; and others, because they are discontented fools" (*Redgauntlet*, 261). In *Waverley* Scott makes no reference to those chieftains and Scottish lords with substantial property and wealth who once imbued the Jacobite cause with stature, depicting rather the attraction to that cause of the marginalized and discontented. *Redgauntlet* is peopled with outcasts from society, thieves, outlaws, hypocrites and villains over whom Redgauntlet believes his dynasty can rule, as the chieftains did two decades earlier. The social landscape of the Jacobite cause is as reduced as the Royal Wanderer himself and the breadth of support afforded him throughout Great Britain.

Redgauntlet's vision of the political topography is very different from that of his nephew. While Darsie Latimer also interprets his world as political and geographical landscapes, he sees "a settled government—an established authority—a born Briton on the throne—the very Highland mountaineers, upon whom alone the trust of the exiled family reposed, assembled into regiments which act under the orders of the existing dynasty" (*Redgauntlet*, 317). To Darsie, the Chevalier's cause appears a mere vestige of outmoded air-dreaming,

and not, as Redgauntlet believes, the basis of an "enterprize, for which [his] oppressed country calls with the voice of a parent, entreating her children for
aid—or [a] noble revenge which [his] father's blood demands" (*Redgauntlet*,
317). Not until Alan Fairford is taken to Fairladies is anything actually seen of
this political ghost, Charles Edward. Even there, having been smuggled into
the country, he is not only confined within a household, his wellbeing and
safety due to two old maids, but, disguised as Father Buonaventure, is unrecognizable as an aspiring monarch. This inability to recognize the Chevalier of
former days extends well beyond his person. In *Waverley*, the Chevalier is at
the head of an army of four to six thousand men moving from Holyrood to
the Lowlands, into England and back again: a geographical representation of
Charles Edward's attempt to construct himself as the sovereign body politic of
Great Britain. In *Redgauntlet*, a handful of men meets at an inn on the Solway
in England merely to discuss their support for the Jacobite cause. The body
geographical of the Stuart monarchy is indeed reduced. Scott demonstrates a
further diminishment: those few gathered for the Jacobite cause are no more
united than were the chieftains and clansmen in *Waverley*, whose divisiveness
and discord contributed to the failure of Charles Edward's cause in 1745.

Only Redgauntlet, tragically unaware of the equivocal nature of his collabo-
rators' enthusiasm, is resolute. Oblivious of their patent dismay, he rejoices in
Charles Edward's presence in the house, anticipating this will impel them "to
execute as well as to deliberate" (*Redgauntlet*, 347). He then proclaims:

> Charles Edward has instantly complied with the wishes of his faithful
> subjects. [He] is in this country—Charles Edward is in this house!—
> Charles Edward waits but your present decision, to receive the homage
> of those who have ever called themselves his loyal liegemen.
>
> REDGAUNTLET, 349

Redgauntlet remains insensible of the Chevalier's reduced status, both geographically and as the principal of a moribund political cause. Although the
last of the Stuarts, Charles Edward, may well be in the country, in geographical
terms this dynasty is now literally reduced to the confined space of a garret
atop one house—a diminished man representing a futile cause in a restricted
space. The Chevalier descends to the room where his supporters, such as they
are, are gathered only when the conspirators realize their plot has been discov-
ered. Accompanied by General Campbell, a forlorn cavalcade escorts the Royal
Wanderer to the shores of the Solway. Scott's reference to the landscape again
is apposite in the context of the bodies geographical of both the Hanoverian
and the Stuart monarchies: "There was solitude on the landscape, excepting

the small party which now moved towards the rude pier" (*Redgauntlet*, 375). Accompanied by Redgauntlet, Charles Edward Stuart departs, again leaving no impact on Great Britain. Thus, in both *Waverley* and *Redgauntlet*, it is through the places and spaces Charles Edward occupies that Scott represents the inherently anachronistic, marginalized and futile nature of the Stuart cause.

CHAPTER 5

The Royal Presence as Locale: Rehabilitating the Stuart and Hanoverian Monarchies

> By the time of the death of the Virgin Queen, not only the monarchy but the person of the sovereign dominated the public imagination as well as the political constitution and culture of England.
> SHARPE[1]

∵

In the context of this book, the most important locale in each of the six novels—*The Fortunes of Nigel, Woodstock, Peveril of the Peak, The Heart of Mid-Lothian, Waverley* and *Redgauntlet*—is that of the royal presence. In this way Scott explores the character of each sovereign, presenting a historically recognizable and ultimately (to varying degrees) positive representation of James I, Charles II, Queen Caroline, George II and George III. However, the significance of Scott's depictions of the respective royal presences extends beyond this. Individually and collectively, the six novels explore notions and representations of sovereignty that simultaneously suggest the political and social realities of each period and trace the historical changes occurring across the span of the novels.

There is a distinct alignment within these six novels with key Burkean concepts, which of course indicates the inherent counter-revolutionism of Scott's politics.[2] Considered individually but also collectively, the novels portray the idea of a measured societal progress towards a shared and unified future, which underpinned many of Burke and Scott's political beliefs. The Burkean notion that successful governance would enable gradual and sustained societal and (over time) constitutional reform is chiefly upheld in these novels where the

---

1 Kevin Sharpe, *Image Wars: Promoting Kings and Commonwealths in England, 1603–1660* (New Haven and London: Yale University Press, 2010), 11.

2 See David Bromwich's *The Intellectual Life of Edmund Burke: From the Sublime and Beautiful to American Independence* (Cambridge MA: Belknap Press Harvard, 2014) for an excellent assessment of Burkean principles in the context of the times in which he wrote.

monarch ultimately ensures lasting protection against governmental injustice and oppression. The novels are thus each concerned with the practical enactment of justice and the effecting of social benefit and progress. In each novel there operates a counter-revolutionary narrative of historical advancement, a view of societal progress occurring harmoniously, whereby separate cultures and identities are at the last encompassed in a greater whole without divisiveness or irreconcilable conflict.

In *The Fortunes of Nigel, Woodstock,* and *Peveril of the Peak* the king ultimately effects some form of natural justice and creates an emblem of lasting social order by facilitating the protagonist's marriage. In *The Heart of Mid-Lothian,* however, Queen Caroline plays a significantly reduced role. Her involvement in the restoration of justice is limited, in contrast with that achieved by her male counterparts in the other three novels. As such, in that novel Scott appears to harbour some discomfort with the notion of feminine monarchical power and its involvement in, and execution of, justice. In *Waverley* and *Redgauntlet,* Scott portrays the natural body of the sovereign as increasingly distant in contrast with the monarchical presence in *The Fortunes of Nigel, Woodstock, Peveril of the Peak,* and *The Heart of Mid-Lothian.* Considered together, the six novels trace the sovereign's gradual retreat from direct engagement in effecting justice—and a correlative reduction in the need for the monarch to establish representative examples of social order—as societal stability is embedded, buttressed by effective government operating under robust and sustained sovereignty.[3]

A cumulative counter-revolutionary argument can thus be perceived throughout the six novels. This argument moves from a social environment where the personal involvement of the monarch's natural body and body politic is required to ensure justice, to the situation where the sovereign has instituted a degree of social stability that no longer requires the royal presence. In both *Waverley* and *Redgauntlet,* the character, the presence and the cause of Charles Edward are shown to be increasingly anachronistic and superfluous in the context of Hanoverian sovereignty.[4] Equally, the role of the Hanoverian

---

3   C.M. Jackson-Houlston analyses Scott's representation of a number of kings and rulers in the Waverley canon in the chapter 'Fathers of Their Countries? Scott, Porter and Male Rulers' of her monograph (C.M. Jackson-Houlston, *Gendering Walter Scott: Sex, Violence and Romantic Period Writing* (New York and Oxon: Routledge, 2017), 122–42).

4   Stuart Kelly comments that while Scott created memorable portraits of Mary, Queen of Scots, Elizabeth I (both of whom fall outside the scope of this book), James VI and I, Cromwell and Charles II, and even Charles Edward Stuart, he never depicted a ruling Hanoverian monarch in his novels (with Queen Caroline in *The Heart of Mid-Lothian* coming nearest to that state.) See: Stuart Kelly, *Scott-Land: The Man Who Invented a Nation* (Edinburgh: Polygon, 2010), 174.

sovereign no longer necessitates his actual presence. In *Waverley*, Edward Waverley receives a royal pardon from the hands and the interventions of Colonel Talbot, not from George II. Similarly, in *Redgauntlet* the threat posed by the (fictitious) Jacobite rebellion is of such slight consequence to the monarchy that Colonel Campbell, a representative of George III's government, can summarily dismiss it, and indeed ignore it, with impunity. Ultimately, George III's monarchy is so secure that his actual presence is unnecessary to ensure that the social order operating under Hanoverian rule will continue.

It is in the context of analysing the literal body and the presence of the monarch as a physical site in the six novels that Sharpe's concepts of political authority's being creating through public images become so useful. Scott's own construction of the image of the monarch—and of the monarchy—through both portraiture and place, and through positioning within the broader physical, political and social landscapes of each novels, is fundamental to his consistent counter-revolutionism. Scott and Sharpe focus alike on images of political regimes as created through performances of rulership—via the actions of the sovereign and the multifarious representations of their monarchies.

As will be clear from what has been argued so far, Scott displays a constant curiosity about how the various monarchs sought to establish, consolidate and legitimate their respective authorities in the dynamic politico-religious environments (and the resultant widespread social instability) they presided over. James VI and I and Charles II are cases in point. In *The Fortunes of Nigel* James' personal mannerisms, habits and obsessions lead to significant diminution— and much disparagement—of his kingly authority. In *Woodstock* and *Peveril of the Peak*, Scott assesses Charles II as a monarch-in-waiting with nascent authority—and as a royal authority after 1660 in England only. In *The Heart of Mid-Lothian*, Scott considers the role of regency and Caroline as the directly representative monarch but George II as the ultimate sovereign figure. In *Waverley* and *Redgauntlet* the literal immediacy of the monarch is replaced with that of his military and governmental representatives, themselves portraying the image of the Hanoverian monarchs.

It can be seen, then, that Scott's interest in and use of portraiture is of critical importance in the analysis of his counter-revolutionary depiction of the various Stuart and Hanoverian monarchs. This he seeks to bring to life by way of his descriptions of portrait paintings and his own detailed characterizations of each monarch and of other related characters. By considering Scott's astute verbal and visual construction of each monarch, and their images in each of the six novels, the importance of the royal presence as a site can be fully appreciated.

James I: *"I shall never see such another king"*
NIGEL, 363

Sharpe reasonably contends that "[a]s a man, king, legitimate heir, and successor, husband and father, James from the moment of his proclamation, represented a nation's hope of stable, good government".[5] One could summarize this as the desire for a decorous king and a government of administrative as well as financial decorum. Although James may have represented the hope of a nation for both of these things, it cannot be argued that this hope is represented as being realized in *The Fortunes of Nigel*. There, Scott considers a number of questions regarding decorum and sovereignty in his portrait of James I, whom he represents as the most indecorous of English monarchs. Yet, drawing on an extensive array of historical representations of James, Scott adroitly seeks to rehabilitate both the king and his reign by exploring various notions of physicality, by playing with the verisimilitude of the roles James plays, and by deploying redirection and reinterpretation as he constructs James' 'character.'

Scott's portrait of James, and its purpose, have been the subject of varied critical interpretation. Many critics have commented on Scott's portrait of James being the most vibrant and detailed of all the monarchs he represented across the Waverley Novels, with Jordan and Robert C. Gordon suggesting Scott was fascinated by the quirks and conflicts in James' nature.[6] Hart argues that Scott's James, intriguing as his representation is, stands separate from his surrounds, for the Jacobean "world is neither cause nor effective nor symbolic extension of him," while John J. Burke, Jr. opines that Scott's motivation was defensive, seeking to counter popular misconceptions of James and prejudices against his Scottishness.[7] Some, as Drake has also noted, consider James in the context of the Civil Wars; yet others consider that, in James' character, Scott encapsulated his concerns regarding the state of the Jacobean aristocracy and its lack of morality.[8]

---

5 Sharpe, *Image Wars*, 16.

6 See: Frank Jordan, 'Essay on the Text,' *The Fortunes of Nigel*, ed. Frank Jordan (Edinburgh: Edinburgh University Press, 2004), 418, and Robert C. Gordon, *Under Which King?* (Edinburgh and London: Oliver & Boyd, 1969), 129.

7 See: Francis R. Hart, *Scott's Novels: The Plotting of Historic Survival* (Charlottesville: University Press of Virginia, 1966), 198, and John J. Burke, Jr., 'The Homoerotic Subtext in Scott's *The Fortunes of Nigel*: The Question of Evidence,' CLIO, 29 (2000), 300.

8 See: George A. Drake, "'The Ordinary Rules of the Pave': Urban Spaces in Scott's *Fortunes of Nigel*," *Studies in the Novel*, 33 (Winter 2001), 416–29. Regarding Scott's focus on James and links to the Civil Wars, see, for example: C. Hugh Holman. '*Nigel* and the Historical Imagination,'

My focus is somewhat different, for I suggest that Scott's representation of James' 'character' is intrinsic to one of his primary purposes in *The Fortunes of Nigel*—the rehabilitation of the Stuart monarchy (and thus James as a Stuart and a monarch). Without wishing to downplay or avoid the issues raised by other critics, I argue that Scott's purpose simultaneously incorporates and transcends those concerns. Thus, I will explore the historical documents on which Scott drew—and on which he chose not to draw—in his portrait of James, before considering how Scott seeks to construct James' 'character' with particular reference to ideas of decorum. Ultimately, I contend that Scott attempts to circumvent the limitations of James' character, as well as the values and notions of decorum itself, to posit a (partial) rehabilitation of this flawed sovereign.

It may be helpful to recall that many histories of the Enlightenment, including David Hume's *History of England* which resided in the Abbotsford library, contained character portraits of famous historical figures, in accordance with Hume's belief that history's main function was to reveal and to assess the nature of man and the characters of 'men.'[9] Scott had no shortage of sources, historical and historiographical, on which to base the 'character' of James VI and I in *The Fortunes of Nigel.* James provoked extensive historical appraisal— both critical and defensive—and most of the assessments and representations of James written in the century after his death were to be found in the library at Abbotsford.[10] They of course included Scott's own edition of the representations of James by Weldon, Osborne, Heylyn and Peyton in his *Secret History of the Court of James I* (1811). Because Scott made use of so many critical representations of James, many scholars have argued that, as these historical depictions of the king foregrounded his myriad negative characteristics, Scott was

---

    The Classic British Novel, ed. Howard M. Harper, Jr. and Charles Edge (Athens: University of Georgia Press, 1972), 73; and Harry E. Shaw. *The Forms of Historical Fiction: Sir Walter Scott and His Successors* (Ithaca: Cornell University Press, 1983), 174. For an assessment of James as representation of aristocratic decay, see, for example: Gordon, *Under Which King?*, 134, and Fiona Robertson, *Legitimate Histories: Scott, Gothic, and the Authorities of Fiction* (Oxford: Clarendon Press, 1994), 229, and her 'Disfigurement and Disability: Walter Scott's Bodies,' *Otranto*, 003 (2013) http://www.otranto.co.uk/index.php/publication/view/54.

9   See, for example, David Hume's *A Treatise of Human Nature*, ed. Ernest C. Mossner (Harmondsworth: Penguin, 1984).

10   Refer to 'Appendix: Sources for Scott's Characterization of James I' later in this monograph for the histories specifically referring to James VI and I included in the *Catalogue of the Library at Abbotsford* (1838).

therefore positing his own similarly critical portrait of James and his reign.[11] Indeed, Scott's own assessment of the decorum of James' person and his sovereignty is frequently scathing and never wholeheartedly positive. It is true that, as Jordan emphasizes, "to an unusual degree in the Waverley series, the historical characters in *Nigel* are major players, their characters (and not the historical events that reveal them) front and centre in this novel".[12] However, while Scott describes James in far more detail than he does sovereigns, say, Charles II, Caroline, George II or George III in other Waverley Novels, that depiction can hardly be interpreted as glowing. How then can one argue that Scott sought to present this monarch in a positive light, when clearly to do so successfully would constitute the resuscitation rather than the mere rehabilitation of a king whom Scott himself deemed the "least talented of the Stuarts"? (*Nigel*, 67).

Ina Ferris suggests that Isaac D'Israeli (whose portrait of James Scott slights in the 'Introduction' to *The Fortunes of Nigel*) "was less concerned with recreating James as an historical representation than with challenging his representation in national histories as a degraded stylized 'character'".[13] I want to argue that, by way of contrast, Scott was more concerned with recreating James as an historically recognizable 'character', the representation of whom would enable the positing of (albeit heavily qualified) support of his sovereignty. As John J. Burke astutely notes, "What better way to defend James than to create a

---

11   Scott's *Secret History of the Court of James I* comprised critical representations of James—Osborne's *Traditional Memoirs*, Weldon's *Court and Character of King James* and Peyton's *Divine Catastrophe of the House of Stuarts*—and a more approving one, *Aulicus Coquinariae* (attributed variously to Heylyn and Sanderson while also referencing Goodman, and written in reply to Weldon's assessment, hence the sub-title 'A Vindication in Answer to a Pamphlet entitled The Court and Character of James I'). In addition to other contemporary histories, Scott appears to have drawn on aspects of Weldon and Osborne's representation of the monarch rather than on the more favourably inclined *Aulicus Coquinariae* in the construction of his 'character' of James I. It is interesting to note that Arthur Wilson's *The History of Great Britain, Being the Life and Reign of King James I* (London, 1653), another highly influential and negative portrait of James I, is not included in the *Catalogue of the Library at Abbotsford* (1838), although Marc L. Schwarz suggests that the views of both Weldon and Wilson "were, of course, retold, with all their color retained, in the nineteenth century by Sir Walter Scott [...] [in] *Secret History* and his novel *The Fortunes of Nigel*" (Marc L. Schwarz. 'James I and the Historians: Towards a Reconciliation,' *The Journal of British Studies*, 13 (May 1974), 116).

12   Jordan. 'Essay on the Text,' *The Fortunes of Nigel*, 531. For descriptions of James in the novel, see *Nigel*, 66–7, 109, 397–8.

13   Ina Ferris, 'The "Character" of James the First and Antiquarian Secret History,' *Wordsworth Circle*, 37 (Spring 2006), 73.

portrait that would acknowledge all his weaknesses yet show that on balance
he still deserved a place in the nation's affection?".[14] Thus, Scott exerts considerable ingenuity in his creation of James by embedding his qualified approval
within the parameters of the most popular, biased and critical historical assessments of this monarch.[15]

Various aspects of Scott's 'character' of James become clear when we examine how he describes the king's physique, his physical surrounds and his
physical presence. While Sharpe draws attention to James constructing his
monarchical identity through his writings, it is interesting to note how carefully Scott confines his 'character' of James to his physical appearance and
his actions, and how he does not allow us to hear James' actual words at any
point. Indeed, it is remarkable how completely Scott denies James his historical voice. While allowing him a garrulousness that simultaneously reveals his
being "deeply learned, without possessing useful knowledge," "a wit, though
a pedant; and a scholar, though fond of the conversation of the ignorant and
uneducated," Scott negates his written voice, reducing *Basilikon Doron*—
intended, as Jenny Wormald notes, to "be a persuasive, instructive handbook
of imperial kingship for Prince Henry, his intimates, and (later) a wider audience" and *Trew Law* ("more than a claim of divine right; it was a restatement
of imperial kingship")—to "notes of unmercifully long orations, and essays on
king-craft" (*Nigel*, 66) and consigning them to historical silence.[16] It is not inconceivable that James' personal beliefs regarding 'king-craft' would scupper
the most ingenious of arguments implicitly supporting James' reign.

---

14   Burke, 'The Homoerotic Subtext,' 314.

15   Ralph Houlbrooke emphasizes that "[p]ublished in 1650 and 1658 respectively, the accounts attributed to Sir Anthony Weldon (c.1583–1648) and written by Francis Osborne
(1593–1659) shared a dry, ironic, cynical tone that would have a lasting influence on
subsequent histories of James' reign. These authors relied heavily on court gossip and
rumours. They emphasized James' timidity, his extravagance, and his male favourites"
(Ralph Houlbrooke. 'James' Reputation, 1625–2005,' *James VI and I: Ideas, Authority, and
Government* ed. Ralph Houlbrooke (Aldershot and Burlington: Ashgate Publishing Company, 2006), 171). Weldon's representation especially is notable for his cruel representation of James' physical appearance. Robert Ashton also questions the probity of various
harsh assessments of James by a number of contemporary historians (notably Weldon
and Osborne) in his 'Introduction' to *James I by His Contemporaries* ed. Robert Ashton
(London: Hutchinson & Co, 1969).

16   Jenny Wormald, 'James VI and I, *Basilikon Doron* and *The Trew Law of Free Monarchies*: the
Scottish context and the English translation,' *The Mental World of the Jacobean Court*, ed.
Linda Levy Peck (Cambridge: Cambridge University Press, 1991), 49, 48.

Although James speaks a great deal (and usually nonsense) in the novel, it is the various indecorums committed in both his appearance and his actions that Scott predominantly uses to portray him:

> The King's dress was of green velvet, quilted so full as to be dagger-proof—which gave him the appearance of clumsy and ungainly protu-berance; while its being buttoned awry communicated to his figure an air of distortion. Over his green doublet he wore a sad-coloured night-gown, out of the pocket of which peeped his hunting-horn. His high-crowned grey hat lay on the floor, covered with dust, but encircled by a carkanet of large balas rubies; and he wore a blue velvet night-cap, in the front of which was placed the plume of a heron, which had been struck down by a favourite hawk in some critical moment of the flight, for remembrance of which the King wore this highly honoured feather.
>
> But such inconsistencies in dress and appointments were mere out-ward types of those which existed in the royal character, rendering it a subject of doubt amongst his contemporaries, and bequeathing it as a problem to future historians.
>
> *NIGEL*, 66

So Scott depicts James in all his tarnished sovereignty. He minimizes the cruel exaggeration and suggestion of deformity in Weldon's physical 'character' of James, focusing rather on his "inconsistencies in dress and appointments," the "appearance of clumsy and ungainly protuberance" and the mistaken button-ing that "communicated to his figure an air of distortion." Although seeming to portray James' physical characteristics accurately, Scott thus transfers to his dress and appearance those idiosyncratic aspects for which James was famed, and by doing so distances those attributes from James' own body. Yet Scott makes no attempt to dissociate James' external peculiarities of appearance from his personal qualities. In fact he links them overtly: "such inconsistencies in dress and appointments were mere outward types of those which existed in the royal character".

Scott then extends this representation of James' 'character' to a broader physical canvas. In the immediate vicinity, James' inner sanctum also acts as a facsimile of his psyche:

> The scene of confusion amid which he found the King seated, was no bad picture of the state and quality of James's own mind. There was much that was rich and costly in cabinet pictures and valuable ornaments, but they were slovenly arranged, covered with dust, and lost half their value,

or at least their effect, from the manner in which they were presented to
the eye.

NIGEL, 66

Again Scott shows James' worth and merit being obscured and diminished
by indecorous and inappropriate self-presentation and uncouth appearance.
What could be called Scott's careful overwriting of Weldon can be readily seen,
in sources similarly scathing of James, to be neither baseless nor without historical precedent. Colonel John Hutchinson, for example, suggests that similar
overwriting of James' character took place at court:

> The poore king [was told] he was Salomon, that his sloth and cowardize,
> by which he betrey'd the cause of God and honor of the nation, was Gos-
> pell meekenesse and peaceablenesse, for which they rays'd him up above
> the heavens, while he lay wallowing like a swine in the mire of his Lust.
> He had a little learning, and this they call'd the spiritt of wisedome, and
> so magnified him, so falsely flatter'd him, that he could not endure the
> words of truth and soundnesse but rewarded these base, wicked, unfaith-
> fulle fawnes with rich preferments, attended by pomp and titles.[17]

It is useful to note the very similar language Scott uses in his descriptions of
James:

> The temper of the King, peaceable even to timidity, inclined him per-
> petually to interfere as mediator amongst the contending factions, whose
> brawls disturbed his court.
>
> *NIGEL*, 19

> He was deeply learned, without possessing useful knowledge; sagacious
> in many individual cases, without having real wisdom; fond of his power,
> and desirous to maintain and augment it, yet willing to resign the direc-
> tion of that and of himself, to the most unworthy favourites.
>
> *NIGEL*, 66–7

What this process of overwriting suggests, of course, is that Scott uses the
physical presence of James to image and negotiate the imbalances of James'
character.

---

17   John Sutherland, *Memoirs of the Life of Colonel Hutchinson, with the Fragment of an
     Autobiography of Mrs Hutchinson* (Oxford: Oxford University Press, 1973), 43.

At Greenwich, when Nigel seeks to speak with James and assure him of his innocence, Scott's representation of James is worth remarking. James is on horseback, engaged in that most manly of pursuits, hunting; he succeeds in killing the stag, being the first on the scene, as royal protocol dictated. But Scott undermines this representation of physical, manly endeavour when he shows James' cowardice at Nigel's approaching him—again he indicates the conflicting notions of kingly decorum residing in James' 'character.' Scott later inverts this mechanism when he explores the significance of James' presence in the "lugg" in the Tower, that hidden cavity he ordered be built so he could eavesdrop on private conversations. This improper place, which facilitates behaviour unseemly in the king, Scott presents as ultimately enabling James to assume and perform his monarchical responsibilities. By the use of this distasteful and inappropriate mechanism of place and presence, James brings about the justice Nigel merits and begins the partial restoration of the House of Glenvarloch by smoothing the way for the marriage of Margaret and Nigel. James was never, of course, going to be capable of restoring the financial fortunes of the House of Glenvarloch; that task falls to Richie Moniplies and Martha Trapbois. Thus, by referring to the overarching concept of decorum, Scott portrays the physicality of James' 'character.' He does so in a way that enables an apparently rigorous historical accuracy while also softening criticism, for he redirects criticism away from James' physical body. Weldon's criticism of James is emphatically physical; Scott, however, allows at least the possibility of a disparity between James' appearance and the presence of (some) positive attributes. Decorum and an awareness of both positive and negative traits are central to Scott's illustration of James in his 'Tales of a Grandfather':

James VI [...] had more learning than wisdom; and yet, in the course of his future life, it did not appear that he was without good sense so much, as that he was destitute of the power to form manly purposes, and the firmness necessary to maintain them. A certain childishness and meanness of mind rendered his good sense useless, and his learning ridiculous. Even from his infancy he was passionately addicted to favourites, and already, in his thirteenth or fourteenth year, there were two persons so high in his good graces that they could bring him to do any thing they pleased. [...]
[James] was the least dignified and accomplished of all his family; but, at the same time, the most fortunate. [...] He himself alone, without courage, without sound sagacity, without that feeling of dignity which should restrain a prince from foolish indulgences, became King of the great nation which had for ages threatened to subdue that of which he was born monarch; and the good fortune of the Stewart family, which

seems to have existed in his person alone, declined and totally decayed in those of his successors.[18]

In *The Fortunes of Nigel* Scott demonstrates that those different qualities juxtaposed in James' character and his inappropriate behaviour could in fact be the means by which justice is (conditionally) realized.

Nevertheless, there is one important aspect of James' indecorous behaviour as king that Scott does not include in his use of verisimilitude when portraying James' body, physical surrounds or physical presence. Possibly the greatest challenge Scott faces is dealing with the sensitive problem of the king's homosexuality. Seeking neither to deny nor to make a feature of James' sexual preference, Scott attempts sleight-of-hand by obliquely acknowledging it. While John J. Burke opines that "Scott, tolerant and understanding as he seems to have been, had to be careful in broaching this subject, and being careful involved deniability: there could be no obvious fingerprints," I suggest that Scott uses erasure rather than "deniability" in his depiction of James' sexuality.[19] More important, rather than Scott "demasculiniz[ing] James through a series of equivocal references to his bisexuality," as Jackson-Houlston argues, or James' sexuality being "a central feature in his representation of King James and the court in England" as Burke contends, the homosexuality in the novel is sidelined by being overlaid in a number of ways.[20] Scott treads lightly around this contentious issue, although he does not ignore it. Chief among his techniques is the deployment of allusion. His wary acknowledgement of the king's homoeroticism is quite literally the identification of a love which Scott will not conceal but which he will not name. It is not insignificant that Scott refrains from using Osborne's graphic descriptions of James' demonstrations of affections for his favourites, such as James "kissing them after so lascivious a mode in publick".[21] In the 'Introduction' to *The Fortunes of Nigel* (added to the text by Scott in 1831 and included in the 1931 Dent edition of the novel), Scott emphasizes that "it was in James I's reign that vice first appeared affecting the better classes in its gross and undisguised depravity".[22] Instead, in his use of allusion

---

18   Walter Scott, 'Tales,' *Prose Works of Sir Walter Scott* (Edinburgh: Robert Caddell,1836), 159, 342–3.
19   Burke, 'The Homoerotic Subtext,' 298.
20   Jackson-Houlston, *Gendering Walter Scott*, 124 ; Burke, 'The Homoerotic Subtext,' 298.
21   Francis Osborne's *Historical Memoires on the Reigns of Queen Elizabeth, and King James*, cited in Michael B. Young. *King James and the History of Homosexuality* (New York: New York University Press, 2000), 125.
22   Walter Scott. *The Fortunes of Nigel* (London and Toronto: J.M. Dent & Sons Ltd, 1931), xi. This edition will be cited subsequently as Scott, *Nigel* (1931). For the entire 'Introduction,' see xv–xiii. It has not been included in all editions of Scott's *Fortunes of Nigel* since then.

he remains as reticent as Weldon, or as Wilson—neither of whom overtly refers to James' known sexual proclivities.

He refers to Harrington, who suggests "the gross debauchery of the period" was "too much encouraged by the example of the monarch, who was in other respects neither without talent nor a good-natured disposition".[23] Although making specific reference to historical sources and frankly conceding the "vice" and "debauchery" of the times, and of the reigning sovereign, Scott does not specify the nature of James' "depravity," submerging it instead under more general representations of men and women engaged in "wild riot, excess and devastation of time and temperance".[24]

Scott addresses the intimacy between James and the Duke of Buckingham (it was well known in Jacobean times, and in Scott's own, that they were lovers) by using the trope that the lovers themselves used throughout their mutual letters, that of father and son. Scott has Buckingham frequently refer to James as his "dear dad and gossip," a phrase James used of himself in his letters to Buckingham.[25] This kind of allusion allows Scott to acknowledge clearly but

---

23 Scott, *Nigel* (1931), xi. Scott refers specifically to Harrington's *Nugae Antique*, Winwood's *Memorials*, Howell's *Letters*, and *Private Letters and Correspondence of Steenie, alias Buckingham* in his vivid depiction of society during in the reign of James I. "It was in James I.'s reign that vice first appeared affecting the better classes in its gross and undisguised depravity [...] In James' reign, [...] the coarsest pleasures were publicly and unlimitedly indulged, since, according to Sir John Harrington, the men wallowed in beastly delights; and even ladies abandoned their delicacy and rolled about in intoxication. [...]" (ibid., xi). Scott's language echoes Colonel Hutchinson's description of the times. However—not unsurprisingly—Scott does not blame these excesses, as Hutchinson does, on the Scots who accompanied James,: "The Court of this king was a nursery of lust and intemperance; he had brought in with him a company of hunger-starved poore Scotts, who comming into this plentiful kingdome surfetted with riott and debaucheries, and gott all the riches of the land only to cast away [...] Then began Murther, incest, Adultery, drunkennesse, swearing, fornication and all sorts of ribaldry to be no conceal'd but countenanced vices, favour'd wherever they were privately practis'd because they held such conformity with the Court example" (John Sutherland, *Memoirs of the Life of Colonel Hutchinson, with the Fragment of an Autobiography of Mrs Hutchinson* (Oxford University Press, 1973), 42).

24 See: David M. Bergeron. *King James and Royal Letters of Homoerotic Desire* (Iowa City: University of Iowa Press, 1999), 147–219 for the most recent and comprehensive collection of James and Buckingham's correspondence.

25 The actual nature of this homoeroticism has been the subject of considerable debate, with a specific focus on whether James and Buckingham's relationship extended beyond desire into behaviour. See: Maurice Lee. *Great Britain's Solomon: James VI and I in his Three Kingdoms* (Urbana: University of Illinois Press, 1990), 249; Roger Lockyer, *Buckingham: The Life and Political Career of George Villiers, First Duke of Buckingham, 1592–1628*

discreetly James' homosexuality.[26] In Chapter 9, he uses another form of allusion. Two courtiers' *sotto voce* responses to James' discourse on his ancestors run as follows:

> "Ay, ay—*Beati pacifi*. My English lieges here may weel make much of me, for I would have them to know, they have gotten the only peaceable man that ever came of my family. If James with the Fiery Face had come amongst you," [James I] said, looking round him, "or my great grandsire, of Flodden memory!"
>
> "We should have sent them back to the north again," whispered one English nobleman.
>
> "At least," said another, in the same inaudible tone, "we should have had a *man* to our sovereign, though it were but a Scotchman."
>
> NIGEL, 110

Scott has James make a doubly unfortunate allusion to his ancestry. Even though the king explicitly disassociates himself from his "great grandsire, of Flodden memory," unavoidably he associates himself with that ancestor by the very act of naming him. The 1513 Battle of Flodden was a disastrous defeat for the Scots following on their invasion of England; in evoking his "great grandsire," James draws attention not only to his own, foreign presence in England but also to his being rather less than a personal success as king. More importantly, his allusion invites the second courtier to remark that James is a failure as a man; the remark implies that, while James' ancestor was merely "a Scotsman," he was at least heterosexual. Scott has the king's naïve reference mark him as diversely flawed in the eyes of those around him.

Two further allusions are noteworthy. In Chapter 33 Scott stresses that the king's interest in Margaret Ramsay occurs as a direct result of his finding her disguised "as a pretty page" (*Nigel*, 369). Scott's narrator makes the point that the "learned and good-humoured monarch [...]" had been much struck (that is, for him, *who was not very accessible to such emotions*,) with the beauty and embarrassment of the pretty Peg-a-Ramsay, as he called her, when he first saw

---

(London: Longman, 1981), 22; Bergeron, *King James and Royal Letters*, 197; and Young, *King James and the History of Homosexuality*, 36–50.

26   Young, in his discussion of Weldon and Wilson's respective descriptions of James I and VI, makes the point that "[m]any of his English subjects found him doubly puzzling because he was both a Scot and a man who loved other males. They viewed him through the distorting lenses of xenophobia *and* homophobia" (Young, *King James and the History of Homosexuality*, 122).

her" (*Nigel*, 397, my emphasis). Moreover, James calling Margaret "his pretty Peg-a-Ramsay" is no accident. Careful readers of the novel will be aware that Margaret Ramsay is not the only character to whom the epithet of Peg-a-Ramsay is applied. Lord Huntinglen's contemptuous dismissal of the Duke of Buckingham ("Mind not Buckingham, he is a Peg-a-Ramsay"—*Nigel*, 119) mirrors the comment by Shakespeare's Sir Toby in *Twelfth Night* that "Malvolio's a Peg-a-Ramsay".[27] In both instances, reference is ironically to a sexually experienced and wanton female. Bonny Peggy Ramsay's trade was lauded in the eponymous ballad:

> Bonny Peggy Ramsay that any Man may see;
> And bonny was her Face with a fair freckl'd Eye;
> Neat is her Body made and she hath good Skill,
> And square is her Wethergig made like a mill
> With a hey trolodol, hey trolodol, hey trolodol lil; [...][28]

James' calling Margaret Ramsay "Peg-a-Ramsay" is not meant to convey his perception of her as a wanton, but it does enable Scott, having first covertly acknowledged the source of James' interest, to signal James' ongoing sexual arousal at Margaret's dressing as "a pretty page". It also draws attention to the heterosexual virility of Buckingham and his amatory pursuit of various women, which Scott further sharpens when he has Dalgarno make sneering reference to his wife, Lady Hermione, joining Buckingham's "harem".[29]

   Thus, Scott was confronted by no shortage of challenges, and expended considerable ingenuity, when fashioning his depiction of the king in such a way as to rehabilitate this scion of the Stuart monarchy. By employing apparently candid (but in fact carefully selective) verisimilitude, and subtly (re)directing our (re)interpretation of James' body, clothing, surroundings, presence, and sexual preferences, Scott succeeds in presenting a construction of James' character that enables a (partial) rehabilitation of this "wisest fool in Christendom" (*Nigel*, 67). Ferris points out that "the awkward figure of the Stuart king

---

27   William Shakespeare, 'Twelfth Night,' *The Arden Shakespeare, Second Series*, ed. J.M. Lothian and T.W. Craik (London: Methuen, 1975), Act II. Scene 3. 76–7.

28   The ballad appears in volume 5 of Thomas D'Urfey's *Wit and Mirth: Or Pills to Purge Melancholy*, 6 vols (London: J. Tonson, 1719–20).

29   John J. Burke makes a slightly different assessment, focusing on Scott's choosing not to present Buckingham as a married man, which he was by the 1620s. However he does note that "Scott portrays him as a promiscuous, heterosexually active bachelor, what we used to call 'a ladies' man.'" (Burke, 'The Homoerotic Subtext,' 308.)

continues to block the recuperative efforts of history, constantly under rehabilitation but somehow never quite rehabilitated".[30] I would argue that Scott
finds James' notions of decorum—his metaphorical and actual "fidling about
his cod-piece"—to be as significant as his "awkward figure" in making sustained rehabilitation of this Stuart monarch an arduous undertaking.[31]

Charles I and Charles II

Although the Waverley canon chronicles the implementation of justice by
several sovereigns, Scott chose not to include a novel featuring Charles I as
sovereign and bringer of justice to his subjects. Rather than draw attention to
Charles' failures in that latter respect—or, at the very least, to controversies
about Charles' personal rule—he deflected attention to Charles' enforced absence as legitimate ruler. Thus he did not omit that fated monarch completely
from his writings about the Stuart dynasty; indeed, Charles I features, along with
Charles II and in varying degrees of detail, in *The Fortunes of Nigel*, *Woodstock*,
and *Peveril of the Peak*, as well as in 'Tales of a Grandfather' and Scott's *Letters*.

Through the representation of Charles I in *The Fortunes of Nigel* and *Woodstock*, and of Charles II in *Woodstock* and *Peveril of the Peak*, Scott traces the
Stuart monarchy's history from the later years of James I's reign to the time of
Charles II's restored sovereignty in England. It is valuable, therefore, to consider Scott's representations of Charles I and Charles II together. One sees that
Scott is making a point of the absence of Charles I's role as sovereign before he
explores Charles II's precarious presence as monarch disguised, and ultimately
positions the restored king as the embodiment of natural justice in the historical context of his reign. I want, therefore, to demonstrate that within *The
Fortunes of Nigel*, *Woodstock* and *Peveril of the Peak* Scott interprets the history
of the sovereign's natural body and body politic to mirror the fate of natural
justice during the periods depicted.

It is generally agreed that *The Fortunes of Nigel* "contains in the portrait of
James I Scott's greatest portrayal of a historical figure".[32] Various critics have
commented on its detail and vivacity.[33] Particularly curious, therefore, is
the contrast between the three-dimensionality and sheer vibrancy of Scott's

---

30   Ferris, 'The "Character" of James the First,' 75.

31   Sir Anthony Weldon. *The Character of King James*, reprinted in vol. II of *Scott's Secret
      History of the Court of King James I* (Edinburgh: James Ballantyne & Co, 1811), 2.

32   Holman, '*Nigel* and the Historical Imagination,' 69.

33   See, for example: Gordon, *Under Which King?*, 129–38; Hart, *Scott's Novels*, 198–203; and
      Burke, 'The Homoerotic Subtext.'

THE ROYAL PRESENCE AS LOCALE

portrait of James and his flat depiction—indeed, it is almost a caricature—of Charles, Prince of Wales. This latter portrait is almost featureless, focusing primarily on Charles' melancholy demeanour, inflated dignity, strict attachment to decorum, and unconscious arrogance. While James lurches haphazardly across the breadth of his sovereign responsibilities, caught between his public and private imperatives, he is at least partly present in his capacity of monarchical body politic:

> George Heriot sighed internally. "O my Master," thought he—"my dear Master, is it then fated you are never to indulge any kingly or noble sentiment, without its being sullied by some afterthought of interested selfishness!"
>
> *NIGEL*, 371

Charles, by contrast, is notably disengaged, almost absent despite the many references—mainly by James—to his physical presence in the novel. Scott's visual rendering of him is cursory:

> The whole train were uncovered excepting the Prince of Wales, afterwards the most unfortunate of British monarchs, who came onward, having his long curled auburn tresses, and his countenance, which, even in early youth, bore a shade of anticipated melancholy, shaded by the Spanish hat and the single ostrich feather which drooped from it.
>
> *NIGEL*, 173

Furthermore, Charles is rarely seen without the Duke of Buckingham, his boon companion.

The influence of "Baby Charles and Steenie" over James' natural body and his body politic is explicitly and frequently demonstrated, as is the negative impact of that unduly self-interested influence. James I, for example, chides George Heriot for accommodating Charles and Steenie's demands despite his own command to do so:

> "Respecting the Duke of Buckingham's plate," said the goldsmith, "your Majesty was pleased to direct that no expence should be spared, and"—
>
> "What signifies what I desired, man? when a wise man is with fules and bairns, he maun e'en play at the chucks. But you should have had mair sense and consideration than to gie Babie Charles and Steenie their ain gate; they wad hae floored the very rooms wi' silver, and I wonder they didna."
>
> *NIGEL*, 68

Similarly, Charles and Buckingham's dislike of Nigel, and their desire to appropriate his property as a hunting ground, are major impediments to James' fulfilling his monarchical responsibilities and effecting justice for his loyal subject:

> "[...] Steenie and Baby Charles cannot abide him—neither can your own son, my lord; and so, methinks, he had better go down to Scotland before he comes to ill luck by them."
>
> "My son, an it please your Majesty, so far as he is concerned, shall not direct my doings," said the Earl [of Huntinglen], "nor any wild-headed young man of them all."
>
> "Why, neither shall they mine," replied the Monarch; "by my father's saul, none of them all shall play Rex with me—I will do what I will, and what I aught, like a free king."
>
> *NIGEL*, 113–4

However, James' autonomous stance is short-lived:

> "To grant the truth," he said, after he had finished his hasty perusal, "this is a hard case; and harder than it was represented to me, though I had some inkling of it before. And so the lad only wants payment of the siller due from us, in order to reclaim his paternal estate? But then, Huntinglen, the lad will have other debts—and for what burthen himsell with sae mony acres of barren woodland? let the land gang, man—let the land gang; Steenie has the promise of it from our Scottish Chancellor—it is the best hunting ground in Scotland—and Baby Charles and Steenie want to kill a buck there this next year—they mun hae the land—they mun hae the land."
>
> *NIGEL*, 114

Although Scott depicts Charles' negative influence on his father's performance of his duties as the sovereign body politic, there is no compensatory portrayal of Charles' disinterestedly undertaking any positive action befitting either a monarch-in-training or a prince. Charles is shown to be a creature of the court, on whom courtiers such as Dalgarno fawn. Scott's depiction of his one engagement in the righting of the wrongs suffered by a subject (Lady Hermione) is coloured with deep irony. The malefactor is his intimate, as James makes clear: "I grieve to say it, but your son Dalgarno, whom I thought a very saint, as he was so much with Steenie and Baby Charles, hath turned out a very villain" (*Nigel*, 357). Charles and the Duke of Buckingham then attempt to distance themselves from Dalgarno's infamy by aligning themselves with the formal institutions of James' court: "[I]t is the opinion of our council and ourself, as weel as of Baby Charles and Steenie, that your son maun amend his wrong by wedding this lady, or undergo such disgrace and discountenance as we can bestow" (*Nigel*, 359). Even James, ever the fond father, is simultaneously conscious of Charles' inappropriate influence over his own majesty, and the incongruity of Charles engaging in the restitution of justice:

> [...] I left Baby Charles and Steenie laying [Dalgarno's] duty before him; and if he can resist doing what they desire him, why I wish he would teach me the gate of it. O Geordie, Jingling Geordie, it was grand to hear Baby Charles laying down the guilt of dissimulation, and Steenie lecturing on the turpitude of incontinence!
>
> NIGEL, 362

Scott makes no attempt, then, to portray Charles as an emblem of judicial efficacy. He represents the prince as either an impediment to justice or a deeply flawed instrument of official retribution, and as in fact aligned with the most self-interested politician in James' court. Through Charles, Scott demonstrates the increasing absence of the sovereign body politic's will and capacity to effect justice. Although Scott can only give a heavily qualified approval of him as an institutional means of justice, James is still shown to be both able and willing to bring about natural justice for Nigel, despite the fact that he must in the end depend on such lowly entities as Richie Moniplies and Martha Trapbois to secure Nigel's birthright in the face of Dalgarno's stratagems. Yet, as Scott makes clear, *The Fortunes of Nigel* is set in the latter years of James' reign and Charles is the ascendant monarchical body.

The significance of this is underlined by Scott's juxtaposition of James' and Charles' respective characters. It might seem that Charles contrasts favourably with James' foibles, absurdities and lack of kingly decorum, for, as I argued earlier, Scott constructs James' 'character' with particular reference to notions of decorum or the lack thereof. So, for example, we read:

> Charles, as strict in his notions of decorum, as his father was indifferent to it, fixed himself in an attitude of rigid and respectful attention, while the haughty favourite, conscious of his power over both father and son, stretched himself more easily on his seat, and in assuming an appearance of listening, seemed to pay a debt to ceremonial rather than to duty.
>
> NIGEL, 367

In focusing on Charles' dignity, formality and resolve, Scott may appear to be demonstrating Charles' superior monarchical qualities, especially when considered in the light of the embarrassing way in which James established Nigel's right to a free pardon—from "a lurking-place called the king's lugg" (*Nigel*, 368):

> "I am happy your gracious Majesty," said the Duke of Buckingham, "has arrived at that conclusion, though I could never have guessed at the road by which you attained it."
>
> "I trust," said Prince Charles, "that it is not a path which your Majesty will think it consistent with your high dignity to tread frequently."
>
> "Never while I live again, Baby Charles, that I give you my royal word on."
>
> NIGEL, 370

Yet Scott implicitly identifies Charles' exaggerated dignity, formality, and strength of will not as the attributes of an effective sovereign, but as causes of the looming Civil Wars and Charles' own demise. Commentators have considered the coming conflict a central concern in *The Fortunes of Nigel*. Robertson suggests that the "action of *The Fortunes of Nigel* is overshadowed by the crisis of 1649," and notes the many references Scott makes anticipating the Civil Wars, and thereby "foreshortening and distorting historical process".[34] In this context, Scott discreetly positions Charles to indicate further how the sovereign body politic is becoming increasingly absent from the affairs of government and to foreshadow its erasure. Charles is not shown as superior to James, whom Scott has laboured hard to represent in a positive light. Rather, Charles' focus on sovereign will, even when he considers monarchical engagement in justice, serves to reveal the commitment to absolutism that will effect his downfall:

> "What your Majesty says," replied Prince Charles, "is marked with your usual wisdom—the precincts of palaces must be sacred as well as the persons of kings, which are respected even in the most barbarous nations, as being one step only beneath their divinities. But your Majesty's will can control the severity of this and every other law, and it is in your power, on consideration of his case, to grant the rash young man a free pardon."
>
> NIGEL, 368

---

34   Robertson, *Legitimate Histories*, 229. See also: Shaw, *The Forms of Historical Fiction*, 174; Holman, '*Nigel* and the Historical Imagination,' 69; cf. Drake, "'The Ordinary Rules of the Pave,'" 426; Hart, *Scott's Novels*, 198.

A further example of the difference between Charles and James occurs in James' almost prophetic speech to Charles at Greenwich in Chapter 28 and Charles' response:

> "Ay, ay," continued the monarch; "take them to ye *per aversionem*, bairns—the one pouch stuffed with petitions, t'other with pasquina-does—a fine time we have on it. On my conscience, I believe the tale of Cadmus was hieroglyphical, and that the dragon's teeth whilk he sowed were the letters he invented. Ye are laughing, Baby Charles?—Mind what I say—when I came here first frae our ain country, where the men are as rude as the weather, by my conscience, England was a bieldy bit— one would have thought the King had little to do but to walk by quiet waters, *per aquam refectionis*. But I kenna how or why, the place is sair changed—read that libel upon us and on our regimen. The dragon's teeth are sown, Baby Charles; I pray God they bearna their armed harvest in your day, if I suld not live to see it. God forbid I should, for there will be an awful day's kemping at the shearing of them."
>
> "I shall know how to stifle the crop in the blade,—ha, George?" said the Prince, turning to the favourite with a look expressive of some con- tempt for his father's apprehensions, and full of confidence in the supe- rior firmness and decision of his own counsels.
>
> *NIGEL*, 310–1

James, that most indecorous of kings who wrote in *Basilikon Doron* and *The Trew Law of Free Monarchies* assertions of divine right and imperial sovereign- ty, is yet depicted as a far more astute and responsive monarch than his blithely arrogant and rigidly decorous son.

Scott's representation of Charles I in his *Letters* is similar to that in *The For- tunes of Nigel*: he even alludes to Charles' reaping what he has sown, in eerie duplication of James' prophetic words in Chapter 28.[35] On the other hand, the difference between the depiction of Charles I in *The Fortunes of Nigel* and that in *Woodstock* is nothing less than a transformation. The sympathetic hues of Charles' portrait in *Woodstock* (and also in 'Tales') are in stark contrast to the harsh tones used in the earlier novel. This may be because in *The Fortunes of Nigel* and *Letters*, Scott's attention is focused on Charles I's capacity as the as- cendant sovereign body politic, whereas in *Woodstock* and 'Tales' his analysis

---

35   Scott refers in his correspondence to Charles' virtue in "a private capacity" but consid- ers him to have "sow[n] the wind [and thus] God knows he reaped the whirlwind." See: *Letters*, 5.310–2.

is confined to the person—the natural body—of the monarch. Charles I is represented as a tragic figure in *Woodstock*—as "the royal Martyr" or "the Blessed Martyr"—and the descriptions of him are almost entirely focused on his personal qualities, not his public stature (*Woodstock*, 340, 361).

When, in that novel, Cromwell accidentally turns over Charles I's painting, he focuses on the physical features of his person:

> "That Flemish painter" he said—"that Antonio Vandyke—what a power was his! Steel may mutilate, worms may waste and destroy—still the King stands uninjured by time; and our grandchildren, while they read his history, may look on his image, and compare the melancholy features with the woful tale.—It was a stern necessity—it was an awful deed! The calm pride of that eye might have ruled worlds of crouching Frenchmen, or supple Italians, or formal Spaniards; but its glances only roused the native courage of the stern Englishman [...]—Verily he hath his reward—Then, what is that piece of painted canvas to me more than others? No—let him show to others the reproaches of that cold, calm face, that proud yet complaining eye—Those who have acted on higher respects have no cause to start at painted shadows."
>
> WOODSTOCK, 94

Similarly Scott refers to Charles' natural body in positive terms in Chapter 41 of 'Tales', but not to his body politic:

> Charles I, who succeeded his father James, was a prince whose personal qualities were excellent. It was said of him justly, that considered as a private gentleman, where was not a more honourable, virtuous, and religious man, in his dominions. He was a kind father, an indulgent master, and even too affectionate a husband [...]
>
> 'TALES', 345

These examples demonstrate how carefully Scott constructs Charles I's 'character' in the context of the natural body. Ironically, earlier in 'Tales' Scott positioned the 1649 destruction of the sovereign's natural body and Charles I's personal response to his execution as enabling the restoration of his son's monarchical body politic:

> [T]he King's serene and religious behaviour at his trial and execution excited the sympathy and sorrow of many who had been his enemies when in power; the injustice and brutality which he bore with so much dignity,

overpowered the remembrance of the errors of which he had been guilty; and the almost universal sense of the iniquity of his sentence, was a principal cause of the subsequent restoration of his family to the throne.

'TALES', 69

However, it is important to note that by this sympathetic reconstruction Scott does not seek to reposition Charles as an emblem of effective sovereignty. On the contrary, for Scott, the truncation of Charles' reign signifies the erasure of natural justice from England, and it remains erased for the entire period of the Interregnum. Just as Charles is associated with the waning of natural justice by his not functioning as an effective body politic in *The Fortunes of Nigel*, so the execution of his natural body symbolizes the lack of justice operating in the Commonwealth under Cromwell and officials like the Commissioners.

Scott, therefore, positions Charles II very differently from his father as both the private body and the body politic of sovereignty in *Woodstock*. Avrom Fleishman suggests a negative comparison: "To contrast with the 'royal martyr'—whose spirit hovers even in Cromwell's study, in the form of a Van Dyck portrait—there is his son, whose libertinism generates the later complications of the plot".[36] The politically naïve Alice also juxtaposes Charles II's monarchical role and Charles I's personal qualities in her rapturous 'eulogium':

> He shall have all the chivalrous courage, all the warlike skill, of Henry of France, his grandfather, in order to place him on the throne;—all his benevolence, love of his people, patience even of unpleasing advice, sacrifice of his own wishes and pleasures to the commonweal, that, seated there, he may be blest while living, and so long remembered when dead, that for ages after it shall be thought sacrilege to breathe an aspersion against the throne which he had occupied! [...]
>
> For the man, [...] need I wish him more than the paternal virtues of his unhappy father, of whom his worst enemies have recorded, that if moral virtues and religious faith were to be selected as the qualities which merited a crown, no man could plead the possession of them in a higher or more indisputable degree.
>
> *WOODSTOCK*, 246

While the fulsomeness of Alice's wishes for her sovereign emphasizes her personal and political innocence and idealism, Scott makes Charles' wrestling

---

36   Avrom Fleishman, *The English Historical Novel: Walter Scott to Virginia Woolf* (Baltimore and London: Johns Hopkins Press, 1971), 65.

with his private inclinations and his public duties pivotal to his counter-revolutionary argument for the restoration of the monarchy.[37] Indeed, it is only when Charles II subordinates the private desires of his natural body to the obligations of the sovereign body politic that he begins to assume the role of England's monarch.

Certainly, Markham Everard, upon recognizing Charles, is conscious of the latter's personal and public roles, as this necessarily substantial excerpt suggests:

> "Sire," he said, bowing low, and with profound deference, "if I do not offer you the homage of a subject with knee and sword, it is because God, by whom kings reign, has denied you for the present the power of ascending your throne without rekindling civil war. For your safety being endangered by me, let not such an imagination for an instant cross your mind. Had I not respected your person—were I not bound to you for the candour with which your noble avowal has prevented the misery of my future life, your misfortunes would have rendered your person as sacred, so far as I can protect it, as it could be esteemed by the most devoted royalist in the kingdom. If your plans are soundly considered, and securely laid, think that all which is now passed is but a dream. If they are in such a state that I can aid them, saving my duty to the Commonwealth, which will permit me to be privy to no schemes of actual violence, your Majesty may command my services."
>
> *WOODSTOCK*, 313

Charles II himself makes a point of both his monarchical bodies in his subsequent communication to Sir Henry Lee: "Loyal and much esteemed friend, our trusty subject," which he duly signs 'C[arolus]. R[ex].' (*Woodstock*, 407).

Nevertheless, as several critics have noted, at no time in *Woodstock* does Scott unequivocally approve of Charles' character.[38] Indeed, Scott only once applauds Charles' actions wholeheartedly, when Charles throws off his

---

37 Hart notes Charles' "education" at Woodstock and his resultant engagement with his sovereign responsibilities (Hart, *Scott's Novels*, 101).

38 See, for example: Daniel Cottom, 'Violence and Law in the Waverley Novels.' *Studies in Romanticism*, 1 (Spring 1981), 78, 80; Hart, *Scott's Novels*, 94, 97, 98–101, 102–3; Graham McMaster, (Cambridge: Cambridge University Press, 1981), 128–9, 135, 226; Robertson, *Legitimate Histories*, 188–95, 265–73; Kenneth M. Sroka, 'Fairy Castles and Character in Woodstock,' *Essays in Literature*, 14 (Fall 1987), 197, 200–3; and Judith Wilt, *Secret Leaves: The Novels of Walter Scott* (Chicago: University of Chicago Press, 1985), 164–76.

disguise to announce his identity and assume his disinterested monarchical responsibilities:

> Meanwhile, the disguised Prince had beheld the whole in silence, but with an agitation to which he was unwonted, and which his swarthy features, and still more his motions, began to betray [...]. [H]e was strongly agitated by contending feelings, was on the point, too, of forming some sudden resolution, and yet still in uncertainty what course he should pursue.
>
> But when he saw Markham Everard, after one look of unspeakable anguish towards Alice, turning his back to depart, he broke out into his familiar ejaculation, "Oddsfish! this must not be." In three strides he overtook the slowly-retiring Everard, tapped him smartly on the shoulder, and, as he turned round, said, with an air of command, which he well knew how to adopt at pleasure, "One word with you, sir [...] Colonel Everard, I am CHARLES STUART!"
>
> *WOODSTOCK*, 311–2

Sroka suggests that Charles' shedding his disguise to involve himself in Alice and Everard's reconciliation is one step towards his redemption that sees him return to England and secure his throne.[39] Charles ascending the throne is, I suggest, a restoration of his better self and thus of his right to rule.

Woodstock, therefore, having signalled the erasure of natural justice with the execution of the natural body of Charles I, articulates the dawning of a rehabilitated monarchy by having Charles II embrace the role and responsibilities of the sovereign body politic. *Peveril of the Peak* ultimately establishes Charles II as the embodiment of natural justice. Yet, for all that, Scott does not seek at any time in this novel to portray Charles as the ideal monarch of Alice Lee's imagination. Inglis, Hewitt and Lumsden comment that in this novel, "Scott presents an uncomplicated picture of the king as a man of good nature, fundamentally good impulses, sincerity, generosity, sociability, and ready wit partly vitiated by weakness of character".[40] This is true, for Scott depicts Charles as a sovereign with several flaws: a voluptuary "who often formed manly and sensible resolutions, though he was too easily diverted from them by indolence or pleasure," with yet "that kindness, which was a redeeming point of his character" (*Peveril*, 410, 411). However, similarly to the way in which Dryden skirts

---

39   Sroka, 'Fairy Castles,' 202.

40   Inglis, et al, 'Historical Note,' *Woodstock*, 544. See for a more detailed assessment of Scott's sources for and representations of Charles II in *Woodstock* and *Peveril of the Peak*.

negative aspects of Charles' character by drawing parallels between Charles and King David in his 'Absalom and Achitophel' (1681), Scott astutely delineates the known, private Charles but dissociates him from any involvement in gross abrogation of law and justice, especially with regard to the Popish Plot.[41] It is his courtiers, notably Buckingham and Chiffinch, who drive the Plot on in the hope of achieving political advantage, just as they attempt to capitalize politically on the appetites of Charles' natural body. It is not Charles' personal desires that pose a threat to the functioning of justice in Restoration England, says Scott; rather, his courtiers' exploitation of his personal inclinations imperils the true application of law and justice. While Charles may at times be a victim of his appetite for pleasure, he at least endeavours to keep that aspect of his private life distinct from his public role—whether or not he is successful in this, his ambition is not be manipulated in political affairs through entanglements with women.

One of the most telling discourses in the novel occurs when Charles confronts the social impact of the Popish Plot and decides that he must ensure the operation of natural justice by assuming consciously the role of the sovereign body politic. This is not, however, a simple undertaking, particularly in the aftermath of Charles I's fateful attempts at sovereignty. The climactic moment occurs as follows:

> "[...] I have borne, and borne with it—I have seen blood flow on the scaffold, fearing to thwart the nation in its fury—and I pray to God that I or mine be not called on to answer for it. I will no longer swim with the torrent, which Honour and Conscience call upon me to stem—I will act the part of a Sovereign, and save my people from doing injustice, even in their own despite."
>
> Charles walked hastily up and down the room as he expressed these unwonted sentiments, with energy equally unwonted. After a momentary pause, the Duke answered him gravely, "Spoken like a Royal King, sir, but—pardon me—not like a King of England."
>
> Charles paused, as the Duke spoke, beside a window which looked full on Whitehall, and his eye was involuntarily attracted by the fatal window of the Banquetting House, out of which his unhappy father was conducted to execution. [...] "Our Council must decide in this matter," he said, looking to the Duke; "and be assured, young man," he added, addressing

---

41   John Dryden, *Selected Poems*. ed. Steven N. Zwicker and David Bywaters (London: Penguin, 2001), 111–41.

Julian, "your father shall not want an intercessor in his King, so far as the
laws will permit my interference in his behalf."

PEVERIL, 329

Charles, in his vehemence speaking from the position of his natural, private
body, confronts the need for himself to operate as the king's body politic.
Natural justice must be achieved at one level by the king's engagement with
the institutions of law and justice, rather than by the king's person acting for
an individual's good at the expense of, or in defiance of, the nation's laws and
justice systems, as indeed Charles I did in his attempts to rule independently
of such restraints. It is in this context that Scott depicts two instances of the
justice that Charles achieves.

The first is his involvement in the trial of Sir Geoffrey and Julian Peveril,
where they are found to be not guilty. Scott is at pains to illustrate the need
for the monarch's body politic, and not his natural body, to be involved in the
workings of justice:

> Such was the singular termination of this trial. Charles himself was desir-
> ous to have taken considerable credit with the Duke of Ormond for the
> evasion of the law, which had been thus effected by his private conniv-
> ance; and was both surprised and mortified at the coldness with which
> his Grace replied, that he was rejoiced at the poor gentleman's safety, but
> would rather have had the King redeem them like a prince, by his royal
> prerogative of mercy, than that his Judge should convey them out of the
> power of the law, like a juggler with his cups and balls.
>
> *PEVERIL*, 428

Here, Scott directs attention not to Charles' constitutional or legal authority, but to his personal authority to effect the appropriate regulation of civil
matters. Scott has comprehensively shown that the various laws and forms of
justice operating during Charles' reign do not fulfil their (generally perceived)
purpose. Charles is thereby shown to be the only person, in his time, who can
execute the initial act of natural justice that absolves the Peverils of any involvement in the Popish Plot. But although this situation of natural justice supports Scott's defence of Charles' restoration, Scott's argument that Charles is
the embodiment of natural justice requires more than this one achievement
of justice by his natural, private body. While Charles' intervention achieves an
individual instance of justice, a second instance, more lasting and with greater
social ramifications, must yet be achieved by Charles' monarchical body politic.

This second instance is Charles' effecting the marriage of Alice and Julian, and thus the creation of Martindale-Moultrassie. Martindale-Moultrassie is a permanent and concrete example of the restoration of social order and of natural justice, signified by the rekindling of the Peveril Pole-star—the symbol of triumphant natural justice. Scott describes the union in these terms:

> "[Alice and Julian] love each other like lovers of the last age," said the Countess; "but the stout old Knight likes not the round-headed alliance."
>
> "Our royal recommendation shall put that to rights," said the King; "Sir Geoffrey Peveril has not suffered hardship so often at our command, that he will refuse our recommendation when it comes to make him amends for all his losses."
>
> "It may be supposed the King did not speak without being fully aware of the unlimited ascendancy which he possessed over the old Tory; for within four weeks afterwards, the bells of Martindale-Moultrassie were ringing for the union of the families, from whose estates it takes its compound name, and the beacon-light of the Castle blazed high over hill and dale."
>
> PEVERIL, 494–5

Thus, Scott shows Charles' ultimate achievement of reconciliation and restoration of social order in his capacity as the monarchical body politic to be the final proof required that he is indeed the embodiment of natural justice, and is capable of achieving widespread social reconciliation—should he so wish.

Caroline: *"But I am a woman and you are a man"*
MID-LOTHIAN, 108

The Fortunes of Nigel, Woodstock, Peveril of the Peak and *The Heart of Mid-Lothian* have at their centres a very similar plot. In each of these novels, the protagonists and their immediate families face situations that require the interventions of the respective monarchs if natural justice is to be done.[42] Once justice has been achieved, the hero or heroine then marries, thereby signalling the creation of an harmonious social order based on reconciliation and traditional values. However, despite the similarities of plot and of the role of the monarch in the four novels, there exist significant disparities. These are most effectively realized by exploring Scott's treatment of Caroline in *The Heart of*

---

42   In *Woodstock*, of course, Charles is not the recognized British monarch until the closing chapter.

Midlothian and contrasting this with his characterizations of James I in *The Fortunes of Nigel* and of Charles II in *Woodstock* and *Peveril of the Peak*. Lumsden suggests there are a number of "reasons consistent with the impulses of the fiction for including the Queen within it":

> For one thing, it moves the site of Effie's pardon into the hands of women keeping alive the play of feminine discourse; significantly, it also allows the Queen the opportunity of alluding to the Porteous Riots, thus also referring to the Scottish questions at work here, as Jeanie pleads the unique circumstances of religion and morality with Scotland which give rise to her sister's situation.[43]

These are valid and persuasive reasons, yet they do not account for the fact that Scott depicts Caroline and her sovereignty very differently from James and Charles II and their respective rules over Great Britain. It is interesting to note how the presence of James and of Charles II suffuses their novels. Both are significant characters throughout, physically present in many chapters and engaged in the plot developments and resolutions. But Caroline, while mentioned at various points in *The Heart of Mid-Lothian*, is absent for much of the novel, only appearing in one (albeit climactic) chapter of the novel depicting her interview with Jeanie Deans. Despite emphasizing that "Queen Caroline possessed the masculine soul of the other sex" (*Mid-Lothian*, 331), Scott seems to be at pains to differentiate her from those kingly counterparts preceding her rule (alongside George II) in a number of ways—an approach that may be consistent with a more generalized discomfort with feminine power displayed by Scott and commented upon by critics.[44]

First, he emphasizes the fact that Caroline rules not in her own right but as George II's regent. He then shows her to engage actively in the judicial policies affecting Edinburgh in the wake of Wilson's hanging, thereby contributing directly to the injustice perceived to be visited on the Scottish populace. Scott next limits Caroline's success as a monarch and as an institution of justice to

---

43   Lumsden, *Walter Scott and the Limits of Language*, 129.

44   See: James P. Carson, 'Popular vs Legitimate Authority in Scott's *The Heart of Midlothian*' in Carson's *Populism, Gender, and Sympathy in the Romantic Novel*, 45–75. Susan Broomhall and David G. Barrie, 'Changing of the Guard: Governance, Policing, Masculinity, and Class in the Porteous Affair and Walter Scott's *Heart of Midlothian*,' *Parergon*, 28 (2011), 65–90; and C.M. Jackson-Houlston's chapter, '"Hardly Any Women At All"? Gender and Genre,' which suggests that Scott's limited inclusion of women in his "historized fiction" reveals a degree of discomfort with feminine autonomy (Jackson-Houlston, *Gendering Walter Scott*, 26).

the essentially domestic issue of Effie Deans' child-murder charge. He also underscores a threat to Caroline's official queenly authority and her public standing, that being the presence at court of Lady Suffolk, George II's mistress. Finally, although Caroline does indeed bring about an instance of justice—the pardon for Effie Deans—she is never allowed to be the agent of creation of a new, idealized social order, as are James (albeit nominally) in *The Fortunes of Nigel* and Charles in both *Woodstock* and *Peveril of the Peak*. This new order is achieved in *The Heart of Mid-Lothian*, but not by the Queen as the (pen)ultimate figure of justice in Britain. Instead it is achieved by the Duke of Argyle, that idealized, patriarchal figure of "traditional loyalties, and the landlord of active humane concern".[45] Thus, Scott qualifies, implicitly and explicitly, the justice that Caroline—as Queen and as regent, as public and private personage—can effect, an approach that was not evident when he was representing the power of James I, Charles II, or indeed of the Duke of Argyle.[46]

Intrinsic to *The Fortunes of Nigel, Woodstock*, and *Peveril of the Peak* is the notion of the monarch's supreme authority. While Scott may question the monarch's ability to wield that authority appropriately—James is the "least talented of the Stuarts" (*Nigel*, 67) and Charles a voluptuary "too easily diverted from [his royal duties] by indolence or pleasure" (*Peveril*, 410)—their rightful positions as sovereigns are maintained and, indeed, asserted throughout the novels.[47] Early in *The Heart of Midlothian*, however, Scott introduces Caroline, and immediately points out that her sovereignty is not of the same supremacy—the monarch is "Queen Caroline, (regent of the kingdom during the absence of George II. on the continent,)" (*Mid-Lothian*, 35). She is merely representative of the monarch's body politic in the absence of his natural body. As Duncan points out, feminine sovereignty does not exist in its own right: "female power is produced by an absence of patriarchy [...] Queen Caroline wields power in the absence of her husband".[48] While she can assume the responsibilities and authority of the monarch, she remains positioned as less than he.

---

45   Hart, *Scott's Novels*, 145.

46   Even though, as I have argued earlier, James' role in effecting social order is limited to creating an aristocratic Scottish title for Margaret and to promoting the marriage of Nigel and Margaret, and does not extend to the fiscal restoration of Glenvarloch, he is still involved in constructing a microcosm of social harmony, as Caroline is not.

47   Scott's positioning of Charles as the rightful sovereign is implicit throughout *Woodstock*, although Charles' monarchical rights are only restored in the closing chapter of the novel.

48   Ian Duncan, *Modern Romance and Transformations of the Novel: The Gothic, Scott, Dickens*, (Cambridge: Cambridge University Press, 1992), 161.

Moreover, Scott, while apparently lauding Caroline's political prowess, indicates that her abilities are only required because of George II's own lack of monarchical capabilities and, indeed, his lack of interest in ruling England.[49] As we read:

> Since Margaret of Anjou, no queen-consort had exercised such weight in the political affairs of England, and the personal address which she displayed on many occasions, had no small share in reclaiming from their political heresy many of those determined tories, who, after the reign of the Stuarts had been extinguished in the person of Queen Anne, were disposed rather to transfer their allegiance to her brother the Chevalier de Saint George, then to acquiesce in the settlement of the crown on the Hanover family.
>
> *MID-LOTHIAN*, 331

Caroline's power exists only in the absence of the rightful monarch—whether that be the lack of his physical presence or of his sovereign qualities and capabilities. In this context of qualified regency, Scott then explores the nature of the justice that Caroline effects in *The Heart of Mid-Lothian*.

Earlier in this chapter and in Chapter 3, I argued that a common plot existed in *The Fortunes of Nigel*, *Peveril of the Peak*, and *The Heart of Mid-Lothian*: the legitimate monarch is roused to pursue justice, then transcends the abuse of the current legal authority being exercised, and effects an instance of natural justice. In each instance, the monarch's decision whether to involve himself or herself in the pursuit of justice is made according to the strengths and weaknesses of that monarch's personality. James in *The Fortunes of Nigel* is shown to be lazy in his performance of his sovereign duties, rejecting myriad minor petitions from his Scottish subjects and ignoring other, more significant claims. The combined efforts of George Heriot and the Earl of Huntinglen are required to engage James in making restitution to Nigel Olifaunt and giving him the sign-manual essential to his continued ownership of Glenvarloch. Even then, James' initial response is to encourage Nigel to relinquish his ancestral inheritance, and to "let the land gang, man, let the land gang"; and it is James' failure to address Nigel's legal issues in a timely manner that enables Dalgarno to traduce Nigel at court (*Nigel*, 114). This slander results in Nigel striking Dalgarno in St James Park, "in the precincts of the court," where such conflict is "Star-Chamber business" (*Nigel*, 180). Nigel, by necessity, descends into the lawlessness intrinsic to Alsatia, and once there loses the precious sign-manual.

---

49   It should be noted that both Caroline and George are absent monarchs of Scotland.

In despair, he goes to Greenwich to plead his case to James, who misinterprets his accosting him for an attempt at murder. Nigel is then confined to Newgate, from which James extricates him, albeit in his own unique style. While James' tardiness in addressing Nigel's situation is the catalyst for Nigel's adventures, Scott makes it clear that James does not himself instigate legal activities that can be generally perceived as unjust.

Charles II in *Woodstock*—a monarch both disguised and unrecognized— is in no position to engage with the legal processes of the Interregnum that wreak such injustice on Woodstock. His involvement in the processes of justice is confined to the private domain. Thus, while his attempts to seduce Alice would, were they successful, result in a moral injustice in that they would exploit the loyalty of the Royalist Lees, he does not, and cannot, publicly bring about judicial policy. Ultimately, of course, he elects not to engage in this travesty of moral justice, and thus signals his acceptance of the responsibilities inherent in his assumption of kingship. In *Peveril of the Peak*, Charles is estab- lished in his role as sovereign. Just as James is remiss in his tardy addressing of Nigel's supplication, so Charles fails to stand against the tide of popular hysteria sweeping across England. Charles' inaction in the face of the injus- tice being wrought as a result of the Popish Plot is deplorable; however, Scott makes it clear that it is his inactivity, a lesser sin than the active creation of an injustice, for which Charles should be held accountable.

In *The Heart of Mid-Lothian*, however, Scott shows Caroline's initial engage- ment in the processes of justice to be very different from that of James in *The Fortunes of Nigel* and of Charles in *Peveril of the Peak*. Caroline, by contrast, is seen to engage actively in the legal processes affecting Scotland. In the wake of Wilson's hanging, her decision to grant Captain Porteous a reprieve, thus overturning the Edinburgh court's decision to sentence him to death, leads to the Porteous Riots, as a direct and vehement reaction to that perceived injus- tice. Thus, Scott establishes Caroline's involvement in the public performance of justice as a comprehensive failure. Not only does she manifest injustice by her involvement, she also inflames discord between various elements of her sovereignty, namely England and Scotland. The reprieve she grants Captain Porteous is perceived by the Scots as a blatant disregard and contempt for not just the authority of the law generally, but of Scottish law specifically. Her ac- tion in pardoning Porteous acts as a lightning rod, exacerbating existing re- sentment of the effects of the Union and the English dominance over Scottish law and society. As such, Caroline is the only monarch in *The Fortunes of Nigel*, *Woodstock*, *Peveril of the Peak* and *The Heart of Midlothian* to engage in deter- mining a judicial outcome that is unjust and results in social disruption. In the context of this failed engagement in judicial proceedings and the ensuing riots, Scott has Jeanie Deans plead with the Queen to grant Effie a reprieve.

Against the public, the political and the masculine, Scott positions the private, the domestic and the feminine. Caroline's engagement in the achievement of justice is confined to dealing with a private request for mercy in a conversation that takes place in a secluded garden at Richmond, far removed from the court environment. It is, then, only in the domestic realm that Caroline effects an instance of justice. Her public reprieve of Porteous was an injustice, her private pardoning of Effie restores justice. There is, of course, a qualification to be noted here. Earlier, I discussed Scott's emphasis on the Queen's lesser stature as regent rather than ruler in her own right. In the interview with Jeanie Deans, it becomes clear that even in her capacity as regent, Caroline can only do so much for Jeanie. As Beth Newman argues, "[t]he Queen's power is limited to that of an intermediary between the Scottish courts and the English king".[50] Caroline herself tells Jeanie: "I cannot grant a pardon to your sister": while she can instigate the pardon, she cannot herself grant it—her authority is (ostensibly) confined to "warm intercession with his Majesty" (*Mid-Lothian*, 341). Both Newman and Michael Cohen draw attention to Scott's apparent discomfort in this novel with the notion of a woman having power. Cohen suggests that Scott's "first novel to recognize the heroic possibilities of sisterhood [...] fights the idea of female empowerment every step of the way"; this antagonistic response to "female empowerment" extending to Scott's representation of Queen Caroline.[51] Cohen argues that Scott adapts a salacious bit of Georgian history when he brings into his story the king's mistress, Henrietta Howard, Lady Suffolk, as the companion of Queen Caroline when Jeanie Dean makes her appeal for a royal pardon. While this assertion is disproportionate to Scott's subtle use of Lady Suffolk, Scott does consciously allow a certain confusion of the Queen's private affairs and her public persona. Lady Suffolk's being present at the interview between Caroline and Jeanie Deans reminds us that the Queen, while the predominant influence over the king, is not his sole advisor; Lady Suffolk also enjoys intimacy with, and influence over, the sovereign. While apparently applauding Caroline's adroit risk management, Scott makes this rivalry and Caroline's inherently humiliating position overt:

> It was not the least instance of the Queen's address, that she had contrived that one of her principal attendants, Lady Suffolk, should unite in her own person the two apparently inconsistent characters of her husband's mistress, and her own very obsequious and complaisant confidant.

---

50   Beth Newman, '*The Heart of Midlothian* and the Masculinization of Fiction,' *Criticism: A Quarterly for Literature and the Arts*, 36 (Fall 1994), 533.

51   Michael Cohen, 'Empowering the Sister: Female Rescue and Authorial Resistance in *The Heart of Midlothian*', *College Literature*, 20 (June 1993), 59.

> By this dexterous management the Queen secured her power against the
> danger which might most have threatened it—the thwarting influence
> of an ambitious rival; and if she submitted to the mortification of being
> obliged to connive at her husband's infidelity, she was at least guarded
> against what she might think its most dangerous effects.
>
> MID-LOTHIAN, 333

So Scott diminishes Caroline's stature again, as a monarchical figure and as a woman. Despite her magnificent decorum in responding to this unpleasant situation, she is helpless against encroachments on her status by so small a matter as the sexual preferences of George II.

It is interesting to note that in *The Fortunes of Nigel* Scott considers it important, if not imperative, to divert attention from James' own sexual preferences and his homoerotic relationship with Buckingham so as not to diminish his monarchical status. Moreover, as I have argued earlier, Scott goes to significant effort throughout the entire novel to maintain this diversion. It is obviously far less important to him to uphold Caroline's status as Queen and regent of Britain in *The Heart of Midlothian*; he has little hesitation in drawing the reader's attention to George II's infidelity and the need for Caroline not only to accommodate this privately, but also to befriend her husband's mistress publicly. Scott seems to have little regard for Caroline's public standing being diminished by this aspect of his character portrait. By contrast, Scott's representations of Charles' sexual proclivities and adventures do not reflect poorly on the latter's sovereignty, despite his being depicted as susceptible to undue political influence from his mistresses, and thus as vulnerable to manipulation by those positioned behind these paramours. It appears that it is only Caroline whose sovereignty can be compromised by the sexual politics of the court.

Common to *The Fortunes of Nigel*, *Peveril of the Peak*, *Woodstock* and *The Heart of Mid-Lothian* is Scott's use of the protagonist's marriage to signify the creation of a new, idealized social order. A significant difference exists, however, in the agency of the monarch between *The Heart of Mid-Lothian* and the other novels. In *The Fortunes of Nigel*, *Woodstock* and *Peveril of the Peak* the king is essential to effecting the marriage between the hero and his beloved; in both *The Fortunes of Nigel* and *Peveril of the Peak*, the sovereign is also central to the subsequent creation of the locale symbolizing social reconciliation—Glenvarloch and Martindale-Moultrassie, respectively. In *The Heart of Mid-Lothian*, however, just as Caroline's physical presence in the novel is confined to a single chapter, her engagement as monarch in the creation of justice is confined to the instance of securing Effie's reprieve.

In *The Fortunes of Nigel* James takes great pleasure in bringing about the marriage of Nigel Olifaunt and Margaret Ramsay. He then goes on to orchestrate, albeit with the financial assistance of Richie and Martha Moniplies, Nigel's regaining of his ancestral lands. Thus, Scott intimates, this flawed monarch, this least masculine of the Stuart kings, is still able to effect both an instance of justice and a representative forging of a new social order at Glenvarloch, in which the aristocracy and the bourgeoisie meld to achieve social and economic stability. In *Woodstock*, Charles facilitates the marriage of Markham Everard and Alice Lee, symbolizing the reconciliation of Roundhead and Cavalier loyalties that will come about with his subsequent restoration. In *Peveril of the Peak* Charles first influences the acquittal of the Peverils at their trial, signalling a return to legal probity as a result of monarchical intervention in the justice process. He next engages directly in overcoming the difficulties surrounding Julian's marriage to Alice Bridgenorth, and the locale of Martindale-Moultrassie is thereby created—another emblem of the social reconciliation the monarch can achieve. In *The Heart of Mid-Lothian*, however, the Queen does not engage in any form of societal melding or reconciliation. Austin points out despite the Duke of Argyle suggesting to Caroline that her sympathetic resolution of Effie's plight may propitiate her Scottish subjects inflamed by the Porteous affair, this does not appear to eventuate.[52] I contend that while Caroline's reprieve of Effie Deans' death sentence mirrors that granted previously to John Porteous, it does not signal that Caroline acknowledges that earlier injustice; nor does it undo the social damage caused by the Porteous Riots.

It is the Duke of Argyle—whom the Queen cannot afford to disdain, as his power in Scotland exceeds her own—who effects a symbol of lasting societal reconciliation. Indeed, Scott depicts him as having a *de facto* monarchical role in his own, Scottish environment:

> In thus maintaining occasional intercourse with several persons who seemed most alienated from the crown, it may readily be supposed, that Queen Caroline had taken care not to break entirely with the Duke of Argyle. His high birth, his great talents, the estimation in which he was held in his own country, the great services which he had rendered the house of Brunswick in 1715, placed him high in that rank of persons who were not to be rashly neglected. He had, almost by his single and unassisted talents, stopped the eruption of the banded force of all the

---

52   Carolyn F. Austin, 'Home and Nation in *The Heart of Midlothian*,' SEL: *Studies in English Literature, 1500–1900*, 40 (Autumn 2000), 628–9.

Highland chiefs; there was little doubt that with the slightest encouragement, he could put them all in motion, and renew a civil war; and it was
well known that the most flattering overtures had been transmitted to
the Duke from the court of Saint Germains. The character and temper of
Scotland was still little known, and it was considered as a volcano, which
might, indeed, slumber for a series of years, but was still liable, at a moment the most unexpected, to break out into a wasteful eruption. It was,
therefore, of the highest importance to retain some hold over so important a personage as the Duke of Argyle.

MID-LOTHIAN, 332

However, for all that, the success of this interview, which Gottlieb suggests
has benefits for Argyle as well as for his protege and the Queen, is limited and
qualified in both societal and temporal terms for Jeanie.[53] Caroline effects
an intervention in Effie's individual case; it is the Duke of Argyle who brings
about the familial reconciliation necessary for Jeanie Deans and Reuben Butler's marriage to take place. His role in the novel is indeed, as Gottlieb suggests,
inherently conservative. However, he does not "reintegrate the Deans family
into the social fabric from which they have been torn"; rather he creates an
idealized domestic and social environment for Jeanie, her father and Reuben
at Knocktarlitie.[54] The commencement of Jeanie and Reuben's life together
thus signals the creation of a microcosmic social order within Scotland constructed by a figure who is himself committed to Scotland's welfare and a self-
nominated representative of the Hanoverian sovereignty. Whether or not the
Duke of Argyle functions as a *deus ex machina*, his role in creating a lasting
emblem of conservative harmony is undeniable.[55] Yet again, Scott portrays
Caroline's role as monarch as a marginalized one: only masculine figures of
sovereignty, whether James, Charles or the Duke of Argyle, have the desire and
the power to reconstruct society so that it is harmonious and naturally just.

Scott, therefore, diminishes the stature of Caroline's sovereignty in several ways. She functions only as regent of George II, and even in that capacity
she does not have the requisite authority to pardon Effie. She can only adjure
the king to do so. By showing her initial intervention in the trial of Captain

---

53   Evan Gottlieb, *Walter Scott and Contemporary Theory* (London: Bloomsbury Academic,
      2013), 82.

54   Ibid., 82.

55   Hart argues that "[f]ar from being a *deus ex machina*, Argyle's emergence as resolution of
      Jeanie's speculative dilemma is prepared for by the entire book. To see how is to recognize
      the novel's most comprehensive and significant coherences" (Hart, *Scott's Novels*, 144–5).

Porteous to result in social upheaval, Scott brings her success as a monarch into question; then he limits her efficacy in restoring justice to the essentially private and domestic matter of Effie Deans' child-murder charge. In addition, Caroline's status at court is compromised by the presence of Lady Suffolk and Scott's own explanation of the Queen's need to make her husband's mistress her own confidante. Finally, Scott implicitly questions Caroline's capacities by having the Duke of Argyle, rather than the Queen, be the agent of larger social reconciliation. In the wider context of Scott's representations of masculine governance—James I, Charles II and the Duke of Argyle—it becomes clear that in *The Heart of Midlothian* at least, Scott considers a woman's sovereignty to be significantly less august.

Charles Edward Stuart, George II and George III

There is no shortage of monarchs, or indeed monarchies, in *Waverley* and *Redgauntlet*. Concepts of, and questions about, sovereignty saturate both novels; the weary reader, having traversed various geographical and political landscapes alongside Edward Waverley and Darsie Latimer, may well consider there to be a surfeit of monarchs. However, I suggest that throughout these two novels a recession of kingship takes place, which becomes particularly clear when considered beside Scott's representations of the immediate, personal presence of the monarch in *The Fortunes of Nigel, Woodstock, Peveril of the Peak* and *The Heart of Mid-Lothian*. I have noted elsewhere the centrality of James VI and I in *The Fortunes of Nigel*. Scott makes him the focal point of the novel; while he is hardly an ideal monarch, he is critical to Nigel's receiving natural justice, instrumental in restoring Nigel's ancestral property, and deeply interested in promoting Nigel's marriage to Margaret Ramsay. Similarly, the plot of *Woodstock* revolves around Charles, whose engagement in effecting an instance of social reconciliation is pivotal to the novel and to Scott's argument for his restoration. In *Peveril of the Peak*, although Charles does not appear as frequently as he did in *Woodstock*, his engagement in Julian's affairs is still critical to their successful conclusion.

Through Charles' direct intervention, Julian is found innocent of the charges against him and marries Alice Bridgenorth. Thus, the King is shown to be able to restore social order by reconciling conflicting ideologies, even if he is not always inclined to do so. In *The Heart of Mid-Lothian*, as I have just argued, with George II's absence the monarchy is split between two characters. Caroline, as George II's regent, engineers a pardon for Effie Deans, but it is the Duke of Argyle who creates a microcosm of a new, idealized social order. While Caroline only appears in one crucial scene, the Duke of Argyle is frequently centre stage, ensuring that the monarchy is comprehensively represented throughout the novel. In clear contrast, neither the Stuart nor the Hanoverian monarchy acts in these personal ways either to effect natural justice for the protagonist or establish social order through a marriage in *Waverley* and *Redgauntlet*. Charles Edward Stuart, while he takes an interest in Edward Waverley's matrimonial prospects, is not positioned—and nor does he have the power—to ensure that Edward obtains natural justice. As Sharpe might put it, he has none of the 'imaging' of a monarch in *Waverley*. He has even less in *Redgauntlet*, where Charles Edward himself receives the Hanoverian monarchy's clemency at the hands of an imaged, military and judicial representative of that monarch. In both novels, the Hanoverian monarchs are represented by men of unimpeachable integrity. In *Waverley*, Colonel Talbot initiates George II's pardon of Waverley's treasonable actions and ensures a restoration of social order at Tully-Veolan. Although Colonel Talbot displays some of the less than exemplary prejudices of the typical English officer—D'Arcy, for instance, notes his "racial bigotry towards the Highlanders"—he is nevertheless positioned by Scott as an inherently decent, revered and upstanding representative of the Hanoverian monarchy.[56] In *Redgauntlet*, it is General Campbell who effects justice on behalf of the monarchy.

One can see this change clearly by considering the representation of each monarch in quantitative terms. James VI and I appears in seven chapters of *The Fortunes of Nigel*, Charles II in thirteen chapters of *Woodstock* and eight of *Peveril of the Peak*, and Caroline is present in one and the Duke of Argyle in eight chapters of *The Heart of Mid-Lothian*. Charles Edward Stuart appears in six chapters in *Waverley* (in some only fleetingly) and in three in *Redgauntlet* (one as Father Buonaventure and two as himself). By contrast, George II is not physically present at any point in *Waverley*, and neither is George III in *Redgauntlet*.

What, then, is the significance of this gradual disappearance of the king? How can it be argued that Scott positions an overarching counter-revolutionary argument in the six novels, premised primarily on the presence of the monarch, if the reigning monarch is demonstrably absent from the later two novels? How

---

56   Julian Meldon D'Arcy, *Subversive Scott: The Waverley Novels and Scottish Nationalism* (Reykjavík: Stofnun Vigdísar Finnbogadóttur í erlendum tungumálum: Háskólaútgáfan, 2005), 49. Cf. David Brown. *Walter Scott and the Historical Imagination* (London: Routledge & Paul Kegan, 1979), 23; David Daiches. 'Scott and Scotland' in *Scott: Bicentenary Essays* ed. Alan Bell (Edinburgh and London: Scottish Academic Press, 1973), 54.

is the marginalization of the Stuart monarchy to be interpreted in the context of the Hanoverian monarchs' absence in *Waverley* and *Redgauntlet*? I suggest that Scott's tactics for representing the Stuart and Hanoverian monarchies are astutely different. The Stuart monarch, Charles Edward, appears in both novels solely in his capacity as natural body, while the Hanoverians—George II in *Waverley* and George III in *Redgauntlet*—are portrayed only as the sovereign body politic. This is significant in two ways. First, the Chevalier's representation only as the natural body, and his diminishing stature over time, constitute a sustained negation of the Stuart monarchy's relevance. Second, the absence of the natural bodies of the Hanoverian monarchy is Scott's way of asserting that the immediate presence of the monarch is no longer required to sustain social stability in Georgian England. The government, representative of the monarch's body politic, is charged with, and capable of, effecting justice on behalf of the monarch.

By these means, Scott writes his support for the notion of monarchy deeply into both these novels. With *Waverley* and *Redgauntlet* Scott's counter-revolutionary argument reaches its culmination. As part of both novels demonstrating a sustained commitment to a united Britain, Scott in *Waverley* and *Redgauntlet* moves away from insisting—as he did in the novels discussed earlier—that the monarch engage personally in the administration of justice to conceding that the body politic of the British sovereign is so entrenched that the royal presence is no longer needed for natural justice to occur.[57]

I have argued that in *The Fortunes of Nigel, Woodstock, Peveril of the Peak*, and *The Heart of Midlothian* Scott makes the protagonist's meeting with the monarch critical to the alleviation of injustice and (or) the establishment of social order. However, the interactions between Charles Edward Stuart and each of the heroes—Edward Waverley in *Waverley* and Darsie Latimer in *Redgauntlet*—demonstrate the increasing irrelevance of the Stuart monarchy. It is important to note that Scott represents Charles Edward entirely through his relationship with these protagonists. The Chevalier is present only when either Edward Waverley or Darsie Latimer is also present. In each novel, the hero's encounter with this notional emblem of superseded sovereignty is fundamental to Scott's depiction of the legitimacy and relevance of the Stuart monarchy.

---

57   See, for example, Gottlieb's position with regards *Waverley* in his *Feeling British*, 178, and
      Yoon Sun Lee's in reference to *Redgauntlet* in 'Giants in the North: Douglas, the Scottish
      Enlightenment, and Scott's *Redgauntlet*,' *Studies in Romanticism*, 40 (Spring 2001), 109–21.

These are not the only two novels where Scott shows a monarch in hiding, unrecognized in his capacity as king.[58] Charles II's equivocal status as monarch is pivotal to the plot and themes of *Woodstock*, a novel preoccupied with notions of sovereignty and the restoration of social order. Yet Scott does not seek to represent Charles Edward Stuart as either the lawful king or the potential embodiment of natural justice, as he does with Charles II in *Woodstock*. Yet this is not to imply that Scott's depiction of Charles Edward is insignificant in *Waverley*, despite Hart's suggestion that his relevance to the novel is limited, comparable to Cromwell's minimal importance in *Woodstock*—itself another debatable proposition.[59] Rather, just as Cromwell's role is essential to Scott's counter-revolutionary argument in *Woodstock*, so too is Charles Edward Stuart's in *Waverley*.

Indeed, Charles Edward holds a unique position in the Waverley corpus. As Edward Mornin reminds us, he is "the main historical figure in what is generally acknowledged to have been the first real historical novel" and is initially depicted in his "aura of enchantment, glamour and romance".[60] Aspects of Scott's portrait of Charles Edward reflect the glorified image depicted in popular works such as *Ascanius, or The Young Adventurer* (1747).[61] However, his representation of Charles Edward is uniformly focused on his character and on his adventures, rather than on his capacity to embrace monarchical responsibilities. The Chevalier's main concern is to establish his own rights of sovereignty, rather than to rectify the (assumed) injustices being suffered by his Highland (and other) subjects under Hanoverian rule:

> You have, however, heard of my landing in the remote district of Moidart, with only seven attendants, and of the numerous chiefs and clans whose loyal enthusiasm at once placed a solitary adventurer at the head of a gallant army.
>
> *WAVERLEY*, 207

---

58   While *The Black Dwarf, Rob Roy, The Abbot* and *Ivanhoe* also refer to a distant or disguised monarch, the significance of that royal presence is not integral to those novels, as it is in *Woodstock*.

59   Hart, *Scott's Novels*, 92.

60   Edward Mornin, "'Bonnie Charlie's now awa'" …: Charles Edward Stuart after the '45: On the Uses of History in Fiction,' *Forum for Modern Language Studies*, 24 (April 1988), 98, 97.

61   'Ascanius, or The Young Adventurer, a True History, &c. Translated from a MS. privately handed about the Court of Versailles, &c. sm. 8vo . ib. 1747' is included in the *Catalogue of the Library at Abbotsford* (at page 89).

Similarly, Scott emphasizes the fact that Edward Waverley's loyalty is pledged, not to the body politic of the Stuart monarchy, but to Charles Edward, a charismatic individual with engaging manners and a pleasing demeanour:

> [Charles'] words and his kindness penetrated the heart of our hero, and easily outweighed all prudential motives. To be thus personally solicited for assistance by a prince, whose form and manners, as well as the spirit which he displayed in this singular enterprise, answered his ideas of a hero of romance—to be courted by him in the ancient halls of his paternal palace, recovered by the sword which he was already bending towards other conquests, gave Edward, in his own eyes, the dignity and importance which he had ceased to consider as his attributes. Rejected, slandered, and threatened upon the one side, he was irresistibly attracted to the cause which the prejudices of education, and the political principles of his family, had already recommended as the most just. [...] Waverley, kneeling to Charles Edward, devoted his heart and sword to the vindication of his rights!
>
> *WAVERLEY*, 206

Thus, Waverley's devotion of "heart and sword" to the Chevalier and to his cause is an emotional response to Charles Edward's person, and to the monarch's personal request for his "affection" and friendship.

It is interesting that Fergus Mac-Ivor also queries Waverley's response to this potential monarch solely in terms of his natural body:

> "How do you like him?" was Fergus's first question, as they descended the large stone staircase.
>
> "A prince to live and die under," was Waverley's enthusiastic answer.
>
> *WAVERLEY*, 209

In *Waverley*, Scott depicts Charles Edward as possessing many good qualities, yet none of these is aligned with the notion of the sovereign body politic; they are merely the characteristics of an individual. Scott underlines this in several instances, the two most notable being the Chevalier's release of Colonel Talbot and his promotion of Waverley's relationship with Rose. Scott brings Charles Edward's nobility to the fore when he frees Colonel Talbot, a prisoner of war, and thereby enables him to return to his ailing wife. The Chevalier initially refuses Waverley's request on the grounds of political expediency, but accedes when Waverley reconstructs his petition as a personal one. Waverley recounts his conversation with the Chevalier to Colonel Talbot:

"I told him my own story and yours; and asked him to judge what my feelings must be by his own. He has a heart, and a kind one, Colonel Talbot, you may say what you please. He took a sheet of paper, and wrote the pass with his own hand. 'I will not trust myself with my council,' he said, 'they will argue me out of what is right. I will not endure that a friend, valued as I value you, should be loaded with the painful reflections which must afflict you in case of further misfortune in Colonel Talbot's family; nor will I keep a brave enemy a prisoner under such circumstances. Besides,' said he, 'I think I can justify myself to my prudent advisers by pleading the good effect such lenity will produce on the minds of the great English families with whom Colonel Talbot is connected.'"

"There the politician peeped out," said the Colonel.

"Well, at least he concluded like a king's son;—'Take the passport; I have added a condition for form's sake; but if the Colonel objects to it, let him depart without giving any parole whatever. I come here to war with men, but not to distress or endanger women.'"

WAVERLEY, 277–8

Thus, it can be seen, that while Charles Edward tries to assert that freeing Talbot is the astute decision of a sovereign body politic, his removing the conditions of parole is actually a personal kindness for a friend and a foe, not a political stratagem.

Another significant instance demonstrating the emphasis on the natural body, rather than the body politic, of the Chevalier is his involvement in the dispute between Edward Waverley and Fergus Mac-Ivor over Rose Bradwardine as potential bride. This member of the Stuart dynasty explicitly refuses to exercise his powers as sovereign, emphasizing instead his role as brother-in-arms to his two comrades:

The Chevalier was silent for a moment, looking steadily at them both, and then said, "Upon my word, Mr. Waverley, you are a less happy man than I conceived I had very good reason to believe you. But now, gentlemen, allow me to be umpire in this matter, not as Prince Regent but as Charles Stuart, a brother adventurer with you in the same gallant cause. Lay my pretensions to be obeyed by you entirely out of view, and consider your own honour, and how far it is well or becoming to give our enemies the advantage and our friends the scandal of showing that, few as we are, we are not united."

WAVERLEY, 291

THE ROYAL PRESENCE AS LOCALE

Thus, Scott is at pains to construct Charles Edward in *Waverley* as "[t]he generous, the courteous, the noble-minded Adventurer" of historical and contemporary romantic prose and poetry, but not as the sovereign body politic at any
point (*Waverley*, 312).

Indeed, the one instance in which the Chevalier is afforded the traditional
trappings of his position is comprehensive in its absurdity. In the aftermath
of the Highland army's initial battle victory, the Baron of Bradwardine con-
sults Edward Waverley and Fergus Mac-Ivor on a most important matter: the
traditional requisite for a titled subject to remove the sovereign's boots after
battle.[62] Yet again, this discussion about the finer points of such an act, while
acknowledging the homage due to the monarch, focuses rather on his person:

> "Why, he is Prince Regent," answered Mac-Ivor, with laudable com-
> posure of countenance; "and in the court of France all the honours are
> rendered to the person of the Regent which are due to that of the King.
> Besides, were I to pull off either of their boots, I would render that service
> to the young Chevalier ten times more willingly than to his father."
>
> "Ay, but I talk not of personal predilections," [replied the Baron of
> Bradwardine] "[D]oubtless the Prince, as alter ego, may have a right to
> claim the homagium of the great tenants of the crown, since all faithful
> subjects are commanded, in the commission of regency, to respect him
> as the King's own person."
>
> WAVERLEY, 245

This valiant attempt by the Baron to establish Charles Edward's claim to authority in the context of his body politic is undermined in two ways. First, the
attempt is made by "the most absurd original that exists north of the Tweed"
(*Waverley*, 247). Second, a ludicrous discussion then ensues about difficulties
regarding the nature of the sovereign's footwear—"the Prince wears no boots,
but simply brogues and trews"—that further diminishes any grandeur of sovereignty surrounding Charles Edward (*Waverley*, 245).

As the novel progresses, the Chevalier becomes increasingly irrelevant, for
Edward Waverley grapples with the issues surrounding his attempt to return
to his rightful geographic and social place—which is in England and Scotland,

---

62   See: P.D. Garside's 'Historical Note' in Walter Scott, *Waverley*, ed. P.D. Garside (Edinburgh:
      Edinburgh University Press, 2007), 498, for Garside's commentary on the broader signifi-
      cance of the relationship between the Baron of Bradwardine and Fergus Mac-Ivor and, for
      a more detailed analysis of these two characters, see 514–9.

under Hanoverian rule. Yet again, Waverley refers to Charles Edward's natural body when he explains to Colonel Talbot the reason for the rebels' wintering in the Highlands: "Indeed, it seems likely that they only prolong the war to place the Chevalier's person out of danger" (*Waverley*, 309). From then on, only fleeting reference is made to the Adventurer's escape, and he simply evaporates from the closing chapters of *Waverley*, to reappear (fictitiously) some twenty years later in the abortive rebellion of *Redgauntlet*.

Charles Edward's presence in *Redgauntlet* is even less substantial than in *Waverley*, but it has the same significance. Again, his relationship with the protagonist defines the role of the Stuart monarchy, illustrating its increasing irrelevance. Darsie Latimer is no Edward Waverley, transfixed by a charismatic adventurer; rather, he has been kidnapped by his fanatical uncle so that his fortune and familial prestige can be commandeered to assist the Stuart cause. Darsie, resisting involvement in the doomed rebellion and standing aloof from both the Chevalier and his adherents, demonstrates how increasingly peripheral is Charles Edward's cause to Hanoverian England. Scott signals Charles Edward's, and thus the Stuarts', decreasing significance in *Redgauntlet* in another way. Just as he did in *Waverley*, Scott depicts the Chevalier in terms of his natural body, and in so doing shows us both Charles Edward's diminishment as an individual and his having no claim to being a sovereign body politic. While in *Waverley* Scott represented the Chevalier as a man of some extraordinary ability and charisma, in *Redgauntlet* he presents the aging Pretender as a considerably reduced character. Scott overtly tracks the Prince's degradation over time. He shows Charles Edward to be obstinate, self-important and petty-minded; and he draws a connection with the limitations of his Stuart ancestors.

Through Scott's representation of Charles Edward Stuart in *Waverley* and in *Redgauntlet*, then, the diminishment of the Stuart dynasty becomes apparent. Scott first focuses on the depredations of time and thwarted ambition on the one-time Adventurer in the 'Introduction' to *Redgauntlet*:

> Their Prince, young, valiant, patient of fatigue, and despising danger, heading his army on foot in the most toilsome marches, and defeating a regular force in three battles [...] proved to be one of those personages who distinguish themselves during some single and extraordinarily brilliant period of their lives, like the course of a shooting star, at which men wonder, as well on account of the briefness, as the brilliancy of its splendour. A long tract of darkness overshadowed the subsequent life of a man who, in his youth, showed himself so capable of great undertakings; and, without the painful task of tracing his course further, we may

say the latter pursuits and habits of this unhappy Prince, are those pain-
fully evincing a broken heart, which seeks refuge from its own thoughts
in sordid enjoyments.

Still, however, it was long ere Charles Edward appeared to be, perhaps
it was long ere he altogether became, so much degraded from his original
self; as he enjoyed for a time the lustre attending the progress and termi-
nation of his enterprise.[63]

This is not to suggest that Scott portrays Charles Edward in entirely negative
terms in *Redgauntlet*. Yet as Mornin notes, the admirable qualities he does
display—such as his kindness to Alan Fairford while disguised as Father Buonaventure, and his moments of "'sweetness', 'courtesy' and 'kindness'"—these,
says Scott, "recall the Young Chevalier of former days."[64] Scott makes it clear that
Charles Edward has diminished in stature since the halcyon days of Gladsmuir
nostalgically recalled by his adherents. In *Waverley*, one can sympathize with
Edward Waverley's youthful enthusiasm and emotion-driven loyalty to a charismatic prince and adventurer. Similarly, one can—at a stretch—understand,
if not empathize with, Flora Mac-Ivor's devotion to Charles Edward Stuart,
pre-figuring her devotion to Christ after Charles' failed rebellion. Twenty years
on, it is far more difficult to understand why Redgauntlet is so fanatically attached to the cause of a peevish, obstinate monarch. It is in *Redgauntlet* that
this would-be sovereign proudly announces his nobility in answering a call
from his loyal followers, conceives of his sovereignty as "personal aggrandize-
ment" and then asks of his adherents what he, as monarch, should now do.
Scott's representation of the Stuart monarchy's reduced stature is masterly, not
least because it comes out of the Young Pretender's mouth:

It is the call of my faithful and suffering people which alone could have
induced me to take once more the sword in my hand. [...] But since so
many men of worth and honour conceive the cause of England and Scotland to be linked with that of Charles Stuart, I must follow their brave
example, and, laying aside all other considerations, once more stand for-
ward as their deliverer. I am, however, come hither upon your invitation;
and as you are so completely acquainted with circumstances to which my

---

63   Walter Scott, *Redgauntlet* (London and Toronto: J.M. Dent & Sons Ltd, 1931), 3. This edition
     will be cited subsequently as Scott, *Redgauntlet* (1931). For the entire 'Introduction' which
     was added to the text by Scott in 1832, see 3–12. It has not been included in all editions of
     Scott's *Redgauntlet* since then.
64   Mornin, 'Bonnie Charlie,' 101–2.

> absence must necessarily have rendered me a stranger, I must be a mere tool in the hands of my friends. [...] Give me your advice, then, how we are to proceed, and decide upon the fate of Charles Edward.
>
> REDGAUNTLET, 354–5

Such sentiments are unlikely to inspire confidence in one's monarch as either a military leader or a sovereign. Moreover, throughout *Redgauntlet*, Scott explicitly links Charles Edward's weaknesses with his Stuart ancestry. The Pretender overtly aligns himself with the Royal Martyrdom of Charles I, the notion of royal absolutism, and the enormity of the issues that led to Charles' beheading in 1649:

> Is it in these circumstances of personal danger in which you expect to overcome a resolution, which is founded on a sense of what is due to me as a man or a prince? If the axe and scaffold were ready before the windows of Whitehall, I would rather tread the same path with my great-grandfather, than concede the slightest point in which my honour is concerned.
>
> REDGAUNTLET, 357

Similarly but less overtly, Charles Edward also sees in the reticence of his followers to engage in military action on his behalf a mirroring of the betrayal of Charles I by his Scottish subjects, who gave him up to the English Parliamentary authorities in January 1647. His accusation that his followers "who have been ready to assume arms in my behalf, will atone for their treason to the Elector, by delivering me up to the fate for which so many proclamations have destined me" makes indirect reference to that scenario where "the Scots were accused of selling their King as Judas had sold Christ—a first step towards Charles' later status as an Anglican martyr" (*Redgauntlet*, 358).[65]

In both instances, Charles Edward's coupling of his situation with that of Charles I does him little credit. The Chevalier's obstinate refusal to sever his sexual relationship with a woman suspected of treachery is hardly an appropriate cause around which to trumpet elevated concepts of monarchical divine right and Christic mythology. His doing so merely serves to call attention to the lessened status of the Stuart monarchy. That Charles Edward lacks the

---

65   Tony Inglis, J.H. Alexander, David Hewitt and Alison Lumsden's 'Essay on the Text,' *Woodstock*, ed. Tony Inglis, J.H. Alexander, David Hewitt and Alison Lumsden (Edinburgh: Edinburgh University Press, 2009), 536. See also Austin Woolrych. *Britain in Revolution 1625–1660* (Oxford: Oxford University Press, 2002), 349.

judgment and other qualities required of a successful sovereign is also Scott's point here.

Interestingly, Graham McMaster links this "Charles Stuart" not with Charles I, but with Charles II:

> Scott allowed his people, fables and symbols to accrete meaning and emotional charge, to be transmitted as ready-made units from one work to another. "Charles Stuart," as we have seen, is one example: the Pretender of *Redgauntlet* is the successor only slightly of the same historical person shown in *Waverley*, much more of his ancestor and namesake, Charles II, of *Peveril of the Peak* and *Woodstock*. "Charles Stuart" had come to mean to Scott a father/king whose weaknesses induce disastrous failures of trust in his subjects/children.[66]

However, Scott himself, in several instances, overtly links the Pretender, not with Charles I or with Charles II but with Charles Edward's undistinguished grandfather, James II.

James II is hardly the heroic and principled figure of sovereignty that Charles I has been represented as being by various historians. Similarly, I suggested earlier that Scott, while not whitewashing Charles II's pursuit of pleasure at the expense of his monarchical duties, ultimately presents his reign as a qualified, yet positive chapter in English history. It is, again, in the 1832 'Introduction' to *Redgauntlet* that Scott first draws attention to the similarities between Charles Edward and James II:

> [T]he principal fault of Charles Edward's temper is sufficiently obvious. It was a high sense of his own importance, and an obstinate adherence to what he had once determined on—qualities which, if he had succeeded in his bold attempt, gave the nation little room to hope that he would have been found free from the love of prerogative and desire of arbitrary power, which characterized his unhappy grandfather.[67]

Redgauntlet himself also refers to similarities between Charles Edward Stuart and James II: "But what is to be done if Charles should refuse, with the inflexibility of his grandfather, to comply with this request of yours? Do you mean to abandon him to his fate?" (*Redgauntlet*, 352).

---

66   McMaster, *Scott and Society*, 226.
67   Scott, *Redgauntlet* (1931), 8.

Charles Edward's inheritance of the Stuart dynasty's less felicitous qualities is underscored several times in the novel. As Scott recounts, when France was, as a condition of suing for peace with England, required to evict the Chevalier from the French dominions, "[i]nspired, however, by the spirit of hereditary obstinacy, Charles preferred a useless resistance to a dignified submission".[68] And much later in the novel Sir Richard Glendale, a loyal supporter of the Pretender and his cause, decries not just Charles Edward himself, but his entire Stuart lineage: "of what great and inexpiable crime can your Majesty's [Stuart] ancestors have been guilty, that they have been punished by the infliction of judicial blindness on their whole generation!" (*Redgauntlet*, 358).

Thus, Scott provides no opportunity for us to see the Chevalier as a worthy potential monarch in *Redgauntlet*. He gives us a character whose innate princely qualities and abilities have withered and whose assumption of the sovereign body politic is inconceivable. Mornin suggests that "[t]he failure of this plot (ludicrous in its ineffectiveness) is perceived even by the fanatical Redgauntlet truly to mark the end of any hope of another Jacobite uprising".[69] I propound rather that it is the failure of Charles Edward to demonstrate any form of monarchical capability—which everyone recognizes, except the fanatical Redgauntlet—that truly marks the end of any hope of another Jacobite uprising. The Chevalier's supporters have, to inspire them, only a petty figure of outmoded sovereignty, so attached to his honour that his will is not to be questioned, and so deficient in ability that he has no ambitions or thoughts of his own. *Redgauntlet* closes with a bleak portrait of this last representative of the Stuart monarchy—in terms of both the natural body and the sovereign body politic. It also closes with a comprehensive representation of Hanoverian strength, as does *Waverley*. In both novels Scott achieves this, I contend, primarily by literally absenting the natural body of the respective monarch—whether George II or George III—and presenting the Hanoverian sovereign body politic as its substitute.

Scott's reliance on the protagonist's meeting with the monarch, who subsequently functions as a *deus ex machina*, is a feature of many of the Waverley Novels. Perhaps the most notable feature of Scott's use of the Hanoverians in *Waverley* and *Redgauntlet* is that he chooses not to employ this narrative device. Because he brings Charles Edward Stuart on stage, at first sight it seems strange that Scott excludes the natural bodies of George II and George III from these novels. In *Waverley*, George II is shown indirectly, through Colonel Talbot's letter to Edward Waverley recounting the Colonel's meeting with his monarch.

---

68   Ibid., 8.
69   Mornin, 'Bonnie Charlie,' 100.

George III's voice can be heard only when General Campbell, his representative, quotes him verbatim in *Redgauntlet*. It could be argued that Scott was being politically astute, avoiding any risk of George IV's dissatisfaction with specific portraits of his familial predecessors. This omission serves a number of other purposes, primarily Scott's establishing his support for the Hanoverians, and monarchy generally, in each of these novels. First, Scott circumvents the reader's (potentially) sympathetic response to the romantic figure of the Stuart monarchy being notionally 'usurped' by the Hanoverian sovereigns, albeit rather more so in *Waverley* than in *Redgauntlet*. Second, he distances the monarchy from the two most distressing events of the novel, the brutal response to the battle of Culloden and the sentencing to death of Fergus Mac-Ivor and Evan Dhu Maccombich. Third, Colonel Talbot and General Campbell, spokesmen for the Hanoverian monarchy, simultaneously demonstrate the integrity, justice and clemency of the reigning monarchs. Finally, Scott is able to represent the Hanoverian monarchs in their capacity as sovereign body politic, in contrast to his portrayal of Charles Edward Stuart merely as the natural body of a 'prince.'

I have already discussed Scott's representation of Charles Edward as the debonair, charming adventurer, and Edward Waverley's response to that charismatic figure. Mack remarks that "[a]ware as he was of the emotional appeal of Jacobitism, Scott in *Waverley* created a fiction which expresses some sympathy with its hero's openness to the appeal of the cause of Prince Charles".[70] Similarly aware of the attraction of Charles Edward as an individual, Scott does not create an opportunity for us to compare the two sovereign figures, one a romantic and disadvantaged underdog, the other a mundane character advantaged by monarchical incumbency. Indeed, Scott is at pains to demonstrate that the appeal of both Charles Edward and the Jacobite cause is inherently romantic, immature and emotional, while support of the Hanoverian monarchy, although prosaic, is both rational and progressive.

Claire Lamont comments, as does Mack, on Scott's consigning the battle of Culloden to the background of *Waverley* by separating Edward Waverley physically from the Highland army after Preston.[71] Equally, by not foregrounding the natural body of George II, Scott is able to relegate other members of the Hanoverian monarchy, most specifically George II's younger son, the Duke

---

70   Douglas S. Mack, 'Culloden and After: Scottish Jacobite Novels,' *Eighteenth-Century Life*,
      20 (November 1996), 94.

71   See: Claire Lamont. '*Waverley* and the Battle of Culloden,' *History and the Novel*, ed. Angus
      Easson (Cambridge: D.S. Brewer, 1991), 14–26; Lamont, 'Introduction,' *Waverley* (Oxford
      and New York: Clarendon Press, 1981); and Mack, 'Culloden and After,' 92–106.

of Cumberland, to the background of the novel. The Duke of Cumberland's brutality and the nature of the atrocities performed under his command after Culloden are scarcely a credit to the Hanoverian monarchy; if highlighted, they would have proved difficult to reconcile with Scott's overarching support for the House of Hanover. Similarly, Scott emphasizes the role of the minions of the law and of the military in Fergus Mac-Ivor's death, surrounding him constantly with minor legal individuals and various lowly soldiers, dragoons and infantrymen.

In one of the most moving parts of the novel, Scott foregrounds the admirable qualities of the Highlanders: Fergus Mac-Ivor's death is conspicuous for its nobility and Evan Dhu Maccombich's for his loyalty to his Chief. However, just as Fergus insists on Edward Waverley's absence from his grisly death—"what a dying man can suffer firmly, may kill a living friend to look upon"—so too does Scott insist on the absence of any emblem of the monarch at the scene (*Waverley*, 348). The Executioner is present in all his gruesomeness, but Colonel Talbot has no place here, and neither does George II. The one comment Scott does allow is Fergus' wry statement that "[t]his same law of high treason [...] is one of the blessings, Edward, with which your free country has accommodated poor old Scotland—her own jurisprudence, as I have heard, was much milder" (*Waverley*, 348). Colonel Talbot in *Waverley* and General Campbell in *Redgauntlet* represent the Hanoverian monarchy—and represent it well. They are similar characters, though Talbot is far more significant in *Waverley* than is General Campbell in *Redgauntlet*. As we read:

> [T]he character of the Colonel rose in Waverley's estimation. There seemed at first something harsh in his strong expressions of dislike and censure, although no one was in the general case more open to conviction. The habit of authority had also given his manners some peremptory hardness, notwithstanding the polish which they had received from his intimate acquaintance with the higher circles. As a specimen of the military character, he differed from all whom Waverley had as yet seen. [...] Colonel Talbot was in every point the English soldier. His whole soul was devoted to the service of his king and country, without feeling any pride in knowing the theory of his art with the Baron, or its practical minutiae with the Major, or in applying his science to his own particular plans of ambition, like the Chieftain of Glennaquoich. Added to this, he was a man of extended knowledge and cultivated taste, although strongly tinged, as we have already observed, with those prejudices which are peculiarly English.
>
> WAVERLEY, 262

Scott describes General Campbell in more succinct terms.

> [A] gentleman, plainly dressed in a riding-habit, with a black cockade in
> his hat, but without any arms except a couteau-de-chasse, walked into
> the apartment without ceremony. He was a tall, thin, gentlemanly man,
> with a look and bearing decidedly military.
>
> *REDGAUNTLET*, 371

However, General Campbell is well known to the Chevalier's supporters, several of whom make overt reference to his being a man of honour: Charles Stuart himself refers to the general as his "friendly foe" (*Redgauntlet*, 374). Readers
of *The Heart of Mid-Lothian* would also find themselves acquainted, not with
General Campbell himself, but with his noble ancestor. As Mack notes, "[t]he
general is a modern representative of the powerful clan Campbell, the clan
of the earls and later the dukes of Argyll, the clan so long in the forefront of
the forces that developed into the anti-Jacobite faction in the political life of
Scotland".[72] Kathryn Sutherland, as Mack mentions, also links General Campbell with his famous relative, John Campbell, Fourth Duke of Argyll—as does
Charles Edward himself.[73] However, I find it considerably more significant that
General Campbell is the direct descendant of John Campbell, Second Duke
of Argyle, that representative of the Hanoverian monarchy whose interest in
justice and social order is pivotal to the events of *The Heart of Mid-Lothian*.

In *Waverley* and *Redgauntlet*, the Hanoverian monarchs speak directly, but
through a spokesman, to both Edward Waverley and the Chevalier. The use
of Colonel Talbot and General Campbell allows Scott to represent each monarch in his capacity as sovereign body politic. They are present without being present—as opposed to Charles Edward Stuart, who is actually present in
the natural body of a 'prince.' Quoting the respective monarch verbatim fulfils
three functions: it demonstrates that the sovereign is engaged in the process of
justice, reinforces the social stability that supports the monarchy, and obviates
the need for the king's actual presence.

In *Waverley*, just as Edward Waverley earlier recounted his conversation
with the Chevalier to Colonel Talbot, so does Colonel Talbot also quote His
Majesty. However, it is important to note that George II is not influenced by

---

72   Mack, 'Culloden and After,' 103.

73   Ibid., 103. Charles Edward makes pointed reference to General Campbell's ancestry:
      "Our ancestors, nevertheless, have been well acquainted," said Charles, unable to sup-
      press, even in that hour of dread and danger, the painful recollections of fallen royalty"
      (*Redgauntlet*, 372).

the personal factors of Edward Waverley's case. An appeal to friendship and good-will, such as was successful with Charles Edward, makes no impression on George II, and neither does the notion of personal obligation. He agrees to Waverley's pardon only when Colonel Talbot threatens to resign as a representative of the sovereign body politic, as Talbot recounts:

> I said I was rejoiced to learn that his Royal Highness was in the course of granting such requests, as it emboldened me to present one of the like nature in my own name. He was very angry, but I persisted; I mentioned the uniform support of our three votes in the house, touched modestly on services abroad, though valuable only in his Royal Highness having been pleased kindly to accept them, and founded pretty strongly on his own expressions of friendship and good-will. He was embarrassed, but obstinate. I hinted the policy of detaching, on all future occasions, the heir of such a fortune as your uncle's from the machinations of the disaffected. But I made no impression. I mentioned the obligations which I lay under to Sir Everard, and to you personally, and claimed, as the sole reward of my services, that he would be pleased to afford me the means of evincing my gratitude. I perceived that he still meditated a refusal, and, taking my commission from my pocket, I said, as a last resource, that as his Royal Highness did not, under these pressing circumstances, think me worthy of a favour which he had not scrupled to grant to other gentlemen, whose services I could hardly judge more important than my own, I must beg leave to deposit, with all humility, my commission in his Royal Highness's hands, and to retire from the service. He was not prepared for this; he told me to take up my commission; said some handsome things of my services, and granted my request. [...] Thus you see *my* prince can be as generous as *yours*. [...][T]he evident reluctance with which he grants your request, indicates the sacrifice which he makes of his own inclination to your wishes.
>
> WAVERLEY, 334

Indeed, George II's reluctance to grant Waverley's pardon demonstrates, not the sacrifice of "his own inclination to Waverley's wishes," but rather the subordination of his inclinations as the monarch's natural body to the requirements of the sovereign body politic.

Ironically, General Campbell's speech as George III's mouthpiece in *Redgauntlet* seeks to attribute to Charles Edward the morality and motives of the sovereign body politic. George III assumes that the Pretender will withdraw from England because, as a monarch, the Chevalier's concern for his adherents' well-being would naturally outweigh his own (delusional) ambitions of kingship.

> "I speak the King's very words, from his very lips," replied the general. "'I will,' said his Majesty, 'deserve the confidence of my subjects, by reposing my security in the fidelity of the millions who acknowledge my title—in the good sense and prudence of the few who continue, from the errors of education, to disown it.'—His Majesty will not even believe that the most zealous Jacobites who yet remain can nourish a thought of exciting a civil war, which must be fatal to their families and themselves, besides spreading bloodshed and ruin through a peaceful land. He cannot even believe of his Kinsman, that he would engage brave and generous, though mistaken men, in an attempt must ruin all who have escaped former calamities; and he is convinced, that, did curiosity or any other motive lead that Person to visit this country, he would soon see it was his wisest course to return to the continent; and his Majesty compassionates his situation too much to offer any obstacle to his doing so."
>
> *REDGAUNTLET*, 373

It is interesting to note how closely this speech resembles Charles Stuart's own words earlier in the novel when he seeks to profile his own nobility in returning to England:

> [W]hen I have reflected how many of my loyal and devoted friends perished by the sword and by proscription, or died indigent and neglected in a foreign land, I have often sworn that no view to my personal aggrandizement should again induce me to agitate a title which has cost my followers so dear.
>
> *REDGAUNTLET*, 354

Scott's point is clear: a true monarch does not engage in acts of rebellion to the detriment of his adherents and dominions, with the sole purpose of realizing the ambitions (possibly futile) of his natural body. Scott's support is ultimately for a monarchy that functions in the capacity of sovereign body politic, placing the needs of its subjects and the stability of the nation above personal inclinations.

By tracing the increasing distance of the natural body of the Stuart and Hanoverian sovereigns in *Waverley* and *Redgauntlet*, Scott posits two counter-revolutionary arguments. The first is that the Stuart monarchy is so inherently irrelevant in eighteenth-century Georgian England that its presence ultimately achieves the same thing as its absence: failure and inconsequentiality. The second is that the Hanoverian monarchy is so secure that the presence of the monarch's natural body is unnecessary to assure the continued social order. Both of these arguments are present in the closing chapter of *Redgauntlet*; Charles Edward's presence is of such slight consequence to the Hanoverian monarchy that it can be summarily dismissed with impunity by the government, in the absence of the reigning monarch's natural body. As Stuart Kelly points out, this "kind of benevolence [is] made only possible by absolute victory".[74]

Tracing Scott's representations of the royal presence throughout the six novels—*The Fortunes of Nigel, Woodstock, Peveril of the Peak, The Heart of Mid-Lothian, Waverley* and *Redgauntlet*—reveals his cumulative counter-revolutionary support for the notion of monarchy itself and for the Hanoverian monarchy specifically. Scott's depictions of the natural body and the sovereign body politic of the monarch, when viewed as a continuum throughout the six novels, document a transition from a society dependent on the personal involvement of the monarch for true justice to one with such a degree of social stability and order that the royal personal presence is no longer necessary. I suggest that the notion of the royal presence as a locale is thus fundamental to Scott's staunch counter-revolutionism within *The Fortunes of Nigel, Woodstock, Peveril of the Peak, The Heart of Mid-Lothian, Waverley* and *Redgauntlet*, considered singly and as a group. Indeed, the royal presence is arguably the most important locale in each novel. Its use enables Scott to explore each sovereign's character and to craft a historically recognizable and ultimately positive representation of James VI and I, Charles II, Queen Caroline, George II, and George III. In addition, this notion allows Scott to demonstrate just how varied were concepts of sovereignty throughout the monarchical dynasties he depicts and the historical periods in which they reigned.

Scott's representation of the concept of monarchy and his portraits of specific monarchs clearly demonstrate his nuanced, politically conservative position, especially when viewed in the framework of his broader use of place. Locale in Scott is a complex and, as the preceding chapters have argued, ingenious literary apparatus. Scott uses it to build, throughout the six novels, an overarching argumentation dedicated to the rehabilitation of both the Stuart and Hanoverian dynasties. *The Fortunes of Nigel, Woodstock* and *Peveril of the Peak* speak in support of the Stuarts in their historical contexts, while *The Heart of Mid-Lothian, Waverley* and *Redgauntlet* do the same for the Hanoverians, with *Waverley* and *Redgauntlet* additionally commenting on the increasing superfluity of the Stuarts to British society and politics.

---

74   Kelly, *Scott-Land*, 238.

Homecoming, Return and Journey's End

In 1822, a year after his coronation, George IV visited Scotland, the first reigning English monarch to do so since Charles II. The visit served two immediate purposes: diverting King George's intention to engage in international diplomacy at the Congress of Verona, and addressing a groundswell of Scottish radicalism in the wake of the Radical War (or the Scottish Insurrection) of 1820. Scott, having been actively involved in attempts to quell that rioting across Scotland and now engaged to oversee his monarch's visit, saw a means of countering the rebellious spirit seeping across Scotland. Ambitiously, in arranging the royal visit—some contemporaries, including Macauley, saw it more as an engineering—Scott sought also to effect the historical rehabilitation of the Stuart monarchy and to reinforce the then-current legitimacy of the Hanoverian monarchy. His doing so took place against two potent historico-political backdrops: the disrepute associated with George IV's sovereignty and the dominance of Whig historiography.

Although George IV has ascended the throne a bare year before the proposed visit to Scotland, he had ruled over Britain in the capacity of Prince Regent for some ten years as the result of George III's precarious mental health. This period had seen the Prince Regent metamorphose from a handsome, romantic and popular royal figure to an obese, wildly unpopular bigamist whose poor treatment of his wife, acrimonious divorce proceedings, and gross pecuniary and sexual indecorum had alienated swathes of his subjects. At the same time, Scott had been writing his politico-historical literature against a backdrop of assertively Whig historiography. Since the publication of Hume's *History of England* (1754–61)—widely although not universally considered Tory in perspective—Burke's *Reflections on the Revolution in France* (1790) defined the historical literary landscape, together with Whig histories such as George Brodie's *History of the British Empire from the Accession of Charles I to the Restoration* (1822), which were followed some years later by Henry Hallam's *Constitutional History of England* (1827) and William Godwin's *History of the Commonwealth of England* (1824–8).[1] That is to say, the royal visit occurred at a time when the interpretation of history was dominated by the Whig premise that the Glorious

---

1 The following scholarly works, among others, provide useful insight into the nature of Whig and Tory historiographies of that time: Herbert Butterfield's *The Whig Interpretation of History* (London: Bell, 1931); Jenifer Hart's 'Nineteenth-Century Social Reform: a Tory

Revolution heralded, in fact was, the exordium to British modern history, from which time the country had continued in progress towards measured constitutional monarchical reform and socio-political enlightenment. This historiographical presumption rested upon the idea that the period immediately prior, that of the Stuart monarchy, was one of political and civil oppression at the hands of the monarchy—what Thomas Babington Macaulay was later to term "a state of ignominious vassalage"—from which Britain had been freed only by the Whig-enabled parliamentary monarchy of William and Mary of Orange.[2]

Against this background, Scott was able to position the royal visit as a conservative historiographical discourse that conflated Whig notions of historiography with Tory ones through his careful reinterpretation of George IV's bloodline to establish his legitimacy as a Stuart king while incorporating his Hanoverian lineage. While the artificiality of such constructs horrified the (primarily) Highland purists of Scottish descent, the wider context of Scott's recreation of Scotland in his role of the father of the historical novel (and thus, by definition, a creator of fictions around and about Scotland) defied and defies much of the criticism—then and since. As Anne Frey points out, "Scott simultaneously plays the roles of Scottish antiquarian and British patriot: he employs local knowledge both to celebrate Scottish history and to serve the British government".[3] It is fascinating to see Scott's use of the King's natural body to ameliorate radicalized aversion to his body politic, and his body politic to mitigate the damage to the sovereignty by the monarch's natural body. Further, as Stuart Kelly notes, the interwoven nature of the monarch's natural body and body politic encompassed the interrelations between the two dynasties, especially as *The Fortunes of Nigel* was published at the time of George IV coming to Scotland (thereby notionally completing the journey commenced by James VI in that novel).[4]

It is, therefore, through the topoi of homecoming, return and journey's end that Scott enacts the historical rehabilitation of the Stuart monarchy and the espousal of the then-contemporary Hanoverian monarchy's legitimacy. To that end, as Gottlieb points out, in organizing the 'King's Jaunt' Scott was faced with the challenge of "construct[ing] a British identity, [and] also the dilemma of

Interpretation of History,' *Past & Present*, 31 (1965), 39–61; and Ernst Mayr's 'When is Historiography Whiggish?,' *Journal of the History of Ideas*, 51 (1990), 301–9.

2   Thomas Babington Macaulay, *The History of England from the Accession of James II*, Vol 1 (London: Macmillan and Co., 1914), 1.

3   Anne Frey, *British State Romanticism: Authorship, Agency, and Bureaucratic Nationalism* (Stanford: Stanford University Press, 2009), 88.

4   Stuart Kelly, *Scott-Land: The Man Who Invented a Nation* (Edinburgh: Polygon, 2010), 228.

how to configure Scotland's various cultural identities while vindicating the necessity of the Union and the social order it entailed".[5] To this, I would add that, against that background of intent, the imaging and legitimation of political authority were priorities throughout Scott's stage management of the royal visit. Hence, as he did in the six novels previously discussed, Scott positioned this celebration of monarchy as the fitting representation of both an individual monarch and a dynastic sovereignty—again rehabilitating a specific monarch and positing a staunchly (if consciously qualified) counter-revolutionism.

In contriving and staging the elaborate spectacle of George IV's visit, Scott used many of the same literary and theatrical constructs and mechanisms by which he established his arguments supporting the notion of sovereignty as a superior form of national governance and of the Stuart and Hanoverian monarchies respectively in those novels. In other words, Scott applied those tools of royal image construction that Kevin Sharpe identifies in his work on the Stuart dynasty to both George IV and his beloved Scotland. As in the six novels, ultimately the most important locale is that of the sovereign: with the focus here being foregrounding the sovereign body politic while attempting to minimize (as much as possible) the formidable girth of George IV's natural body. This undertaking was not without challenges. As Lumsden notes, the event was freighted with significance: not only was it the first monarchical visit since the mid-seventeenth century one by the restored Stuart Charles II, but also the first visit by the Hanoverian royal family since the Duke of Cumberland— the infamous 'Butcher' Cumberland who savagely suppressed the Jacobite rebellion of 1745—had wreaked such bloody retribution for that uprising.[6] Additionally, Scott was given little notice of his monarch's intention and thus had only two weeks in which to organize this pageant.[7] More particularly, in this contracted period, Scott needed to construct George IV positively as a ruler and convincingly trace his lineage from Robert Bruce through the Stuart monarchy. He also had to traverse, and in many instances, elide historical

5   Gottlieb, *Feeling British*, 189.
6   See: Lumsden's "'Beyond the Dusky Barrier:' Perceptions of the Highlands in the Waverley Novels,' *Mìorun mòr nan Gall, 'The great ill-will of the Lowlander'?: Lowland perceptions of the Highlands, medieval and modern*, ed. Dauvit Broun and Martin MacGregor (Glasgow: University of Glasgow, Centre for Scottish and Celtic Studies, 2007), 161. See also: Hugh Trevor-Roper, 'The Invention of Tradition: The Highland Tradition of Scotland,' *The Invention of Tradition*, ed. Eric Hobsbawn and Terence Ranger (Cambridge: Cambridge University Press, 2012), 15–42.
7   See: Lumsden's 'Essay on the Text,' *Peveril of the Peak*, 502.

incidents over the past two centuries. Additionally, he sought to celebrate Scotland—ancient and modern—and commemorate (or rather, re-establish) its significance within Great Britain. In planning such an ambitious endeavour, his exploration through his novels of how various monarchs sought to establish, consolidate and legitimate authority in dynamic politico-religious environments stood him in good stead.

Just as Scott's descriptions of portrait paintings and his own detailed depiction of various monarchs in his novels were aimed at positioning monarchical images and their respective causes—current and retrospective—within the broader significances of the physical, political and social landscapes of the novels, so too did his representation of George IV and of Scotland itself. McCracken-Flesher astutely notes that

> Scott carefully deployed Scottish signs to raise the King's value, but in so doing quietly subjected the monarch to a Scotland constructed as transcendental Sign. He turned the King to Scottish use. How could Scott determine George IV as the nation's dominant term, but Scotland as his site of meaning? The author locked King and people in a dynamic of mutual valuation through the narrative of 'return.' Neither George nor any other Hanoverian king had ever set foot north of the border, and the stream of Stuart blood ran thin in the King's German veins, yet in the texts that set the tone for the visit, particularly in his manual for the Scottish reception, Scott insisted that "this remote part of the empire" received him home (Hints, 7).[8]

Thus, George IV (assured by Scott of his having both Stuart blood and links to the Jacobite Highlanders) stood garbed in red Royal Tartan (Royal Stuart, as it was later named). Scott manufactured the image of a sturdily built, gracious and benevolent ruler reclaiming and proudly acknowledging his Scottish heritage.

This construction of the much-caricatured ruler was broadly, if not universally, well received. Macaulay, for one, was not enamoured of the spectacle created:

> The last British King who held a court at Holyrood thought that he could not give a more striking proof of his respect for the usages which had prevailed in Scotland before the Union, than by disguising himself in what, before the Union, was considered by nine Scotchmen out of ten as a dress of a thief.

---

8   McCracken-Flesher, *Possible Scotlands*, 79.

The Entrance of George IV at the Palace of Holyroodhouse: Sir David Wilkie.
REPRODUCED BY PERMISSION OF ROYAL COLLECTION TRUST / © HER MAJESTY QUEEN
ELIZABETH II 2018.

> Thus it has chanced that the old Gaelic institutions and manners have
> never been exhibited in the simple light of truth. [...] The time when a
> perfectly fair picture could have painted has now passed away. [...] all
> that is possible is to product an imperfect likeness by the help of two
> portraits, one a coarse caricature and the other a masterpiece of flattery.[9]

Macauley voiced an overt regret that the opportunity for accurate imaging and
portraiture of Scotland was now lost; for just as Scott was refashioning a portrait of his sovereign, so he was doing the same to his homeland.

This legitimating of the monarch and his dynasty in the context of Scottish
nationalist discourses was effected with the result that images come to depend
largely upon each other. Scott was melding two sets of images of monarchy: an
authentic (or at least, somewhat recognizable) image of personal and dynastic
monarchical legitimacy; a Jacobite infused image of that same monarch (and
thus dynasty) bearing the historical legitimacy of Stuart lineage. At the same
time, he was crafting the image of Scotland—a nation proud of its unique
landscape, military, ancient heritage and monarchy—through the various pag-
eants and spectacles created in partnership with theatrical manager, William
Henry Murray.

9   Macaulay, *The History of England*, 1591–2.

I have argued throughout this book that Scott's imaging and re-branding of monarchy is effected chiefly through his use of landscape, space and place—pursuing, in the process, how Sharpe's work encourages analysis, in light of recent theories of 'place' and 'space,' of Scott's counter-revolutionism with respect to questions of justice, law and the notion of monarchy itself. It is clear that Scott consciously makes use of a long tradition of developing image and brand through built environments and changes to the landscape throughout his novels. Furthermore, his use of both place and space enables him to produce his own interpretation of the mutability of the individual monarch and the monarchy's status. This is equally true with regards the pageantry of the visit in 1822, as can be seen by the use of Holyrood and the king's natural body, both of which were conscripted in Scott's representation of political and personal homecoming and return. As I have argued across the preceding chapters, concepts are crucially contextualized by place in Scott's fictions: landscape and setting transmit vital political meanings to the story and 'place' is one of the most consistently important elements of the Waverley canon.

A major challenge for Scott in 1822 was to construct Holyrood as a positive symbol of Scottish history and one relevant to the political and social present. This brings us back to representation of Holyrood within the novels considered here. In *The Fortunes of Nigel*, for instance, each mention of Holyrood recalls James as a much valued monarch, supported by and supporting his Scottish subjects. This enabled Scott's deft conflation of the past James-as-Stuart-monarch-of-Scotland (and his then-popularity with his subjects) with the present George-as-Hanoverian-monarch-of-England. While in reality Holyrood is a locale of physical as well as political distance from England (and as such is a curiously penumbral locale in *The Fortunes of Nigel*), its significance arises from its being a place of memory. Just as James appears in that novel to best advantage as sovereign of Scotland when actually there, and when his public as well as private personae are conjoined in enactment of his better self, so too did George IV as he presided so graciously and appreciatively over the ceremonial events situated in Holyrood.

Accordingly, in his careful (if hurried) planning of George IV's royal visit, Scott foregrounded Holyrood as a site of Stuart rule and Scottish history and pride. In so doing, Holyrood was reimaged as a then-current emblem of harmonious Anglo-Scottish cultural identities, constructed as Anglo-Scottish cultural identities. Scott carefully constructs Holyrood as part of a wider imaginative geography emanating from the physical building itself. Eliding his the depiction of Holyrood as it appeared in *Waverley* during the royal visit: he created, rather, a locale capturing and projecting the glory of the Stuart dynasty and Scottish history, a wondrous image of Scottish culture, allegiance to the crown,

and revelry in its proud history. Here indeed was a site befitting acknowledgment of the lineage of a Hanoverian king as including Stuart sovereignty.
In 1822, it was made to blaze as a beacon of restoration, of a king's returning to
his geographical and cultural roots. It housed the majority of the formal events
comprising George IV's visit. These included a preparatory procession where
the Regalia of Scotland was escorted to the palace prior to the king's arrival, a
levee during which the king greeted the most eminent of his Scottish subjects
(himself bedecked in his Highland outfit—the one time he wore it and which
resulted in a field day of caricature in England) and a private visit to the apartments of his ancestor, Mary, Queen of Scots.

Thus both locales—Holyrood and King George IV—were enveloped in mists
of Scottish history and Stuart dynastic lore. Less focus was on the dilapidated
state of both sites: more on the spectacle of the king's returning to his historic
home—both Holyrood and Scotland, where he was rapturously embraced and
welcomed. The king as a microcosmic locale, wearing his 'rightful' Scottish garb,
was situated in a place that was both a shrine to Stuart sovereignty and to monarchy as a model of governance. He was celebrated and feted by his Scottish
subjects, each of those subjects themselves positioned as an emblem of loyalty
to their king and to the monarchy itself. It is interesting to consider the reality
behind the theatrical representation of both Holyrood and George IV. Holyrood, the official site of historic Stuart sovereignty and now of a Hanoverian
monarch returning home, was not, in fact, in suitable condition to house this
newly reclaimed monarch of the Scots, who resided instead at Dalkeith House
in far greater comfort than Holyrood could afford him. Similarly, this monarch
of the day, so besmirched by reputation and such a physical representation of
debauchery and excess, was always only ever going to be a visitor to Scotland.
While his enormously bloated legs were artificially hidden by his wearing of
pink pantaloons with his Scottish regimentals, his 21 day visit to Scotland was
no less artificially reinvented as his return to his 'homeland.' This, then, was
one of the uses to which Scott put the Stuart mythology—demonstrating the
permanence of the bond between the Stuart greyhound and the Hanoverian
elephant, as the imagery of the times captured the two dynasties.[10]

In *Hints Addressed to the Inhabitants of Edinburgh, and Others, in Prospect
of His Majesty's Visit*, Scott notes the difference between Scotland and Ireland
in relation to England and outlines the nature of the relationship between
Scotland and her monarch:

---

10   See Paul Kleber Monad's *Jacobitism and the English People, 1688–1788* (Cambridge: Cam-
      bridge University Press, 1993) for a discussion of the respective imagery of the Stuart and
      Hanoverian dynasties.

No king had ever before set foot on Ireland, but as a warrior, or as a con-
queror, or as a tyrant. King George IV comes hither as the descendant
of a long line of Scottish Kings. The blood of the heroic Robert Bruce—
the blood of the noble, the enlightened, the generous James I is in his
veins. Whatever honour Worth and Genius can confer upon Ancestry,
his Scottish Ancestry possesses. Still more, he is our kinsman. While our
Douglases our Stewarts, our Hamiltons, our Braces, all our high nobility, are his acknowledged relations—it is not too much to say, that there
is scarcely a gentleman of any of the old Scottish families who cannot,
in some way or other, "count kin" with the royal house from which our
Sovereign is descended. Nay, in this small country, blood has been so
much mingled that it is not to be doubted by far the greater part of our
burgesses and yeomen are entitled to entertain similar pretensions. In
short, we are THE CLAN, and our King is THE CHIEF. Let us, on this
happy occasion, remember that if is so; and not only behave towards him
as a father, but to each other, as if we were, in the Words of the old song,
"ae man's bairns."[11]

Scott's merging, or rather melding, of Stuart and Hanoverian as kinsmen in the
'pageant' of the Royal visit of 1822 is a further illustration of Scott's conscious
and deliberate (re)imaging of monarchy in Scotland through the concepts of
return and homecoming that recur in his novels, and are of climactic importance to the novels considered earlier.

It is self-evident that *The Fortunes of Nigel, Woodstock, Peveril of the Peak, The
Heart of Mid-Lothian, Waverley*, and *Redgauntlet* would not be the only Waverley Novels in which Scott's political conservatism and counter-revolutionism
are evidenced. Thus, for example, in *The Tale of Old Mortality* and *Rob Roy* as
well as in Scott's non-fiction (including his *Letters, Journal*, 'Tales of a Grandfather' and many political tracts), the changing nature of the monarchy across
dynasties, countries and socio-political cultures is considered. The scope of
this study does not allow for close assessment of Scott's representations of
his monarchical political views throughout all of his works, engrossing as that
would be. And this leads us to the second omission. The focus on issues of
sovereignty and governance, law and justice, in the context of both the natural body and the body politic of the ruler denies the opportunity of analysing

---

11   Walter Scott, *Hints Addressed to the Inhabitants of Edinburgh, and Others, in Prospect of
     His Majesty's Visit. Facsimile of Printed pamphlet* (Edinburgh: William Blackwood, Waugh
     and Innes, and John Robertson, 1822) downloaded from http://www.spinnet.humanities
     .uva.nl/images/2010-12/scotthints_new.pdf.

the nuances of Scott's insights into legitimacy beyond its pertinence to the notion of monarchical governance. There are many directions and points of departure that could follow this study and build on the current burgeoning interest in Scott. For example, the various political philosophers and historians beyond Burke who also influenced Scott, or the appropriation of political and monarchical mythologies by other governance models are other areas of interest. These areas of research currently remain, however, as the foundation of another study.

Sources for Scott's Characterization of James VI and I

The following histories specifically referring to James VI and I are included in the *Catalogue of the Library at Abbotsford* (1838) and are referenced verbatim from this source:

Howes's (Edmund) *History of England from the invasion of the Romans to King James I., 1614.* With an Appendix, &c., relating to the three Universities of England, &c., 1615. B.L. Wants title page. *fol.*

Williams's (John, Bishop of Lincoln) *Great Britain's Salomon. Funeral Sermon on King James I.* &c. *sm. 4to. Lond.* 1625.

Sanderson's (William) *Life and Raigne of King Charles,* from his cradle to his grave. *fol. ib.* 1658.

Robertson's (Rev. Principal William) *History of Scotland during the reigns of Mary and James VI. 3d edit.* 2 *vols.* 4 *to. ib.* 1760.

Spotswood's (Abp.) *History of the Church of Scotland, from* A.D. *203 to the death of James VI. 4th edit*, with Appendix, *fol. Lond.* 1677.

Calderwood's (Rev. Dav.) *History of the Church of Scotland, from the Reformation to the end of James VI. fol.* 1704.

Coke's (R.) *Detection of the Court and State of England during the reigns of James i. Charles I. and II. And James II.; as also the Interregnum,* &c. 4th edit. 3 *vols. 8vo. Lond.* 1718–19.

Clarendon's (Edward, Earl of) *History of the Rebellion and Civil Wars in England, begun in 1641,* &c.; *with copies of Dean Swift's* MS. *notes. 3 vols. fol. Oxford,* 1702–4. *Complete History of England; with the Lives of all the Kings and Queens thereof, from the earliest Account of Time to the Death of King William III.* &c. (Edited by Bishop Kennett.) 3 *vols. fol. Lond.* 1707.

Scott's (David) *History of Scotland, &c. from the year of the world 3619 to the year of Christ 1726. fol. Westminster,* 1727.

Rapin de Thoyras's. *History of England (translated into English, with additional notes, by Nicholas Tindale.* 2 vols *Lond,* 1732–3—Tindale's (Nicholas) *Continuation of Rapin from the Revolution to the Assession of George II.* &c. 3 *vols. ib.* 1744–75.

Lodge's (Edmund) *Illustrations of British History, Biography, and Manners, in the reigns of Henry* VIII. *Edward* VI. *Mary, Elizabeth, and James I.* &c. 3 *vols. 4to. ib.* 1791.

Hume's (David) *History of England, to the Revolution in 1688.* 8 vols.—

Smollett's (Dr. Tobias) *Continua, of Hist. of Eng. to death of Geo.* II. 5 vols.—13 *vols. 8vo. ib.* 1796–1800.

© KONINKLIJKE BRILL NV, LEIDEN, 2018 | DOI 10.1163/9789004352780_009

Historie and Life of King James the Sext, from a ms. of the 16th Century. Edited by Malcolm Laing. *royal 8vo. ib.* 1804.

Hutchinson's (Mrs.) *Memoirs of the Life of Col. Hutchinson, Governor of Nottingham Castle, &c. With her own Life prefixed.* Published from the Original MSS. by the Rev. Julius Hutchinson. *4to. ib.* 1806.

Secret History of the Court of James I. (Weldon, Osborne, Heylin, and Peyton, &c). Edited by Sir W. Scott 2 vols. *royal 8vo. ib.* 1811.

D'Israeli, I. *Literary and Political Character of James I.* 8vo. London, 1816. Aikin's (Lucy) Memoirs of the Court of King James I. 2 vols. 8vo. *ib.* 1822.

Select Bibliography

A Complete Collection Of State-Trials And Proceedings For High-Treason And Other Crimes and Misdemeanours: Commencing With The Eleventh Year of the Reign of King Richard II. And Ending With The Sixteenth Year of the Reign of King George III: With Two Alphabetical Tables To The Whole, Vol 1 (London: J. Bathurst, et al., 1776).

A Declaration of the Parliament of England, Expressing the Grounds of their late Proceedings, And of Setling the present Government In the way of A Free State (London: Edward Husband, 1648).

Ackroyd, Peter, *London: The Biography* (London: Vintage Random House, 2001).

Adams, Maeve, '"The Force of my Narrative": Persuasion, Nation, and Paratext in Walter Scott's Early Waverley Novels,' *ELH*, 82 (2015), 937–67.

Alexander, Christine, '"For Fiction, Read Scott Alone": The Legacy of Sir Walter Scott on Youthful Artists and Writers,' *The Shadow of the Precursor*, ed. Diana Glenn, Md Rezaul Haque, Ben Kooyman, and Nena Bierbaum (Newcastle upon Tyne: Cambridge Scholars Publishing, 2012), 106–23.

Alighieri, Dante, *The Divine Comedy 2: Purgatory* (London: Penguin, 1995).

Allen, Emily, 'Re-Marking Territory: *Redgauntlet* and the Restoration of Sir Walter Scott,' *Studies in Romanticism*, 37 (Summer 1998), 163–82.

Allentuck, Marcia, 'Scott and the Picturesque: Afforestation and History,' *Scott: Bicentenary Essays*, ed. Alan Bell (Edinburgh and London: Scottish Academic Press, 1973), 188–98.

Armstrong, Nancy, *How Novels Think: The Limits of British Individualism From 1719–1900* (New York: Columbia, 2005).

Armstrong, Nancy, *Desire and Domestic Fiction: A Political History of the Novel* (Oxford: Oxford University Press, 1989).

Ascham, Antony, *Of the Confusions and Revolutions of Governments Wherein is examined, How farre a man may lawfully conforme to the Powers and Commands of those who with various successes hold Kingdomes divided by Civill or Forraigne Warrs* (London: W. Wilson, 1649).

Ashton, Robert, (ed.) *James I by His Contemporaries* (London: Hutchinson & Co., 1969).

Austin, Carolyn F., 'Home and Nation in *The Heart of Midlothian*,' *SEL: Studies in English Literature, 1500–1900*, 40 (Autumn 2000), 621–34.

Bachelard, Gaston, *Poetics of Space: The Classic Look at How We Experience Intimate Places* (Boston: Beacon Press, 1994).

Bailey, Rebecca A., 'Staging 'a Queene opprest:' William Habington's Exploration of the Politics of Queenship on the Caroline Stage,' *Theatre Journal*, 65 (2013), 197–214.

Bainbridge, Simon, 'Walter Scott's Picturesque Romance of War, 1805–1814,' *British Poetry and the Revolutionary and Napoleonic Wars* (Oxford: Oxford University Press, 2003), 20–47.

Baker, Samuel, 'Scott's Worlds of War,' *The Edinburgh Companion to Sir Walter Scott*, ed. Fiona Robertson (Edinburgh: Edinburgh University Press, 2012), 70–81.

Bann, Stephen, *The Clothing of Clio: A Study of the Representation of History in Nineteenth-Century Britain and France* (Cambridge, Cambridge University Press: 1984).

Bannet, Eve Tavor, *The Domestic Revolution: Enlightenment Feminisms and the Novel* (Baltimore and London: John Hopkins University Press, 2000).

Barfoot, C.C., (ed.) *Beyond Pug's Tour: National and Ethnic Stereotyping in Theory and Literary Practice* (Amsterdam and Atlanta: Rodopi, 1997).

Beiderwell, Bruce, 'Romantic Enlightenment: Sir Walter Scott and the Politics of History,' *European Romantic Review*, 13 (September 2002), 223–4.

Beiderwell, Bruce, *Power and Punishment in Scott's Novels* (Athens: University of Georgia, 1992).

Beiderwell, Bruce, 'Scott's *Redgauntlet* as a Romance of Power,' *Studies in Romanticism*, 28 (Summer 1989), 273–89.

Bender, John, *Imagining the Penitentiary: Fiction and the Architecture of Mind in Eighteenth-Century England* (Chicago and London: University of Chicago Press, 1987).

Bergeron, David M., *King James and Royal Letters of Homoerotic Desire* (Iowa City: University of Iowa Press, 1999).

Berndt, Katrin, 'Civic Virtues in the Restless Polity: Sir Walter Scott's Fergusonian Vision of British Civil Society in *Redgauntlet* (1824),' *Studies in Eighteenth-Century Culture*, 41 (2012), 115–35.

Bevir, Mark, *The Logic of the History of Ideas* (Cambridge: Cambridge University Press, 2002).

Bevir, Mark and R.A.W. Rhodes, (eds.) *Routledge Handbook of Interpretive Political Science* (Abingdon, Oxon: Routledge, 2016).

Bhabha, Homi K., *The Location of Culture* (New York and London: Routledge, 1994).

Bhabha, Homi K., *Nation and Narration* (New York and London: Routledge, 1990).

Black, Eugene Charlton, (ed.) *British Politics in the Nineteenth Century* (London: Palgrave Macmillan, 1969).

Blair, David, 'Scott, Cartography, and the Appropriation of Scottish Place,' *Literature and Place, 1800–2000*, ed. Peter Brown and Michael Irwin (Bern: Peter Lang, 2006), 87–107.

Blomley, Nicholas K., *Law, Space, and the Geographies of Power* (New York: Guildford Press, 1994).

Bold, Alan, (ed.) *Sir Walter Scott: The Long-Forgotten Melody* (London and Totowa: Vision and Barnes & Noble, 1983).

Bouma-Prediger, Steven and Brian J. Walsh, *Beyond Homelessness: Christian Faith in a Culture of Displacement* (Grand Rapids: Eerdmans, 2008).

Bourke, R., 'Liberty, Authority and Trust in Burke's Idea of Empire,' *Journal of the History of Ideas*, 61 (2000), 453–71.

Bourke, R., 'Edmund Burke and the Politics of Conquest,' *Modern Intellectual History*, 4 (2007), 403–32.

Braddick, Michael J., *State Formation in Early Modern England c.1550–1700* (Cambridge: Cambridge University Press, 2000).

Bradshaw, Brendan and Peter Roberts, (eds.) *British Consciousness and Identity: The Making of Britain, 1533–1707* (Cambridge: Cambridge University Press, 2003).

Bragg, Tom, 'Scott's Elementals: Vanishing Points between Space and Narrative in the Waverley Novels,' *Studies in the Novel*, 42 (2010), 205–26.

Brantlinger, Patrick, *The Spirit of Reform: British Literature and Politics, 1832–1867* (Cambridge: Harvard University Press, 1977).

Breisach, Ernst, *Historiography: Ancient, Medieval, and Modern* (Chicago: University of Chicago Press, 1994).

Broadie, Alexander, (ed.) *The Cambridge Companion to the Scottish Enlightenment* (Cambridge: Cambridge University Press, 2003).

Bromwich, David, *The Intellectual Life of Edmund Burke: From the Sublime and Beautiful to American Independence* (Cambridge MA: Belknap Press Harvard, 2014).

Bromwich, David, *Hazlitt: The Mind of a Critic* (NewYork: Oxford University Press, 1983).

Broomhall, Susan and David G. Barrie. 'Changing of the Guard: Governance, Policing, Masculinity, and Class in the Porteous Affair and Walter Scott's *Heart of Midlothian*,' *Parergon*, 28 (2011), 65–90.

Brown, David, *Walter Scott and the Historical Imagination* (London: Routledge & Kegan Paul, 1979).

Brown, Iain G., (ed.) *Abbotsford and Sir Walter Scott: The Image and the Influence* (Edinburgh: Society of Antiquaries of Scotland, 2003).

Brown, Ian, (ed.) *Literary Tourism, the Trossachs and Walter Scott* (Glasgow: Scottish Literature International, 2012a).

Brown, Ian, 'Literary Pilgrimage as Cultural imperialism and "Scott-land,"' *Literary Tourism, the Trossachs, and Walter Scott*, ed. Ian Brown (Glasgow: Scottish Literature International, 2012b), 1–28.

Browning, Reed, 'The Origin of Burke's Ideas Revisited,' *Eighteenth-Century Studies*, 18 (Autumn, 1984), 57–71.

Bulman, William J, 'The Practice of Politics: The English Civil War and the "Resolution" of Henrietta Maria and Charles I,' *Past & Present*, 206 (Feb 2010), 43–79.

Burghclere, Winifred, (ed.) *George Villiers, Second Duke of Buckingham, 1628–1687: A study in the history of the Restoration* (Whitefish: Kessinger Publishing, LLC, 2007).

Burgess, Miranda J., *British Fiction and the Production of Social Order, 1740–1830* (Cambridge: Cambridge University Press, 2000).

Burke, John J. Jr, 'The Homoerotic Subtext in Scott's *The Fortunes of Nigel*: The Question of Evidence,' *CLIO: A Journal of Literature, History, and the Philosophy of History*, 29 (2000), 295–323.

Burke, Edmund, 'A Proposed Address to the King,' *The Works of Edmund Burke Vol 5.* (Boston: Charles C. Little and James Brown, 1839), 132–49.

Burke, Edmund, *The Speeches of the Right Hon. Edmund Burke, with Memoir and Historical Introductions*, ed. James Burke (Dublin: James Duffy, 1854).

Burke, Edmund, 'Reflections on the Revolution in France,' *The Writings and Speeches of Edmund Burke, Volume VIII: The French Revolution, 1790–1794*, ed. L.G. Mitchell (1998; rpt Oxford: Oxford University Press, 2007).

Burns, J.H., (ed.) *Cambridge History of Political Thought, 1450–1700* (Cambridge: Cambridge University Press, 1991).

Burwick, Frederick, Nancy Moore Goslee, and Diane Long Hoeveler, (eds.) *The Encyclopedia of Romantic Literature* (Oxford: Wiley-Blackwell, 2012).

Burwick, Frederick, Nancy Moore Goslee, and Diane Long Hoeveler, 'Competing Histories in the Waverley Novels,' *European Romantic Review*, 13 (September 2002), 261–71.

Butler, Marianne, *Romantics, Rebels and Reactionaries: English Literature and its Background, 1760–1830* (Oxford: Oxford University Press, 1981).

Butterfield, Herbert. *The Whig Interpretation of History* (London: Bell, 1931).

Buzard, James, *Disorienting Fiction: The Autoethnographic Work of Nineteenth-Century British Novels* (Princeton: Princeton University Press, 2005).

Cain, T.G.S. and K. Robinson, (eds.) *Into Another Mould: Change and Continuity in English Culture, 1625–1700* (London and New York: Routledge, 1992).

Calder, Jenni, 'Figures in a Landscape: Scott, Stevenson and Routes to the Past,' *Robert Louis Stevenson: Writer of Boundaries*, ed. Richard Ambrosini and Richard Dury (Madison: University of Wisconsin Press, 2006), 121–32.

Calder, Angus and Jenni Calder, *Scott* (London: Evans Bros, 1969).

Callard, Felicity, 'Iris Marion Young,' *Key Thinkers on Space and Place* 2nd edn, ed. Phil Hubbard, Rob Kitchin and Gill Valentine (London: Sage, 2011), 483–90.

Carlton, Charles, *Charles I: The Personal Monarch* (London, Boston, Melbourne and Henley: Routledge & Kegan Paul, 1983).

Carruthers, Gerard and Liam McIlvanney, (eds.) *The Cambridge Companion to Scottish Literature* (Cambridge: Cambridge University Press, 2012).

Carson, James P., *Populism, Gender, and Sympathy in the Romantic Novel* (Basingstoke: New York: Palgrave Macmillan, 2010).

Case, Alison, 'Against Scott: The Antihistory of Dickens's *Barnaby Rudge*.' *CLIO: A Journal of Literature, History, and the Philosophy of History*, 19 (Winter 1990), 127–45.

Caserio, Robert L. and Clement Hawes, *The Cambridge History of the English Novel* (Cambridge: Cambridge University Press, 2012).

Casey, Edward S., *Representing Place: Landscape Painting and Maps* (Minnesota: University of Minnesota Press, 2002).

Casey, Edward S., *The Fate of Place: A Philosophical History* (Berkeley, Los Angeles and London: University of California Press, 1998).

Casey, Edward S., *Getting Back into Place: Toward a Renewed Understanding of the Place-World* (Bloomington: Indiana University Press, 1993).

Casey, Edward S., 'The World of Nostalgia,' *Man and World*, 20 (1987), 361–84.

Cassirer, Ernst, *The Myth of the State* (New Haven: Yale University Press, 1946).

Chandler, James, (ed.) *The Cambridge History of English Romantic Literature* (Cambridge: Cambridge University Press, 2009).

Chrimes, S.B., *English Constitutional History* (London, Oxford, New York: Oxford University Press, 1967).

Cieraad, Irene, (ed.) *At Home: An Anthropology of Domestic Space* (Syracuse: Syracuse University Press, 2006).

Clarke, Michelle T., 'The Mythologies of Contextualism: Method and Judgment in Skinner's *Visions of Politics,'Political Studies*, 61 (2013), 767–83.

Claybaugh, Amanda, *The Novel of Purpose: Literature and Social Reform in the Anglo–American World* (Ithaca and London: Cornell University Press, 2007).

Cockshut, A.O.J., *The Achievement of Sir Walter Scott* (London: Collins, 1969).

Cohen, Michael, 'Empowering the Sister: Female Rescue and Authorial Resistance in *The Heart of Midlothian,' College Literature*, 20 (June 1993), 58–69.

Colley, Linda, *Britons: Forging the Nation, 1707–1837* (New Haven: Yale University Press, 1992a).

Colley, Linda, 'Britishness and Europeanness: Who Are the British Anyway?' *Journal of British Studies*, 31 (Oct 1992b), 309–29.

Cook, John, *King Charles his Case* (London, 1649).

Cook, John, 'Journal of the Trial of King Charles I,' *A Complete Collection Of State-Trials And Proceedings For High-Treason And Other Crimes and Misdemeanours: Commencing With The Eleventh Year of the Reign of King Richard II. And Ending With The Sixteenth Year of the Reign of King George III. : With Two Alphabetical Tables To The Whole*, Vol 1 (London: J. Bathurst et al., 1776).

Cooper, Joan Garden, 'Scott's Critique of the English Treason Law in *Waverley,' Scottish Studies Review*, 4 (Autumn 2003), 17–36.

Corns, Thomas N., (ed.) *The Royal Image: Representations of Charles I* (Cambridge: Cambridge University Press, 1999).

Cosgrove, Denis, 'Prospect, Perspective and the Evolution of the Landscape Idea,' *Transactions of the Institute of British Geographers*, 10 (1985), 45–62.

Cottom, Daniel, 'Violence and Law in the Waverley Novels.' *Studies in Romanticism*, 1 (Spring 1981), 65–84.

Cottom, Daniel, *The Civilized Imagination: A Study of Ann Radcliffe, Jane Austen, and Sir Walter Scott* (Cambridge: Cambridge University Press, 1985).

Court, Franklin E., 'A Tale of Two Cities: Dickens, Revolution, and the "Other,"' *Victorian Newsletter*, 80 (Fall 1991), 14–8.

Cousins, A.D. *Andrew Marvell: Loss and Aspiration, Home and Homeland* (London; New York: Routledge, 2016).

Cousins, A.D. and Geoffrey Payne, (eds.) *Home and Nation in British Literature from the English to the French Revolutions* (Cambridge: Cambridge University Press, 2015).

Cousins, A.D. and Dani Napton, 'The Sexuality of James I in Scott's *The Fortunes of Nigel' The Explicator*, 68 (Jan–Mar 2010), 9–12.

Cousins, A.D., Dani Napton and Stephanie Russo, (eds.) *The French Revolution and the British Novel in the Romantic Period* (Peiterlen, Switzerland: Peter Lang, 2012).

Cousins, A.D. and Daniella E. Singer, 'Scott's "Character" of Buckingham in *Peveril of the Peak*, XXVIII: Dialogism, Speech/Writing and Law,' *Neophilologus*, 81 (July 1997), 649–57.

Coward, Barry, (ed.) *A Companion to Stuart Britain* (Oxford: Blackwell, 2003).

Coward, Barry, *The Stuart Age: A History of England, 1603–1714* (London and New York: Longman, 1980).

Craig, Cairns, 'Scott's Staging of the Nation,' *Studies in Romanticism*, 40 (2001), 13–28.

Craig, Cairns, *Out of History: Narrative Paradigms in Scottish and English Culture* (Edinburgh: Polygon, 1996).

Cramsie, John. 'The Philosophy of Imperial Kingship and the Interpretation of James IV and I,' *James VI and I: Ideas, Authority, and Government* ed. Ralph Anthony Houlbrooke (Hampshire and Burlington: Ashgate, 2006).

Crawford, Patricia, 'Charles Stuart, That Man of Blood,' *Journal of British Studies*, 16 (Spring 1977), 41–61.

Criscuola, Margaret M., 'Constancy and Change: The Process of History in Scott's *Redgauntlet*,' *Studies in Scottish Literature*, 20 (1985), 123–36.

Croker, John Wilson, 'Diary of the Times of George IV [by Lady Bury],' *The Quarterly Review*, 61, (January 1838), 150–64.

Cullen, Daniel, 'The Personal and the Political in Roger Scruton's Conservatism,' Perspectives on Political Science, 45, (2016), 261–71.

Cullinan, Mary, 'History and Language in Scott's *Redgauntlet*,' *SEL: Studies in English Literature, 1500–1900*, 18 (Autumn 1978), 659–75.

Daiches, David, 'Scott and Scotland,' *Scott: Bicentenary Essays*, ed. Alan Bell (Edinburgh and London: Scottish Academic Press, 1973), 38–60.

Dale, Tom, 'The Shaping of History: Scott's *Life of Napoleon Buonaparte*,' *Scott in Carnival*, ed. J.H. Alexander and David Hewitt (Aberdeen: Association for Scottish Literature Studies, 1993), 393–403.

Daleski, H.M., 'Narrating History in Scott and Dickens,' *Dickens Studies Annual: Essays on Victorian Fiction*, 32 (2002), 37–48.

Daniels, Stephen, 'Political Iconography of Woodland in Later Georgian England,' *The Iconography of Landscape: Essays on the Symbolic Representation, Design, and Use of Past Environments*, ed. Denis E. Cosgrove and Stephen Daniels (Cambridge (England) and New York: Cambridge University Press, 1988), 43–82.

D'Arcy, Julian Meldon, *Subversive Scott: The Waverley Novels and Scottish Nationalism* (Reykjavík: Stofnun Vigdísar Finnbogadóttur í erlendum tungumálum: Háskólaútgáfan, 2005).

D'Arcy, Julian Meldon, 'Roseneath: Scotland or "Scott-Land"? A Reappraisal of *The Heart of Midlothian*,' *Studies in Scottish Literature*, 32 (2001), 26–36.

Davidson, Neil, *The Origins of Scottish Nationhood* (London, Sterling VA: Pluto Press, 2000).

Davis, Leith, *Acts of Union: Scotland and the Literary Negotiation of the British Nation, 1707–1830* (Stanford, CA: Stanford University Press, 1996).

De Groot, Jerome, *The Historical Novel* (Abingdon: Routledge, 2010).

De Groot, H.B., 'History and Fiction: The Case of *Redgauntlet*,' *Scott in Carnival*, ed. J.H. Alexander and David Hewitt (Aberdeen: Association for Scottish Literature Studies, 1993), 358–69.

'Diary Illustrative of the Times of George IV,' *London Quarterly Review* CXXI (1838), 82–90.

Dick, Alexander, 'Scott and Political Economy,' *The Edinburgh Companion to Sir Walter Scott*, ed. Fiona Robertson (Edinburgh: Edinburgh University Press, 2012), 118–29.

Dickson, Beth, 'Sir Walter Scott and the Limits of Toleration,' *Scottish Literary Journal*, xviii (November 1991), 46–62.

Dolin, Kieran, 'Law, Literature and Symbolic Revolution: Bleak House,' *Australasian Victorian Studies Journal*, 12 (2007), 10–8.

Drake, George A., '"The Ordinary Rules of the Pave": Urban Spaces in Scott's *Fortunes of Nigel*,' *Studies in the Novel*, 33 (Winter 2001), 416–29.

Dryden, John, *Selected Poems* ed. Steven N. Zwicker and David Bywaters (London: Penguin, 2001).

Duncan, Ian, 'The Discovery of Scotland: Walter Scott and World Literature in the Age of Union,' *Scotland 2014 and Beyond: Coming of Age and Loss of Innocence?*, ed. Klaus Peter Müller (Frankfurt am Main: Peter Lang, 2015), 301–20.

Duncan, Ian, 'Late Scott,' *The Edinburgh Companion to Sir Walter Scott*, ed. Fiona Robertson (Edinburgh: Edinburgh University Press, 2012a), 130–42.

Duncan, Ian, 'Scott and the Historical Novel: A Scottish Rise of the Novel,' *The Cambridge Companion to Scottish Literature*, ed. Gerard Carruthers and Liam McIlvanney (Cambridge: Cambridge University Press, 2012b), 103–16.

Duncan, Ian, 'The Historical Novel,' *Charles Dickens in Context*, ed. Sally Ledger and Holly Furneaux (Cambridge: Cambridge University Press, 2011a), 158–65.

Duncan, Ian, 'Urban Space and Enlightened Romanticism,' *The Edinburgh Companion to Scottish Romanticism*, ed. Murray Pittock (Edinburgh: Edinburgh University Press, 2011b), 72–83.

Duncan, Ian, 'Edinburgh and Lowland Scotland,' *The Cambridge History of English Romantic Literature*, ed. James Chandler (Cambridge: Cambridge University Press, 2009), 159–81.

Duncan, Ian, 'Scotland and the Novel,' *The Cambridge Companion to Fiction in the Romantic Period*, ed. Richard Maxwell and Katie Trumpener (Cambridge: Cambridge University Press, 2008), 251–64.

Duncan, Ian, *Scott's Shadow: The Novel in Romantic Edinburgh* (Princeton; Oxford: Princeton University Press, 2007).

Duncan, Ian, *Modern Romance and Transformations of the Novel: The Gothic, Scott, Dickens* (Cambridge: Cambridge University Press, 1992).

Dunlop, Eileen, *Sir Walter Scott: A Life in Story* (Scotland: National Museums Scotland, 2016).

D'Urfey, Thomas, *Wit and Mirth: Or Pills to Purge Melancholy*, 6 vols, (first published 1719–20 by J. Tonson, London), prepared from a 1959 facsimile reprint by Folklorem Library Publishers, Inc., New York, of an 1876 reprint (no publisher). http://www.gutenberg.org/files/26679/26679-h/26679-h.htm#Page_139 (Accessed 20 Dec 2016).

Dwan, David and Christopher J. Insole, (eds.) *Cambridge Companion to Edmund Burke* (Cambridge: Cambridge University Press, 2012).

Eagleton, Mary and David Pierce, *Attitudes to Class in the English Novel: From Walter Scott to David Storey* (London: Thames & Hudson, 1979).

Eikon Basilike: The Portraiture of His Sacred Majesty in His Solitudes and Sufferings, ed. Philip A. Knachel (Ithaca: Cornell University Press, 1966).

Eikon Basilike with selections from Eikonklastes, ed. Jim Daems and Holly Faith Nelson (Peterborough, ON: Broadview Press, 2005).

Eagleton, Terry, *Ideology: An Introduction* (London and New York: Verso, 1991).

Elbers, Joan S., 'A Contrast of Fictional Worlds: *Redgauntlet* and *St Ronan's Well*,' *Scottish Literary Journal: A Review of Studies in Scottish Language and Literature*, 7 (1980), 155–66.

Everett, Nigel, *The Tory View of Landscape* (New Haven: Yale University Press, published for the Paul Mellon Centre for Studies in British Art, 1994).

Ewers, Chris, 'Roads as Regions, Networks and Flows: *Waverley* and the "Periphery" of Romance,' *Journal for Eighteenth-Century Studies*, 37 (2014), 97–112.

Faktorovich, Anna, *Rebellion as Genre in the Novels of Scott, Dickens and Stevenson* (Jefferson, NC: McFarland, 2013).

Farrell, John P., *Revolution as Tragedy: The Dilemma of the Moderate from Scott to Arnold* (Ithaca and London: Cornell University Press, 1980).

Ferguson, Stuart, 'The Imaginative Construction of Historical Character: What Georg Lukács and Walter Scott Could Tell Contemporary Novelists,' *Scottish Studies Review*, 6 (Autumn 2005), 32–48.

Ferris, Ina, 'From "National Tale" to "Historical Novel": Edgeworth, Morgan, and Scott,' *British Romanticism: Criticism and Debates*, ed. Mark Canuel (London: Routledge, 2015), 187–97.

Ferris, Ina, 'Transformations of the Novel—II,' *The Cambridge History of English Romantic Literature*, ed. James Chandler (Cambridge: Cambridge University Press, 2009), 473–89.

Ferris, Ina, 'The "Character" of James the First and Antiquarian Secret History' *Wordsworth Circle*, 37 (Spring 2006), 73–7.

Fielding, Penny, 'Curated Regions of the North: Art and Literature in the "Scottish Border" and the "Transpennine Corridor,"' *Visual Culture in Britain*, 15 (2014), 159–72.

Fielding, Penny, 'Usurpt by Cyclops: Rivers, Industry and Environment in Eighteenth-Century Poetry,' *Representing Place in British Literature and Culture, 1660–1830: From Local to Global*, ed. Evan Gottlieb and Juliet Shields (Aldershot: Ashgate, 2013a), 139–54.

Fielding, Penny, 'Scotland: Politics, Religion, Literature,' *Approaches to Teaching the Work of Robert Louis Stevenson*, ed. Caroline McCracken-Flesher (New York: MLA, 2013b), 34–40.

Fielding, Penny, 'Genre, Geography and the Question of the National Tale: P.D. Campbell's *Harley Radington*,' *European Romantic Review*, 23 (2012), 593–611.

Fielding, Penny, (ed.) *The Edinburgh Companion to Robert Louis Stevenson* (Edinburgh: Edinburgh University Press, 2010).

Fielding, Penny, *Scotland and the Fictions of Geography: North Britain, 1760–1830* (Cambridge: Cambridge University Press, 2008).

Fincham, K. and P. Lake, 'The Ecclesiastical Policies of James I and Charles I,' *Early Stuart Church 1603–1642*, ed. K. Fincham (Basingstoke: Macmillan, 1993), 23–49.

Fineberg, Stephen, 'From Improbus to Impius: Jefferson and Buckingham's Epitaph,' *Eighteenth-Century Studies*, 26 (Summer 1993), 595–605.

Firth, C.H., (ed.) *The Memoirs of Edmund Ludlow* (Oxford: Oxford University Press, 1894).

Firth, C.H., 'The Development of the Study of Seventeenth-Century History,' *Transactions of the Royal Historical Society*, 7 (1913), 25–48.

Fischer, Norman Arthur, 'The Modern Meaning of Georg Lukács' Reconstruction of Walter Scott's Novels of Premodern Political Ethics,' *Georg Lukács Reconsidered: Critical Essays in Politics, Philosophy and Aesthetics*, ed. Michael J. Thompson (London: Continuum, 2011), 128–50.

Fisher, P.F., 'Providence, Fate and the Historical Imagination in Scott's *The Heart of Midlothian,*' *Walter Scott: Modern Judgements,* ed. D.D. Devlin (London: Macmillan & Co, 1968), 98–111.

Fleishman, Avrom, *The English Historical Novel: Walter Scott to Virginia Woolf* (Baltimore and London: Johns Hopkins Press, 1971).

Ford, J.D., *Law and Opinion in Scotland during the Seventeenth Century* (Portland, Oregon: Hart Publishing, 2007).

Fradenburg, Louise Olga, *City, Marriage, Tournament: Arts of Rule in Late Medieval Scotland* (Madison: University of Wisconsin Press, 1991).

Fraser, Antonia, *King James I of England, VI of Scotland* (London: Weidenfeld & Nicolson, 1974).

Fraser, Antonia, *Cromwell, Our Chief of Men* (London: Weidenfeld & Nicolson, 1973).

Frey, Anne, 'Romantic Nationalism and the British State,' *European Romantic Review,* 23 (2012), 271–6.

Frey, Anne, *British State Romanticism: Authorship, Agency, and Bureaucratic Nationalism* (Stanford: Stanford University Press, 2009).

Gadamer, Hans-Georg, *Truth and Method,* trans. J. Weinsheimer and D.G. Marshall (London: Sheed & Ward, 1989).

Galaby, Huda A., 'Sir Walter Scott: A Supreme Purveyor of Scottish History and Society,' *International Journal of English and Education,* 4 (2015), 439–45. http://ijee.org/yahoo_site_admin/assets/docs/LT_7.36200745.pdf (Accessed 20 Dec 2016).

García Díaz, E, 'An Overview of Justice in Sir Walter Scott's Waverley Novels: *The Heart of Mid-Lothian,*' *Oñati Socio-legal Series,* 4 (2014), 1167–72.

Gardner, Marilyn, 'Inside Out: The House as Heart of *Barnaby Rudge,*' *Proceedings of the Philological Association of Louisiana* (1992), 53–60.

Garside, P.D., '*Redgauntlet* and the Topography of Progress,' *Southern Review: An Australian Journal of Literary Studies,* 10 (1977a), 155–73.

Garside, P.D., '*Waverley*'s Pictures of the Past,' *ELH,* 44 (Winter 1977b), 659–82.

Garside, Peter, 'Print illustrations and the cultural materialism of Scott's Waverley novels,' *Essays and Studies,* 66 (Annual 2013), 125–57.

Garside, Peter, 'Popular Fiction and National Tale: Hidden Origins of Scott's *Waverley,*' *Nineteenth-Century Fiction,* 46 (June 1991), 30–53.

Garside, Peter, 'The English Novel in the Romantic Period,' *The English Novel, 1770–1829: A Bibliographical Survey of Prose Fiction Published in the British Isles,* Vol 2 ed. Peter Garside, James Raven, and Rainer Schowerling (Oxford: Oxford University Press, 2000), 15–103.

Garside, Peter, James Raven and Rainer Schowerling, (eds.) *The English Novel 1770–1829: A Bibliographical Survey of Prose Fiction Published in the British Isles,* 2 vols, (Oxford: Oxford University Press, 2000).

Gaunt, Peter, *Oliver Cromwell* (Oxford and Massachusetts: Blackwell, 1996).

Gifford, Douglas, 'Scott's Legacy to Scottish Historical Fiction,' *The Bottle Imp*, 16 (2014). https://www.thebottleimp.org.uk/2014/11/scotts-legacy-to-scottish-historical -fiction (Accessed 20 Dec 2016).

Gordon, Robert C., *Under Which King?* (Edinburgh and London: Oliver & Boyd, 1969).

Gottlieb, Evan, *Romantic Realities: Speculative Realism and British Romanticism* (Edinburgh: Edinburgh University Press, 2016).

Gottlieb, Evan, *Romantic Globalism: British Literature and Modern World Order, 1750– 1830* (Columbus: Ohio State University Press, 2014).

Gottlieb, Evan, *Walter Scott and Contemporary Theory* (London: Bloomsbury Academic, 2013a).

Gottlieb, Evan, 'No Place Like Home: From Local to Global and Back Again in the Gothic Novel,' *Representing Place in British Literature and Culture, 1660–1830*, eds. Evan Gottlieb and Juliet Shields (Aldershot and Burlington: Ashgate, 2013b), 85–102.

Gottlieb, Evan, *Feeling British: Sympathy and National Identity in Scottish and English Writing, 1707–1832* (Lewisburg: Bucknell University Press, 2007).

Gottlieb, Evan, '"To be at Once Another and The Same": Walter Scott and the End(s) of Sympathetic Britishness,' *Studies in Romanticism*, 43 (Summer 2004), 187–207.

Gottlieb, Evan, 'Samuel Johnson and London,' *Home and Nation in British Literature from the English to the French Revolutions*, ed. A.D. Cousins and Geoffrey Payne (Cambridge: Cambridge University Press, 2015), 141–53.

Gottlieb, Evan, 'Scott, Walter (Prose),' *Encyclopedia of Romantic Literature*, vol. 3, ed. Frederick Burwick (Oxford and Malden, MA: Wiley-Blackwell, 2012), 1207–13.

Gottlieb, Evan and Juliet Shields, (eds.) *Representing Place in British Literature and Culture, 1660–1830: From Local to Global* (Aldershot and Bloomington, VT: Ashgate, 2013).

Graeber, Wilhelm, 'Nature and Landscape between Exoticism and National Areas of Imagination,' *Romantic Prose Fiction*, ed. Gerald Gillespie, Manfred Engel and Bernard Dieterle (Amsterdam, Netherlands: Benjamins, 2008), 90–106.

Grayling, A.C., *Towards the Light: The Story of the Struggles for Liberty and Rights That Made the Modern West* (London; New York; Berlin: Bloomsbury Publishing. 2007).

Greenblatt, Stephen, *The Norton Anthology of English Literature: The Romantic Period* (New York: W.W. Norton & Company, Inc. 2012).

Grotius, Hugo, *On the Law of War and Peace*, ed. Stephen C. Neff (Cambridge: Cambridge University Press, 2012).

Haakonssen, Knud, 'Natural jurisprudence and the theory of justice,' *The Cambridge Companion to the Scottish Enlightenment*, ed. Alexander Broadie (Cambridge: Cambridge University Press, 2003), 205–21.

Hallam, Henry, *Constitutional History of England* (1827).

Hamilton, Donna B. and Richard Strier, *Religion, Literature, and Politics in Post-Reformation England, 1540–1688* (Cambridge: Cambridge University Press, 2008).

Hamilton, Paul, '*Waverley*: Scott's Romantic Narrative and Revolutionary Historiography,' *Studies in Romanticism*, 33 (Winter 1994), 611–34.

Hampsher-Monk, Ian, 'Edmund Burke's Changing Justification for Intervention,' *The Historical Journal*, 48 (2005), 65–100.

Hannaford, Richard, 'Dumbiedikes, Ratcliffe, and a surprising Jeanie Deans: Comic Alternatives in *The Heart of Midlothian*,' *Studies in the Novel*, 30 (Spring 1998), 1–20.

Harris, Carolyn, *Queenship and Revolution in Early Modern Europe: Henrietta Maria and Marie Antoinette* (New York: Palgrave Macmillan, 2016).

Harris, Robin, *The Conservatives—A History* (London: Bantam, 2011).

Hart, Francis R., 'Scott's Endings: The Fictions of Authority,' *Nineteenth-Century Fiction*, 33 (June 1978), 48–68.

Hart, Francis R., *Scott's Novels: The Plotting of Historic Survival* (Charlottesville: University Press of Virginia, 1966).

Hart, Jenifer, 'Nineteenth-Century Social Reform: a Tory Interpretation of History,' *Past & Present*, 31 (1965), 39–61.

Harvie, Christopher, 'Scott and the Image of Scotland,' *Patriotism and the Making and Unmaking of British National Identity*, vol 2, ed. Raphael Samuel (New York: Routledge, 1989).

Hayden, John O., (ed.) *Scott: The Critical Heritage* (London: Routledge and Kegan Paul, 1970).

Head, Dominic, 'Novelistic complications of spaces and places: the four nations and regionalism,' *The Cambridge History of the English Novel*, ed. Robert L. Caserio and Clement Hawes (Cambridge: Cambridge University Press, 2012), 709–23.

Healy, Thomas and Jonathon Sawday, *Literature and the English Civil War* (Cambridge: Cambridge University Press, 1990).

Helgerson, Richard, 'Milton Reads the King's Book: Print, Performance, and the Making of a Bourgeois Idol,' *Criticism*, 29 (1987), 7–9.

Henry, Patrick Thomas, 'Sir Walter Scott and the Transgression of Anachronistic Borders: The Ideological Fantasy of Westphalian Sovereignty in The Talisman,' *European Romantic Review*, 28 (2017), 203–225.

Hewitt, David, '*Rob Roy*: Trade, Improvement and the Destruction of "Native" Culture,' *Literary Tourism, the Trossachs, and Walter Scott*, ed. Ian Brown (Glasgow: Scottish Literature International, 2012), 85–97.

Hewitt, David, '*The Heart of Mid-Lothian* and "the People,"' *European Romantic Review*, 13 (September 2002), 299–309.

Hewitt, David, *Walter Scott: The History of Scottish Literature*, vol. 3, ed. Cairns Craig (Aberdeen: Aberdeen University Press, 1988).

Hewitt, David, (ed.) *Scott on Himself: A Selection of the Autobiographical Writings of Sir Walter Scott* (Edinburgh: Association for Scottish Literature Studies, 1981).

Hill, Christopher, *The World Turned Upside Down: Radical Ideas During The English Revolution* (London: Penguin, 1991).

Hill, Christopher, *The Century of Revolution, 1603–1714* (London: Thomas Nelson & Sons, 1961).

Hilton, Boyd, *A Mad, Bad, & Dangerous People? England, 1783–1846* (Oxford: Oxford University Press, 2006).

Hoffmeister, Gerhart, 'The French Revolution and Prose Fiction: Allegorization of History and Its Defeat by Romance,' *Romantic Prose Fiction*, ed. Gerald Gillespie, Manfred Engel and Bernard Dieterle (Amsterdam, Netherlands: Benjamins, 2008), 1–21.

Holman, C. Hugh, '*Nigel* and the Historical Imagination,' *The Classic British Novel*, ed. Howard M. Harper, Jr. and Charles Edge (Athens: University of Georgia Press, 1972), 65–84.

Houlbrooke, Ralph, (ed.) *James VI and I: Ideas, Authority, and Government* (Aldershot and Burlington: Ashgate Publishing Company, 2006).

Hubbard, Phil, Rob Kitchin and Gill Valentine, (eds.) *Key Thinkers on Space and Place* 2nd edn (London: Sage, 2011).

Hume, David, *A Treatise of Human Nature*, ed. Ernest C. Mossner (Harmondsworth: Penguin, 1984).

Hutton, Ronald, *The British Republic, 1640–1660* 2nd edn (New York: St Martin's Press, 2000).

Hutton, Ronald, *Charles II: King of England, Scotland and Ireland* (Oxford: Oxford University Press, 1989).

Hutton, Ronald, *The Restoration, 1658–1667: A Political History of England and Wales* (Oxford: Oxford University Press, 1985).

Hyde, William J., 'Jeanie Deans and the Queen: Appearance and Reality,' *Nineteenth-Century Fiction*, 28 (June 1973), 86–92.

Jackson-Houlston, C.M., *Gendering Walter Scott: Sex, Violence and Romantic Period Writing* (New York and Oxon: Routledge, 2017).

Jager, Colin, *Unquiet Things: Secularism in the Romantic Age* (Philadelphia, PA: University of Pennsylvania Press, 2015).

James, David, 'Spaces and Places (II): Around the Globe,' *The Cambridge History of the English Novel*, ed. Robert L. Caserio and Clement Hawes (Cambridge: Cambridge University Press, 2012), 500–16.

Jarrells, Anthony, *Britain's Bloodless Revolutions: 1688 and the Romantic Reform of Literature* (Basingstoke and New York: Palgrave Macmillan, 2005).

Jeffares, A. Norman, (ed.) *Scott's Mind and Art* (Edinburgh: Oliver & Boyd, 1969).

Johnson, Edgar, 'Scott and the Corners of Time,' *Scott: Bicentenary Essays*, ed. Alan Bell (Edinburgh and London: Scottish Academic Press, 1973), 18–37.

Johnson, Edgar, *Sir Walter Scott: The Great Unknown*, 2 vols. (London: Hamish Hamilton, 1970).

Johnson, Samuel, 'The King of Prussia 1756,' *The Works of Samuel Johnson, LL. D.: Lives of the poets*, ed. Arthur Murphy (New York: George Dearborn, 1837), 363.

Johnson, Samuel, *The Rambler*, vol 3, ed. Alex Chalmers (Philadelphia: J.J. Woodwards, 1827).

Jones, Catherine, 'History and Historiography,' *The Edinburgh Companion to Sir Walter Scott*, ed. Fiona Robertson (Edinburgh: Edinburgh University Press, 2012), 59–69.

Jones, J.R., *Liberty Secured? Britain Before and After 1688* (Stanford: Stanford University Press, 1992).

Kalmo, Hent and Quentin Skinner, *Sovereignty in Fragments: The Past, Present and Future of a Contested Concept* (Cambridge: Cambridge University Press, 2010).

Kantorowicz, Ernst Hartwig, *The King's Two Bodies: A Study in Mediaeval Political Theology* (Princeton: Princeton University Press, 1957).

Keeble, N.H., *Literary Culture of Nonconformity in Later Seventeenth-Century England*. (Athens: University of Georgia, 1987).

Keith, Christina, *The Author of Waverley: A Study in the Personality of Sir Walter Scott* (New York: Roy Publishers, 1964).

Kelly, Gary, 'Fiction and the Working Class,' *The Cambridge Companion to Fiction in the Romantic Period*, ed. Richard Maxwell and Katie Trumpener (Cambridge: Cambridge University Press, 2008), 207–34.

Kelly, Gary, *English Fiction of the Romantic Period, 1789–1830*, Longman Literature in English Series (Harlow: Longman, 1989).

Kelly, Stuart, *Scott-Land: The Man Who Invented a Nation* (Edinburgh: Polygon, 2010).

Kelsey, Sean, 'The Trial of Charles I.' *English Historical Review*, 118 (2003), 585–616.

Kelsey, Sean, 'The Death of Charles I,' Historical Journal, 45 (2002), 727–54.

Kelsey, Sean, *Inventing a Republic: The Political Culture of the English Commonwealth, 1649–1653* (Stanford: Stanford University Press, 1997).

Kenyon, J.P., *The Popish Plot* (London: Pelican, 1974).

Kerr, James, *Fiction Against History: Scott as Storyteller* (Cambridge: Cambridge University Press, 1989).

Kerr, James, 'Scott's Fable of Regeneration: *The Heart of Midlothian*,' *ELH*, 53 (Winter 1986), 801–20.

Kipp, Julie, 'Back to the Future: Walter Scott on the Politics of Radical Reform in Ireland and Scotland,' *European Romantic Review*, 16 (2005), 231–42.

Kirk, Russell, *The Conservative Mind: From Burke to Eliot* (7th rev ed) (Washington: Regnery, 1985).

Knoppers, Laura Lunger, (ed.) *Oxford Handbook of Literature and the English Revolution* (Oxford: Oxford University Press, 2012).

Knoppers, Laura Lunger, *Politicizing Domesticity from Henrietta Maria to Milton's Eve* (Cambridge: Cambridge University Press, 2011).

Knoppers, Laura Lunger, *Constructing Cromwell: Ceremony, Portrait, and Print, 1645–1661* (Cambridge: Cambridge University Press, 2000).

Knoppers, Laura Lunger, *Historicizing Milton: Spectacle, Power, and Poetry in Restoration England* (Athens: University of Georgia Press, 1994).

Koelb, Janice Hewlett, *The Poetics of Description: Imagined Places in European Literature* (New York: Palgrave Macmillan, 2006).

Kroeber, Karl, *Romantic Narrative Art* (Madison: University of Wisconsin Press, 1960).

Kroll, Richard, *The Material Word: Literate Culture in the Restoration and Early Eighteenth Century* (Baltimore and London: Johns Hopkins Press, 1991).

Lacey, Andrew, *The Cult of King Charles the Martyr* (Woodbridge: Boydell & Brewer, 2003).

Lackey, Lionel, '"Nigel" and "Peveril": Scott and Gender Roles,' *English Language Notes*, 37 (2000), 36–46.

Lamb, Robert, 'Historicism,' *Routledge Handbook of Interpretive Political Science* ed. Mark Bevir and R.A.W. Rhodes Routledge Handbook of Interpretive Political Science (Abingdon, Oxon: Routledge, 2016), 72–85.

Lamb, Robert, 'Quentin Skinner's Revised Historical Contextualism: A Critique,' *History of the Human Sciences*, 22 (June 2009), 51–73.

Lamont, Claire, 'The Stereotype Scot and the Idea of Britain,' *Beyond Pug's Tour: National and Ethnic Stereotyping in Theory and Literary Practice* (Amsterdam and Atlanta: Rodopi, 1997), 330–50.

Lamont, Claire, 'The Discovery of the Borders: Sir Walter Scott,' *Borders Book*, ed. Donald Omand (Edinburgh: Birlinn, 1995) 147–59.

Lamont, Claire, '*Waverley* and the Battle of Culloden,' *History and the Novel*, ed. Angus Easson (Cambridge: D.S. Brewer, 1991), 14–26.

Lansdown, Richard, *A New Scene of Thought, Studies in Romantic Realism* (Leiden; Boston: Brill, 2016).

Lascelles, Mary, *The Story-teller Retrieves the Past: Historical Fiction and Fictitious History in the Art of Scott, Stevenson, Kipling, and Some Others* (Oxford: Clarendon Press, 1980).

Lauber, John, *Sir Walter Scott* (Boston: Twayne Publishers, 1989).

Ledger, Sally, 'From Queen Caroline to Lady Dedlock: Dickens and the Popular Radical Imagination,' *Victorian Literature and Culture*, 32 (September 2004), 575–600.

Lee, Maurice, *England's Solomon: James VI and I in his Three Kingdoms* (Urbana: University of Illinois Press, 1990).

Lee, Maurice Jr, 'James I and the Historians: Not a Bad King after All?,' *Albion: A Quarterly Journal Concerned with British Studies*, 16 (Summer 1984), 151–63.

Lee, Yoon Sun, *Nationalism and Irony: Burke, Scott, Carlyle* (Oxford: Oxford University Press, 2004).

Lee, Yoon Sun, 'Time, Money, Sanctuary, and Sociality in Scott's *The Fortunes of Nigel*,' *European Romantic Review*, 14 (June 2003), 233–8.

Lee, Yoon Sun, 'Giants in the North: Douglas, the Scottish Enlightenment, and Scott's *Redgauntlet*,' *Studies in Romanticism*, 40 (Spring 2001), 109–21.

Levy, Lindsay, 'Magic, Mind Control, and the Body Electric: "Materia Medica" in Sir Walter Scott's Library at Abbotsford,' *Scottish Medicine and Literary Culture, 1726–1832*, ed. Megan J. Coyer and David E. Shuttleton (Amsterdam; New York: Rodopi, 2014), 216–39.

Lincoln, Andrew, *Walter Scott and Modernity* (Edinburgh: Edinburgh University Press, 2007).

Lincoln, Andrew, 'Conciliation, Resistance and the Unspeakable in *The Heart of Mid-Lothian*,' *Philological Quarterly*, 79 (Winter 2000), 69–90.

Lockhart, John Gibson, *Life of Sir Walter Scott, Bart* (Edinburgh: Adam and Charles Black, 1853). https://archive.org/details/memoirslifesirw85lockgoog (Accessed 20 Dec 2016).

Lockyer, Roger, *The Early Stuarts: A Political History of England, 1603–1642* 2nd edn (London: Longman, 1999).

Lockyer, Roger, *Buckingham: The Life and Political Career of George Villiers, First Duke of Buckingham, 1592–1628* (London: Longman, 1981).

London, April, *The Cambridge Introduction to the Eighteenth-Century Novel* (Cambridge: Cambridge University Press, 2012).

Love, Harold, 'Fixity versus Flexibility in "A Song on Tom of Danby" and Dryden's *Absalom and Achitophel*,' *Agent of Change: Print Culture Studies after Elizabeth L. Eisenstein*, ed. Sabrina Alcorn Baron, Eric N. Lindquist, and Eleanor F. Shevlin (Amherst: University of Massachusetts Publishers, 2007).

Low, Setha M. and Denise Lawrence-Zunigais, *The Anthropology of Space and Place: Locating Culture* (Cambridge: Blackwell, 2003).

Lukács, Georg, *The Historical Novel* (London: Merlin Press, 1989).

Lumsden, Alison, *Walter Scott and the Limits of Language* (Edinburgh: Edinburgh University Press, 2010a).

Lumsden, Alison, 'Stevenson, Scott and Scottish History,' *The Edinburgh Companion to Robert Louis Stevenson, Edinburgh Companions to Scottish Literature*, ed. Penny Fielding (Edinburgh: Edinburgh University Press, 2010b), 70–85.

Lumsden, Alison, '"To Get Leave to Live": Negotiating Regional Identity in the Literature of North-east Scotland,' *Edinburgh History of Scottish Literature, vol 3: Modern Transformations—New Identities (from 1918)*, ed. I. Brown, T.O. Clancy, S. Manning and M.G.H. Pittock (Edinburgh: Edinburgh University Press, 2006), 95–105.

Lumsden, Alison, 'Walter Scott,' *The Cambridge Companion to English Novelists*, ed. Adrian Poole (Cambridge: Cambridge University Press, 2009), 116–31.

Lumsden, Alison, 'Burns, Scott and Intertextuality,' *The Edinburgh Companion to Robert Burns*. Edinburgh Companions to Scottish Literature. ed. G. Carruthers (Edinburgh: Edinburgh University Press, 2009), 125–36.

Lumsden, Alison, '"Beyond the Dusky Barrier": Perceptions of the Highlands in the Waverley Novels,' *Mìorun mòr nan Gall, 'The great ill-will of the Lowlander'?: Lowland perceptions of the Highlands, medieval and modern*, ed. Dauvit Broun and Martin MacGregor (Glasgow: University of Glasgow, Centre for Scottish and Celtic Studies, 2007), 158–86.

Lynch, Deidre, 'Transformations of the Novel—I,' *The Cambridge History of English Romantic Literature*, ed. James Chandler (Cambridge: Cambridge University Press, 2009), 451–72.

Macaulay, Thomas Babington, *Critical, Historical, and Miscellaneous Essays and Poems*, Vol 1 (Boston: Estes and Lauriat, 1880).

Macaulay, Thomas Babington, *The History of England from the Accession of James II*, ed. C.H. Firth (in six volumes) (London: Macmillan and Co., 1914).

MacDonald, Murdo, 'Rethinking Scott, his Literary Predecessors and the Imagery of the Highlands,' *Literary Tourism, the Trossachs, and Walter Scott*, ed. Ian Brown (Glasgow: Scottish Literature International, 2012), 124–32.

MacIntyre, Jean, 'Buckingham the Masquer,' *Renaissance and Reformation/Renaissance et Réforme*, 22 (Summer 1998), 59–81.

Mack, Douglas S., *Scottish Fiction and the British Empire* (Edinburgh: Edinburgh University Press, 2006).

Mack, Douglas S., 'Culloden and After: Scottish Jacobite Novels,' *Eighteenth-Century Life*, 20 (November 1996), 92–106.

Macrae, Lucy, 'Local Explanations: Editing a Sense of Place in Walter Scott's *Minstrelsy of the Scottish Border*,' *Forum*, Special Issue 03 (Winter 2014). http://www.forumjournal.org/article/view/690 (Accessed 20 Dec 2016).

Mahtani, Minelle, 'David Sibley,' *Key Thinkers on Space and Place* 2nd edn, ed. Phil Hubbard, Rob Kitchin and Gill Valentine (London: Sage, 2011), 367–73.

Maitzen, Rohan, '"By No Means an Improbable Fiction": *Redgauntlet*'s Novel Historicism,' *Studies in the Novel*, 25 (Summer 1993), 170–83.

Makdisi, Saree, 'Romantic cultural imperialism,' *The Cambridge History of English Romantic Literature*, ed. James Chandler (Cambridge: Cambridge University Press, 2009), 601–20.

Makdisi, Saree, 'Colonial Space and the Colonisation of Time in Scott's *Waverley*,' *Studies in Romanticism*, 34 (Summer 1995), 155–87.

Mali, Joseph, *Mythistory: The Making of a Modern Historiography* (Chicago: University of Chicago Press, 2003).

Malpas, J., *Heidegger's Topology: Being, Place, World* (Cambridge: MIT Press, 2007).

Malpas, J., *Place and Experience: A Philosophical Topography* (Cambridge: Cambridge University Press, 1999).

Marsh, Jeffrey E., 'Sympathy, Property, and Countenances: Historicising Scott's Reader in the Face of Capitalism,' *Scott in Carnival*, ed. J.H. Alexander and David Hewitt (Aberdeen: Association for Scottish Literature Studies, 1993), 54–70.

Marshall, George, 'Scott and the Reformation of Religion,' *The Edinburgh Companion to Sir Walter Scott*, ed. Fiona Robertson (Edinburgh: Edinburgh University Press, 2012), 82–92.

Maxwell, Richard, *The Historical Novel in Europe, 1650–1950* (Cambridge: Cambridge University Press, 2009).

Maxwell, Richard, 'The Historical Novel,' *The Cambridge Companion to Fiction in the Romantic Period*, ed. Richard Maxwell and Katie Trumpener (Cambridge: Cambridge University Press, 2008a), 55–88.

Maxwell, Richard, 'The Historiography of Fiction in the Romantic Period,' *The Cambridge Companion to Fiction in the Romantic Period*, ed. Richard Maxwell and Katie Trumpener (Cambridge: Cambridge University Press, 2008b), 7–22.

Maxwell, Richard, 'Pretenders in Sanctuary,' *Modern Language Quarterly*, 61 (June 2000), 287–358.

Maxwell, Richard and Katie Trumpener, *The Cambridge Companion to Fiction in the Romantic Period* (Cambridge: Cambridge University Press, 2008).

Mayhead, Robin, '*The Heart of Midlothian*: Scott as Artist,' *Walter Scott: Modern Judgements*, ed. D.D. Devlin (London: Macmillan & Co, 1968), 112–21.

Mayr, Ernst. 'When is Historiography Whiggish?,' *Journal of the History of Ideas*, 51 (1990), 301–9.

Mazlish, Bruce, 'The Conservative Revolution of Edmund Burke,' *The Review of Politics*, 20 (1958), 21–3.

McClelland, John Scott, *History of Western Political Thought* (London and New York: Routledge, 1996).

McCormack, Matthew, *The Independent Man: Citizenship and Gender Politics in Georgian England* (New York: Manchester University Press, 2005).

McCracken-Flesher, Caroline, 'Future Scotts: The Aliens Have Landed,' *The Bottle Imp*, 16 (2014) https://www.thebottleimp.org.uk/2014/11/future-scotts-the-aliens-have-landed/ (Accessed 20 Dec 2016).

McCracken-Flesher, Caroline, 'Scott's Jacobitical Plots,' *The Edinburgh Companion to Sir Walter Scott,* ed. Fiona Robertson (Edinburgh: Edinburgh University Press, 2012), 47–58.

McCracken-Flesher, Caroline, 'Walter Scott's Romanticism: A Theory of Performance,' *The Edinburgh Companion to Scottish Romanticism*, ed. Murray Pittock (Edinburgh: Edinburgh University Press, 2011), 139–49.

McCracken-Flesher, Caroline, *Possible Scotlands: Walter Scott and the Story of Tomorrow* (Oxford: Oxford University Press, 2005).

McCracken-Flesher, Caroline, 'Narrating the (Gendered) Nation in Walter Scott's *The Heart of Midlothian*,' *Nineteenth-Century Contexts*, 24 (September 2002), 291–316.

McFarland, Thomas, *Romanticism and the Form of Ruin: Wordsworth, Coleridge and Modalities of Fragmentation* (Princeton: Princeton University Press, 1981).

McLaren, Moray, *Sir Walter Scott: The Man and Patriot* (London: Heinemann, 1970).

McMahon, Darrin M., *Divine Fury: A History of Genius* (New York: Basic Books (Perseus Books Group), 2013).

McMaster, Graham, *Scott and Society* (Cambridge: Cambridge University Press, 1981).

Melrose, Andrew, 'Writing "The End of Uncertainty": Imaginary Law, Imaginary Jacobites and Imaginary History in Walter Scott's *Heart of Midlothian* and *Redgauntlet*,' *Scottish Literary Journal*, 25 (November 1998), 34–44.

Millgate, Jane, 'Scott and the Law: *The Heart of Midlothian*,' *Rough Justice: Essays on Crime in Literature*, ed. M.L. Friedland (Toronto: University of Toronto, 1991), 95–113.

Millgate, Jane, *Walter Scott: The Making of the Novelist* (Toronto: University of Toronto, 1984).

Milton, John, *Complete Poems and Major Prose*, ed. Merrit Y. Hughes (1957; rpt. Indianapolis: Hackett, 2003).

Milton, John, *The Poems*, ed. John Carey and Alastair Fowler (London: Longmans, 1968).

Mockaitis, Thomas R., 'Sir Walter Scott and the Problem of Revolutions,' *Scott in Carnival*, ed. J.H. Alexander and David Hewitt (Aberdeen: Association for Scottish Literature Studies, 1993), 419–33.

Monad, Paul Kleber, *Jacobitism and the English People, 1688–1788* (Cambridge: Cambridge University Press, 1993).

Monk, Leland, 'The Novel as Prison: Scott's *The Heart of Midlothian*,' *NOVEL: A Forum on Fiction*, 27 (Spring 1994), 287–303.

Monnickendam, Andrew, *The Novels of Walter Scott and his Literary Relations: Mary Brunton, Susan Ferrier, and Christian Johnstone* (Basingstoke; New York: Palgrave Macmillan, 2012).

Montague, F.C., *The Political History of England from the Accession of James I To The Restoration (1603–1660)* ed. William Hunt and Reginald Lane Poole (London: Longmans, Green and Co., 1907).

Mornin, Edward, 'Bonnie Charlie's now awa'...: Charles Edward Stuart after the '45: On the Uses of History in Fiction,' *Forum for Modern Language Studies*, 24 (April 1988), 97–110.

Mornin, Karen M., 'Edward W Said,' *Key Thinkers on Space and Place* 2nd edn, ed. Phil Hubbard, Rob Kitchin and Gill Valentine (London: Sage, 2011), 337–44.

Murray, Molly, *The Poetics of Conversion in Early Modern English Literature: Verse and Change from Donne to Dryden* (Cambridge: Cambridge University Press, 2009).

Napton, Dani, 'Sir Walter Scott: Home, Nation, and the Denial of Revolution,' *Home and Nation in British Literature from the English to the French Revolutions*, ed. A.D. Cousins and Geoffrey Payne (Cambridge: Cambridge University Press, 2015), 250–65.

Napton, Dani, 'Revolutionary and Counter-Revolutionary Agency in Scott's *Woodstock* and *Peveril of the Peak*,' *The French Revolution and the British Novel in the Romantic Period*, ed. A.D. Cousins, Dani Napton and Stephanie Russo (Peiterlen, Switzerland: Peter Lang, 2012), 113–36.

Napton, Dani, 'A Confined Place: The Political Significance of Locale and Language in *Woodstock*,' *AUMLA: Journal of the Australasian Universities Language and Literature Association*, 114 (2010), 23–38.

Napton, Dani and Stephanie Russo, 'Place in Charlotte Smith's *The Banished Man* and Walter Scott's *Woodstock*,' *SEL: Studies in English Literature, 1500–1900*, 52 (2012), 747–63.

Newman, Beth, '*The Heart of Midlothian* and the Masculinization of Fiction,' *Criticism: A Quarterly for Literature and the Arts*, 36 (Fall 1994), 521–41.

Nicol Smith, David, *Characters from the Histories and Memoirs of the Seventeenth Century* (Oxford: Clarendon Press, 1918).

Norbrook, David, *Writing the English Revolution: Poetry, Rhetoric and Politics 1627–1660* (Cambridge: Cambridge University Press, 1999).

Nord, Deborah Epstein, 'Spaces and Places (I): The Four Nations,' *The Cambridge History of the English Novel*, ed. Robert L. Caserio and Clement Hawes (Cambridge: Cambridge University Press, 2012), 325–40.

Oberhelman, David, '*Waverley*, Genealogy, History: Scott's Romance of Fathers and Sons,' *Nineteenth-Century Contexts*, 15 (1991), 29–47.

Oliver, Susan, 'Walter Scott and the Matter of Landscape: Ecologies of Violence for our Time,' *The Bottle Imp*, 16 (2014). https://www.thebottleimp.org.uk/2014/11/walter-scott-and-the-matter-of-landscape-ecologies-of-violence-for-our-time/ (Accessed 20 Dec 2016).

Ollard, Richard, *The Image of the King: Charles I and II* (New York: Atheneum, 1979).

Olwig, Kenneth R., 'Landscape of "Customary" Law versus that of Natural Law,' *Justice, Power and the Political Landscape: From American Space to the European Landscape*, ed. Kenneth R., Olwig and Donald Mitchell (London and New York: Routledge, 2009), 11–32.

Olwig, Kenneth R., *Landscape, Nature, and the Body Politic: From Britain's Renaissance to America's New World* (Madison: University of Wisconsin Press, 2002).

Olwig, Kenneth R., 'Landscape as a Contested Topos of Place, Community and Self,' *Textures of Place*, ed. Steven Hoelscher, Paul Adams and Karen Till (Minneapolis: University of Minneapolis Press, 2001).

Orel, Harold, *The Historical Novel from Scott to Sabatini: Changing Attitudes toward a Literary Genre, 1814–1920* (Basingstoke, London: Macmillan Press, 1995).

Orr, Marilyn, '"Almost Under the Immediate Eye": Framing Displacement,' *Scott in Carnival*, ed. J.H. Alexander and David Hewitt (Aberdeen: Association for Scottish Literature Studies, 1993), 60–71.

Ortiz-Robles, Mario, 'Local Speech, Global Acts: Performative Violence and the Novelization of the World,' *Comparative Literature*, 59 (Winter 2007), 1–22.

Palonen, Kari, *Quentin Skinner: History, Politics, Rhetoric* (Cambridge: Polity, 2003).

Palonen, Kari, 'The History of Concepts as a Style of Political Theorizing: Quentin Skinner's and Reinhart Koselleck's Subversion of Normative Political Theory,' *European Journal of Political Theory*, 1 (2002), 91–106.

Parrinder, Patrick, *Nation and Novel: The English Novel from its Origins to the Present Day* (Oxford: Oxford University Press, 2006).

Peacocke, Emma, 'Facing History: Galleries and Portraits in *Waverley*'s Historiography,' *Romanticism and the Museum* (Basingstoke; New York: Palgrave Macmillan, 2015), 57–86.

Perkins, David, (ed.) *Theoretical Issues in Literary History*, Harvard English Studies. (Cambridge: Harvard University Press, 1991).

Perreau-Saussine, Emile, 'Quentin Skinner in Context,' *The Review of Politics*, 69 (2007), 106–22.

Pittlock, Malcolm, 'Peebles v. Plainstanes: Jarndyce v. Jarndyce: Scott v. Dickens,' *Neophilologus*, 85 (July 2001), 457–75.

Pittock, Murray, 'Sir Walter Scott: Historiography Contested by Fiction,' *The Cambridge History of the English Novel*, ed. Robert L. Caserio and Clement Hawes (Cambridge: Cambridge University Press, 2012a), 277–91.

Pittock, Murray, 'Enlightenment, Romanticism and the Scottish Canon: Cosmopolites or Narrow Nationalists,' *The Cambridge Companion to Scottish Literature*, ed. Gerard Carruthers and Liam McIlvanney (Cambridge: Cambridge University Press, 2012b), 86–102.

Pittock, Murray, (ed.) *The Edinburgh Companion to Scottish Romanticism* (Edinburgh: Edinburgh University Press, 2011).

Pittock, Murray, *The Invention of Scotland: The Stuart Myth and the Scottish Identity, 1638 to the Present* (London: Routledge, 1991).

Pocock, J.G.A., 'Edmund Burke and the Redefinition of Enthusiasm: the Context as Counter-Revolution,' *The French Revolution and the Creation of Modern Political Culture, Vol III: The Transformation of Political Culture 1789–1848* ed. F. Furet and M. Ozouf (Oxford, Pergamon, 1990), 19–43.

Pocock, J.G.A., 'The Political Economy of Burke's Analysis of the French Revolution,' *Virtue, Commerce and History: Essays on Political Thought and History, Chiefly in the Eighteenth Century* (Cambridge: Cambridge University Press, 1985), 193–212.

Pocock, J.G.A., 'Burke and the Ancient Constitution: A Problem in the History of Ideas,' Historical Journal, 3 (1960), 125–43.

Pocock, J.G.A., 'Quentin Skinner: The History of Politics and the Politics of History,' *Common Knowledge*, 10 (2004), 532–50.

Poole, Adrian, (ed.) *The Cambridge Companion to English Novelists* (Cambridge: Cambridge University Press, 2009).

Praz, Mario, *The Hero in Eclipse in Victorian Fiction* (London: Oxford University Press, 1956).

Prebble, John, *The King's Jaunt: George IV in Scotland, August 1822* (London 1988).

Pardoe, James, 'Aura and authenticity and the presentation of UK literary figures through the medium of the home,' *Scrutiny2*, 20 (2015), 65–79.

Rachum, Ilan, 'The Meaning of "Revolution" in the English Revolution (1648–1660),' *Journal of the History of Ideas*, 56 (April 1995), 195–215.

Rangarajan, Padma, 'History's Rank Stew: Walter Scott, James Mill, and the Politics of Time,' *Romanticism*, 21 (2015), 59–71.

Raven, James, 'The Anonymous Novel in Britain and Ireland, 1750–1830,' *Faces of Anonymity: Anonymous and Pseudonymous Publications from the Sixteenth to the Nineteenth Century* ed. Robert J. Griffin (New York: Palgrave Macmillan, 2003), 141–66.

Reed, James, *Sir Walter Scott: Landscape and Locality* (London: Athlone Press, 1980).

Reed, Walter L., *Meditations on the Hero: A Study of the Romantic Hero in Nineteenth Century Fiction* (New Haven and London: Yale University Press, 1974).

Reed Doob, Penelope, *The Idea of the Labyrinth: From Classical Antiquity Through the Middle Ages* (Ithaca and London: Cornell University Press, 1990).

Rezek, Joseph, 'Cooper and Scott in the Anglophone Literary Field: *The Pioneers*, *The Heart of Mid-Lothian*, and the Effects of Provinciality,' *ELH*, 78 (2011), 891–916.

Rigney, Ann, *The Afterlives of Walter Scott: Memory on the Move* (Oxford: Oxford University Press, 2012).

Rigney, Ann, *The Rhetoric of Historical Representation: Three Narrative Histories of the French Revolution* (Cambridge England and New York: Cambridge University Press: 2003).

Rigney, Ann, *Imperfect Histories: The Elusive Past and the Legacy of Romantic Historicism* (Ithaca and London: Cornell University Press, 2001).

Rigney, Ann, 'Portable Monuments: Literature, Cultural Memory, and the Case of Jeanie Deans,' *Poetics Today*, 25 (Summer 2004), 361–96.

Robertson, David, *The Penguin Dictionary of Politics* (London: Penguin, 1987).

Robertson, Fiona, 'Disfigurement and Disability: Walter Scott's Bodies,' *Otranto*, 003 (2013). http://www.otranto.co.uk/index.php/publication/view/54 (Accessed 20 Dec 2016).

Robertson, Fiona, (ed.) *The Edinburgh Companion to Sir Walter Scott* (Edinburgh: Edinburgh University Press, 2012).

Robertson, Fiona, 'Historical Fiction and the Fractured Atlantic,' *Rethinking Romantic History, 1770–1845*, ed. Porsha Femanis and John Regan (Oxford: Oxford University Press, 2014a). 247–70.

Robertson, Fiona, 'Walter Scott and the American Historical Novel,' *American Novels to 1870*, ed. J. Gerald Kennedy and Leland Person (Oxford: Oxford University Press, 2014b), 107–23.

Robertson, Fiona, 'Walter Scott,' *The Edinburgh History of Scottish Literature*, ed. Susan Manning (Edinburgh: Edinburgh University Press, 2007), 183–90.

Robertson, Fiona, 'Romance and the Romantic Novel: Sir Walter Scott,' *A Companion to Romance*, ed. Corinne Saunders (Oxford: Blackwell, 2004), 287–304.

Robertson, Fiona, *Legitimate Histories: Scott, Gothic, and the Authorities of Fiction* (Oxford: Clarendon Press, 1994).

Rommen, Heinrich A., *The Natural Law: A Study in Legal and Social History and Philosophy* (Indianapolis, Liberty Fund, 1998).

Rosen, David, 'A Tale of Two Cities: Theology of Revolution,' *Dickens Studies Annual: Essays on Victorian Fiction*, 27 (1998), 171–85.

Sabine, George, *A History of Political Theory*, 3rd edn, rev. Thomas Landon Thorson (Hinsdale Illinois: Dryden Press, 1973).

Said, Edward W., *Orientalism* (London: Penguin, 1995).

Said, Edward W., *Culture and Imperialism* (New York: Vintage Books, 1994).

Sato, Sora, 'Edmund Burke's Ideas on Historical Change,' *History of European Ideas*, 40 (January 2014), 675–92.

Schor, Hilary M., 'Show-Trials: Character, Conviction and the Law in Victorian Fiction,' *Cardozo Studies in Law and Literature*, 11 (Winter 1999), 179–95.

Schwarz, Marc L., 'James I and the Historians: Towards a Reconciliation,' *Journal of British Studies*, 13 (May 1974), 114–34.

Scott, Walter, *The Antiquary*, ed. David Hewitt (Edinburgh: Edinburgh University Press, 1995).

Scott, Walter, *The Black Dwarf*, ed. P.D. Garside (Edinburgh: Edinburgh University Press, 1993).

Scott, Walter, *The Bride of Lammermoor*, ed. J.H. Alexander (Edinburgh: Edinburgh University Press, 1996).

Scott, Walter, *Catalogue of the Library at Abbotsford*, comp. John George Cochrane. (Edinburgh: T. Constable, 1838). http://books.google.com/books?q=Scott,SirWalter. Catalogue of the Library at Abbotsford (Accessed 20 Dec 2016).

Scott, Walter, *The Fortunes of Nigel*, ed. Frank Jordan (Edinburgh: Edinburgh University Press, 2004).

Scott, Walter, *The Fortunes of Nigel* (London and Toronto: J.M. Dent & Sons Ltd, 1931a).

Scott, Walter, *Guy Mannering*, ed. P.D. Garside (Edinburgh: Edinburgh University Press, 1999).

Scott, Walter, *The Heart of Mid-Lothian*, ed. Alison Lumsden and David Hewitt (Edinburgh: Edinburgh University Press, 2004).

Scott, Walter, *Hints Addressed to the Inhabitants of Edinburgh, and Others, in Prospect of His Majesty's Visit*, Facsimile of Printed pamphlet (Edinburgh: William Blackwood, Waugh and Innes, and John Robertson, 1822). http://www.spinnet.humanities.uva .nl/images/2010-12/scotthints_new.pdf (Accessed 20 Dec 2016).

Scott, Walter, *The Journal of Sir Walter Scott* (New York: Burt Franklin, 1890). http:// www.gutenberg.org/etext/14860 (Accessed 20 Dec 2016).

Scott, Walter, *A Legend of the Wars of Montrose*, ed. J.H. Alexander (Edinburgh: Edinburgh University Press, 1996).

Scott, Walter, *Letters of Sir Walter Scott* 12 vols, ed. H.J.C. Grierson (London: Constable, 1932–37) http://www.walterscott.lib.ed.ac.uk/etexts/etexts/letters.html#etext (Accessed 20 Dec 2016).

Scott, Walter, *Peveril of the Peak*, ed. Alison Lumsden (Edinburgh: Edinburgh University Press, 2007).

Scott, Walter, *The Pirate*, ed. Mark Weinstein and Alison Lumsden (Edinburgh: Edinburgh University Press, 2001).

Scott, Walter, *Redgauntlet*, ed. G.A.M Wood and David Hewitt (Edinburgh: Edinburgh University Press, 1997).

Scott, Walter, *Redgauntlet* (London and Toronto: J.M. Dent & Sons Ltd, 1931b).

Scott, Walter, *Rob Roy*, ed. David Hewitt (Edinburgh: Edinburgh University Press, 2008).

Scott, Walter, *St Ronan's Well*, ed. Mark Weinstein (Edinburgh: Edinburgh University Press, 1995).

Scott, Walter, (ed.) *Secret History of the Court of King James I* vol II, (Edinburgh: James Ballantyne & Co., 1811). https://archive.org/details/secrethistorycoooscotgoog (Accessed 20 Dec 2016).

Scott, Walter, *The Tale of Old Mortality*, ed. Douglas Mack (Edinburgh: Edinburgh University Press, 1993).

Scott, Walter, 'Tales of a Grandfather,' *The Prose Works of Sir Walter Scott* (Edinburgh: Robert Caddell, 1836). http://www.walterscott.lib.ed.ac.uk/etexts/etexts/grandfa ther.html (Accessed 20 Dec 2016).

Scott, Walter, *Waverley*, ed. P.D. Garside (Edinburgh: Edinburgh University Press, 2007).

Scott, Walter, *Waverley*, ed. Claire Lamont (Oxford: Oxford University Press, 1986).

Scott, Walter, *Woodstock*, ed. Tony Inglis, J.H. Alexander, David Hewitt and Alison Lumsden (Edinburgh: Edinburgh University Press, 2009).

Scott, Walter, *Woodstock* (London and Toronto: J.M. Dent & Sons Ltd, 1931c).

Scruton, Roger, *How to be a Conservative* (London: Bloomsbury Continuum, 2014).

Scruton, Roger, *Culture Counts: Faith and Feeling in a World Besieged* (New York: Encounter Books, 2007).

Scruton, Roger, (ed.) *Conservative Thinkers: Essays from the Salisbury Review* (London: Claridge Press, 1988).

Scruton, Roger, *A Dictionary of Political Thought* (London: Macmillan Press, 1982).

Seliger, M., *Ideology and Politics* (London: Allen & Unwin, 1976).

Seymour, Susanne, 'Historical Geographies of Landscape,' *Modern Historical Geographies*, ed. Brian Graham and Catherine Nash (Harlow: Longman, 2000), 193–217.

Sharpe, Kevin, *Reading Authority and Representing Rule in Early Modern England* (New York and London: Bloomsbury Press, 2013a).

Sharpe, Kevin, *Rebranding Rule: The Restoration and Revolution Monarchy, 1660–1714* (New Haven and London: Yale University Press, 2013b).

Sharpe, Kevin, *Image Wars: Promoting Kings and Commonwealths in England, 1603–1660* (New Haven and London: Yale University Press, 2010).

Sharpe, Kevin, *Selling the Tudor Monarchy: Authority and Image in Sixteenth-Century England* (New Haven and London: Yale University Press, 2009).

Sharpe, Kevin, 'So hard a text? Images of Charles I, 1612–1700,' *Historical Journal*, 43 (2000a), 383–405.

Sharpe, Kevin, *Remapping Early Modern England: The Culture of Seventeenth-Century Politics* (Cambridge: Cambridge University Press, 2000b).

Sharpe, Kevin, *The Personal Rule of Charles I* (New Haven: Yale University Press, 1993).

Sharpe, Kevin, *Criticism and Compliment: The Politics of Literature in the England of Charles I* (Cambridge: Cambridge University Press, 1987).

Sharpe, Kevin and Stephen N. Zwicker, (eds.) *Reading, Politics, and Society in Early Modern England* (Cambridge: University of Cambridge, 2003).

Sharpe, Kevin and Stephen N. Zwicker *Refiguring Revolutions: Aesthetics and Politics from the English Revolution to the Romantic Revolution* (Berkeley: University of California Press, 1998).

Sharpe, Kevin and Stephen N. Zwicker *Politics of Discourse: The Literature and History of Seventeenth-Century England* (Berkeley: University of California Press, 1987).

Shaw, Harry E., 'Is There a Problem with Historical Fiction (or with Scott's *Redgauntlet*)?' *Rethinking History*, 9 (June–September 2005), 173–95.

Shaw, Harry E., 'Realities of the Prison: Dickens, Scott, and the Secularization of their Eighteenth-Century Inheritance,' *In the Grip of the Law: Trials, Prisons and the Space Between*, ed. Monika Fludernik and Greta Olson (Frankfurt: Peter Lang, 2004), 169–84.

Shaw, Harry E., *Narrating Reality: Austen, Scott, Eliot* (Ithaca and London: Cornell University Press, 1999).

Shaw, Harry E., (ed.) *Critical Essays on Sir Walter Scott: The Waverley Novels* (New York: G.K. Hall, 1996).

Shaw, Harry E., *The Forms of Historical Fiction: Sir Walter Scott and His Successors* (Ithaca and London: Cornell University Press, 1983).

Sibley, David, *Geographies of Exclusion: Society and Difference in the West* (London and New York: Routledge, 1995).

Simpson, James, *Letters to Sir Walter Scott, Bart., on the moral and political character and effects of the visit to Scotland in August, 1822, of His Majesty King George IV* (Edinburgh: Waugh and Innes: 1822).

Singer, Daniella E., 'Scott's Analysis of Justice, Law, and Equity in *Peveril of the Peak*: The Significance of Martindale,' *Studia Neophilologica*, 68 (1996), 61–71.

Skinner, Quentin, *Regarding Method: Vol. 1 Visions of Politics* (Cambridge: Cambridge University Press, 2002).

Slagle, Judith Bailey, 'Shadwell's Volunteers through the Centuries: Power Structures Adapted in Scott's *Peveril of the Peak* and Churchill's *Serious Money*,' *Restoration: Studies in English Literary Culture*, 20 (Fall 1996), 236–44.

Smith, Marie Hockenhull, '"How Can Ye Criticise What's Plain Law, Man?" The Lawyer, the Novelist, and the Discourse of Authority,' *Law and Literature*, ed. Michael Freeman and Andrew D.E. Lewis. (Oxford: Oxford University Press, 1999), 239–63.

Smuts, Malcolm, 'Cultural Diversity and Cultural Change at the Court of James I,' *The Mental World of the Jacobean Court*, ed. Linda Levy Peck (Cambridge: Cambridge University Press, 1991), 99–112.

Sommerville, Johann P., (ed.) *King James VI and I: Political Writings* (Cambridge: Cambridge University Press, 1994).

Sommerville, Johann P., 'James I and the Divine Right of Kings: English Politics and Continental Theory,' *The Mental World of the Jacobean Court*, ed. Linda Levy Peck. (Cambridge: Cambridge University Press, 1991), 55–70.

Southey, Robert, *Cromwell and Bunyan: Facsimile of the 1844 edition published in London by John Murray* (Boston: Elibron Classics, Adamant Media Corporation, 2006).

Spinner, Jeff, 'Constructing Communities: Edmund Burke on Revolution,' *Polity*, 23 (1991), 395–421.

Sroka, Kenneth M., 'Fairy Castles and Character in *Woodstock*,' *Essays in Literature*, 14 (Fall 1987), 189–205.

Stapleton, Anne McKee, *Pointed Encounters: Dance in Post-Culloden Scottish Literature* (Amsterdam; New York: Rodopi, 2014).

Stovel, Bruce, '*Waverley* and the *Aeneid*: Scott's Art of Allusion,' *Jane Austen & Company: Collected Essays*, ed. Nora Foster Stovel (Edmonton, Alta: University of Alberta, 2011), 55–73.

Sussmann, Charlotte, 'The Emptiness at *The Heart of Midlothian*: Nation, Narration, and Population,' *Eighteenth-Century Fiction*, 15 (2002), 103–26.

Sutherland, John, *The Life of Walter Scott: A Critical Biography* (Cambridge: Blackwell, 1995).

Sutherland, John, *Memoirs of the Life of Colonel Hutchinson, with the Fragment of an Autobiography of Mrs Hutchinson* (Oxford University Press, 1973).

Tessone, Natasha J., *Disputed Titles: Inheritance and the Case of the British Novel, 1798–1832* (Lewisburg: Bucknell University Press, 2015).

Tessone, Natasha, 'Tending to the (National) Economy: Walter Scott's *The Antiquary* and "that happy commerce" of the Enlightenment,' *Eighteenth-Century Fiction*, 26 (Winter 2013–14), 261–80.

Tessone, Natasha, 'Entailing the Nation: Inheritance and History in Walter Scott's *The Antiquary*,' *Studies in Romanticism*, 51, (Summer 2012), 149–77.

Thomson, Michael J., (ed.) *George Lukacs Reconsidered: Critical Essays in Politics, Philosophy and Aesthetics* (London and New York: Continuum International, 2011).

Todo, Fernando, 'The Function of Linguistic Variety in Walter Scott's *The Heart of Mid-Lothian*,' *The Edinburgh Companion to Scottish Romanticism*, ed. Murray Pittock (Edinburgh: Edinburgh University Press, 2011), 190–201.

Trela, D.J., 'Sir Walter Scott on Oliver Cromwell: An Evenhanded Royalist Evaluates a Usurper,' *CLIO: A Journal of Literature, History, and the Philosophy of History*, 27 (Winter 1998), 195–220.

Trevor-Roper, Hugh, 'The Invention of Tradition: The Highland Tradition of Scotland' in *The Invention of Tradition*, ed. Eric Hobsbawn and Terence Ranger (Cambridge: Cambridge University Press, 2012), 15–42.

Trevor-Roper, Hugh, *From Counter-Reformation to Glorious Revolution* (Chicago: University of Chicago Press, 1992).

Trumpener, Katie, *Bardic Nationalism: The Romantic Novel and the British Empire* (Princeton University Press, 1997).

Tysdahl, Bjorn, 'Scott's Imagery: The Beast and the Body,' *Excursions in Fiction: Essays in Honour of Professor Lars Hartveit on His 70th Birthday*, ed. Andrew Kennedy and Andrew Orm Øverland (Oslo: Novus, 1994), 232–54.

Ullmann, Walter, *A History of Political Thought: The Middle Ages* (London: Penguin, 1965).

Vakil, Cyrus, 'Walter Scott and the Historicism of Scottish Enlightenment Philosophical History,' *Scott in Carnival*, ed. J.H. Alexander and David Hewitt (Aberdeen: Association for Scottish Literature Studies, 1993), 404–18.

Van Creval, Martin, *The Rise and Decline of the State* (Cambridge: Cambridge University Press, 1999).

Varey, Simon, *Space and the Eighteenth-Century English Novel* (Cambridge: Cambridge University Press, 1990).

Veeser, H. Aram, (ed.) *The New Historicism* (London: Routledge, 1989).

Veith, David M., (ed.) *Completed Poems of John Wilmot, Earl of Rochester* (New Haven and London: Yale University Press, 1968).

Wallace, Miriam L., 'Nationalism and the Scottish Subject: The Uneasy Marriage of London and Edinburgh in Sir Walter Scott's *The Heart of Midlothian*,' *History of European Ideas*, 16 (1993), 41–7.

Wallace, Tara Ghoshal, 'Historical *Redgauntlet*: Jacobite Delusions and Hanoverian Fantasies,' *Romanticism*, 21 (2015), 145–59.

Wallace, Tara Ghoshal, 'Monarchy and the Middle-Period Novels,' *The Edinburgh Companion to Sir Walter Scott*, ed. Fiona Robertson. (Edinburgh: Edinburgh University Press, 2012), 106–17.

Ward, Ian, 'Scott and the Waverley Constitution: A Study in Literary Constitutionalism,' *English Studies: A Journal of English Language and Literature*, 79 (May 1998), 193–211.

Ward, Ian, 'The Jurisprudential *Heart of Midlothian*,' *Scottish Literary Journal*, 24 (May 1997), 25–39.

Warnke, Georgia, *Gadamer, Hermenuetics, Tradition and Reason* (Stanford: Stanford University Press, 1987).

Watson, J.R., *Romanticism and War: A Study of British Romantic Period Writers and the Napoleonic Wars* (Basingstoke and New York: Palgrave Macmillan, 2003).

Watt, James, 'Orientalism and Empire,' *The Cambridge Companion to Fiction in the Romantic Period*, ed. Richard Maxwell and Katie Trumpener (Cambridge: Cambridge University Press, 2008), 129–42.

Weinstein, Mark A., 'Law, History, and the Nightmare of Romance in *Redgauntlet*,' *Scott and His Influence*, ed. J.H. Alexander, David Hewitt, and Thomas Crawford (Aberdeen: Association for Scottish Literature Studies, 1983), 140–8.

Weinstein, Mark A., 'Sir Walter Scott's French Revolution: The British Conservative View,' *Scottish Literary Journal*, 10 (1980), 31–40.

Welsh, Alexander, *The Hero of the Waverley Novels: With New Essays on Scott* (Princeton: Princeton University Press, 2014).

Welsh, Alexander, 'History; or, The Difference between Scott's *Hamlet* and Goethe's,' *Modern Language Quarterly*, 59 (September 1998), 313–44.

Whyte, Christopher, 'What Walter Scott Can Offer Us Today,' *Gael and Lowlander in Scottish Literature: Cross-Currents in Scottish Writing in the Nineteenth Century*, ed. Christopher MacLachlan and Ronald W. Renton (Glasgow: Scottish Literature International, 2015), 56–71.

Wilkes, Joanne, 'Scott's Use of Scottish Family History in *Redgauntlet*,' *The Review of English Studies*, 41 (May 1990), 200–11.

Williams, Raymond, *The Country and the City* (London: Hogarth Press, 1985).

Williamson, Hugh Ross, *George Villiers First Duke of Buckingham, Study for a Biography* (London: Duckworth, 1940).

Willson, D. Harris, *King James VI and I* (New York: Henry Holt & Co, 1956).

Wilson, A.N., *The Laird of Abbotsford: A View of Sir Walter Scott* (Oxford and New York: Oxford University Press, 1980).

Wilson, John H., *Rake and His Times: George Villiers, 2nd Duke of Buckingham* (London: Frederick Muller Ltd, 1954).

Wilt, Judith, 'Narrative, History, Synthesis,' *The Columbia History of the British Novel*, ed. John Richetti, John Bender, Deirdre David and Michael Seidel (New York: Columbia University Press, 1994), 300–27.

Wilt, Judith, *Secret Leaves: The Novels of Walter Scott* (Chicago: University of Chicago Press, 1985).

Woloch, Alex, *The One vs the Many: Minor Characters and the Space of the Protagonist in the Novel* (Princeton: Princeton University Press, 2003).

Woodford, Benjamin, *Perceptions of a Monarchy Without a King: Reactions to Oliver Cromwell's Power* (Montreal and Kingston: McGill-Queen's University Press, 2013).

Woolrych, Austin, *Britain in Revolution, 1625–1660* (Oxford: Oxford University Press, 2002).

Wootton, David, 'Meaning and Context: Quentin Skinner and his Critics by James Tully.' *Noûs*, 26 (September 1992), 377–9.

Worden, Blair, *Literature and Politics in Cromwellian England: John Milton, Andrew Marvell, Marchamont Nedham* (Oxford: Oxford University Press, 2007).

Wordsworth, Christopher, *Who Wrote Eikon Basilike?* (London, 1824).

Wormald, Jenny, 'James VI and I, *Basilikon Doron* and *The Trew Law of Free Monarchies*: the Scottish Context and the English Translation,' *The Mental World of the Jacobean Court*, ed. Linda Levy Peck (Cambridge: Cambridge University Press, 1991), 36–54.

Worth, Christopher, 'Scott, Story-Telling and Subversion: Dialogism in *Woodstock*,' *Scott in Carnival*, ed. J.H. Alexander and David Hewitt (Aberdeen: Association for Scottish Literature Studies, 1993), 380–92.

Young, Michael B., *King James and the History of Homosexuality* (New York: New York University Press, 2000).

Young, Iris Marion, *Justice and the Politics of Difference* (Princeton: Princeton University Press, 1990).

Zeulow, Eric G.E., '"Kilts versus breeches": the royal visit, tourism and Scottish national memory,' *Journeys*, 7 (Dec 2006), 33–53.

Zimmerman, Everett, 'Personal Identity, Narrative, and History: The Female Quixote and *Redgauntlet*,' *Eighteenth-Century Fiction*, 12 (January–April 2000), 369–90.

Zwicker, Steven N., *Lines of Authority: Politics and English Literary Culture, 1649–1689* (Cornell: Cornell University Press, 1996).

Index